THE KALINGAS

The history of political ideas begins with the assumption that kinship in blood is the sole possible ground of community in political functions; nor is there any of those subversions of feeling which we emphatically call revolutions so startling and complete as the change which is accomplished when some other principle—such as that, for instance, of local contiguity—establishes itself for the first time as the basis of common political action.—SIR HENRY SUMNER MAINE.

PLATE I

A Kalinga Village in the Bangad Region

THE KALINGAS

Their Institutions and Custom Law

By R. F. BARTON

WITH AN INTRODUCTION BY
E. ADAMSON HOEBEL

THE UNIVERSITY OF CHICAGO PRESS
CHICAGO · ILLINOIS

THE UNIVERSITY OF CHICAGO
PUBLICATIONS IN ANTHROPOLOGY

*

SOCIAL ANTHROPOLOGICAL SERIES

THE UNIVERSITY OF CHICAGO PRESS, CHICAGO 37
Cambridge University Press, London, N.W. 1, England
W. J. Gage & Co., Limited, Toronto 2B, Canada

Preface

THE field work for this volume was accomplished during three periods: first, four months in 1916 when the author was Supervising Teacher of Kalinga Subprovince. The second period embraced the first three months of 1941. Professor H. Otley Beyer, head of the Department of Anthropology, University of the Philippines, financed this and the third period. During this second period a rough draft manuscript was prepared, which Mr. E. D. Hester, economic adviser of the High Commissioner, was so good as to get typed for me while I was busy on another project of field work. About two months later I took the more readable typescript back to Kalinga and remained for over a month (the third period); parts of the typescript were read by three educated Kalingas, Pangat Max Dugyang, Mr. Camilo Lammawin, and Mr. Filon Dakauwag. Some of their criticisms led to revisions and some to further investigation and additions.

During both second and third periods I had most excellent living and working conveniences in the Evangelical Mission House and as much advice and assistance as the very busy lives of the missionaries, the Reverend Messrs. C. C. Witmer and J. A. Nagel, allowed time for. My informants among the Kalingas were many; those more or less constantly used were Pangats Dugyang, Galamoy, and Gasatan and Messrs. Dakauwag, Lammawin, and Auwiyao.

Mr. Chester S. Chard, of the Peabody Museum, graciously agreed to see the manuscript through publication, but the outbreak of the war and his immediate entrance into the Navy prevented. I was myself interned by the Japanese for almost the whole period of the war and lost several nearly completed book manuscripts to the enemy. Fortunately, this one had already arrived in the United States.

I am deeply grateful to him who made this work possible and to all those who have helped it along, for in it I have experienced in full measure the joy of ethnographic research and writing. This has been due in part to a rather rare streak of frankness in Kalinga character and in part to the fact that Kalinga institutions illustrate so vividly and incisively the emergence of political organization from pre-existing social units of a quite different character. Thus they afford a close primitive parallel to a cycle of world development very much needed among the world's nations today.

R. F. Barton

Berkeley, California
September 21, 1945

ADDENDUM

At the time of R. F. Barton's death in April, 1947, as a result of complications which set in following an operation for gallstones, he was holding the Lichtstern Fellowship in Anthropology at the University of Chicago. We had already agreed to publish this volume, and Barton was doing the final editing. A preliminary version of his manuscript had reached this country just before the war and had been mimeographed for war use through the efforts of E. D. Hester.

After Barton's death the undersigned took over the responsibilities of final editing and seeing the volume through the Press. Professor E. Adamson Hoebel, one of Barton's friends, and himself a foremost student of primitive legal institutions, has kindly agreed to write an Introduction to this volume. The editor has taken the liberty of adding a few footnotes which are indicated by his initials. Through conversations with Dr. Fay-Cooper Cole and the writer, Barton had begun to appreciate the close connections, in certain aspects of culture, between the Kalinga and the Tinguian; these I hope to document further in forthcoming publications.

Barton lived long enough to learn the good news that his revised manuscript on the Kankanai was not lost, as he had supposed, but had been saved through the efforts of Professor H. Otley Beyer. A recent communication from Professor Beyer states that he is adding some materials to the text, and it is hoped that it will be published in the near future. Together with the Ifugao studies, we will then have an unrivaled series of publications on social institutions and custom law for the Mountain Province.

Barton did not leave a key to his orthography, and his statements in the text suggest that Kalinga phonetics are not easy to master—a conclusion which may be confirmed by glancing at Otto Scheerer's "Kalinga Texts from the Balbalasang-Ginaang Group" (*Philippine Journal of Science*, XIX, No. 2 [1921], 175–207). In the latter paper will be found reference to a bilabial *b* which is characteristic of several Kalinga regions and which Barton writes as *B;* an apparently voiceless *l* which Barton writes as *L;* and a mixed vowel which Barton writes as *E*. Barton also occasionally writes an *R* or *D* which are difficult to interpret; *ng* normally represents the velar *n* of "sing," except in the case of the tribal name, which is pronounced *Kaling-ga*.

The editor has taken the final responsibility for omitting a comparison of the present world situation with the Kalinga state. Barton himself was uncertain as to whether to leave it in or take it out, and he received conflicting advice from various friends who read the manuscript. He asked me to make the decision, and in the interests of unity and coherence I have left it out. But I will gladly furnish a copy to all who may wish it as an appendix. In its place I have added a brief Epilogue.

As I write these words, I have just received a note from Professor Beyer telling of the signing of the Fulbright pact in Manila. Under its generous provisions we can hope for a new era in the study of Philippine life and culture. It is one of the tragedies of anthropology that Barton was not able to live to take advantage of the coming opportunities; but as a pioneer he has presented us with high standards of attainment. He had received generous support from the Guggenheim Foundation just before the war and was looking forward to further field work under its auspices.

It is appropriate that the Department of Anthropology of the University of Chicago should sponsor this volume, not only because of Professor Fay-Cooper Cole's long interest in the Philippines, but also because the late Professor Frederick Starr was acknowledged by Barton as his teacher and friend.

Alfred Harris kindly drew the maps.

FRED EGGAN

CHICAGO, ILLINOIS
April 7, 1948

Table of Contents

List of Illustrations

FIGURES

PLATES

Introduction

WHO among anthropologists has not read Barton's *Ifugao Law?* And who among the readers of that work has not felt intense satisfaction in the contemplation of a rare piece of reporting on a complex and difficult but fascinating subject?

With his first publication, now nearly three decades old, Roy Franklin Barton gave us a work that quickly rose to the status of a classic in Philippine ethnology and the law of primitive peoples. For a quarter of a century it has stood as one of the few shining examples of what can be harvested in the way of legal enlightenment through purposeful and intelligently conceived study of law-ways among primitive peoples.

Now, with this posthumous book on the Kalingas, near-neighbors to the Ifugaos, he has bequeathed to us another first-rate work in behavioristic social science.

When Barton first pushed into the mountains of northern Luzon, he went in as a schoolteacher, but his affinity for people, combined with his perspicacious ability to see what goes on in the realm of human behavior, made of him a natural anthropologist. When, later, his innate talents had been further sharpened and oriented through advanced professional training in anthropology, the scientific world began to enjoy the fruits of his Philippine harvest.

We have learned to expect the highest quality of empirical observation in the works of Barton, spiced with dynamic vitality in writing. He has not disappointed us in this present book on the Kalingas. The reader will find herein a happy combination of narrative analysis of the culture, especially in its legal aspects, along with a rich store of case histories of Kalinga legal actions. Barton has left us no dry systematization of Kalinga law, attractive only to specialists. He had learned well the lesson that law is human behavior. It is not merely a set of hypostasizing rules, of what people think or say they should do in certain hypothetical situations.

Law is what people actually do in cases of violation of their social norms when such violation, or deviation, is punishable by the privileged use of force on the part of the injured party or by a public official. When real behavior in a legal situation is described, there is dramatic stuff in the law. Tension, conflict, clashes of personalities and interests, struggle and the resolution of all these—if the law is a successful system—mark most law cases behavioristically described.

In this book every point of law, every aspect of the system, is illuminated and substantiated with cases. They give flesh-and-blood reality to the legal system the author finds in the society of the Kalingas. The people live in Barton's work!

Barton never undertook to label himself or to claim adherence to this or that school of anthropology or jurisprudence. However, his work made him an anthropological behaviorist and a realist. Wherefore, this and his other contributions will be lasting, because his facts are of enduring worth. They stand in all their unadulterated purity. Students of comparative law may use them as they best see fit.

Although the Kalingas, who are the subject of this book, and the Ifugaos, who were the subject of Barton's earlier publications, are two discrete societies, this and the works on the Ifugao are of a piece. The great theoretical interest that resides in the Ifugao way of life is that it presents us with an anarchistic political organization, i.e., a system controlling intergroup relations within the tribe and between the tribe and the alien world that operates with little or no institutionalization of government. Yet this condition prevails in a technologically sophisticated society whose rice terraces on the rugged mountainsides of Luzon evoke expressions of awe from outside visitors. Further they have developed through the ages a most elaborate system of substantive property law and personal law—a system that operates almost entirely without benefit of government. The Ifugaos are the star example of how far a system of private law can go. They demonstrate that anarchy is not necessarily synonymous with disorder. Their system also shows up nicely the limitations in a legal order that depends primarily upon the kinship group for its operation.

Primitive peoples have usually developed consolidated kinship units as the solidarity group, whose basic function is to give protective security to the individual. The result has found expression in the principles of collective kin responsibility for the acts of relatives and collective kin protection of the individual. The operation of these interacting principles produces the so-called "law of blood revenge," which may be, and usually is, no legal law but merely a sociological one. It is a sociological law in so far as one can predict that, where there has been a killing, there will be a counterkilling. If it stops there, if the kin group of the original killer customarily accepts the action of the avengers as just, and stays its hands from further counterkilling, then we have legal law. The application of the coercive sanction is a socially recognized privilege acknowledged not only by public consensus but also by the kin group of the aggressor. But if the counterkilling leads to feud, the condition is one of an absence of legal law. The condition is one of internecine civil war.

The study of comparative law with anthropological data shows incisively that the mastery of the problem of the feudistic tendencies within primitive society has been one of the great challenges to man's social inventiveness. Primitive man consolidated kinship groups upon the genealogical principle in order to develop a mechanism of protection for the individual. Then he ultimately found to his discomfort that the clan often destroyed the very security it was created to impart. The clan contained the inherent seeds of its own destruction as a social institution.

Historically, clans have been replaced by national states as the security-giving protective groups. Within the more advanced societies public law has supplanted private law in whole or to large degree. Yet this has been no complete solution.

The national state, the very organ that was created to obviate the social disorder growing out of kin-based law, contains the selfsame deficiency that contributed to the desuetude of the clan. Within the world society of today the national state is a feudistically inclined unit of social organization. It arrogates unto itself the social right to apply sanctions to aggressors, real or supposed, and the defendants adhere to the right to retaliate. War is the deadly result. The national state today destroys the very security it was created to give. Contemporary civilization unfortunately blesses its peoples with no great sense of security or prospects for a peaceful future.

The Kalingas, taken with the Ifugaos, represent a type case of the movement from a predominantly kinship organized state over to the territorially organized state. Of particular interest is their elaboration of the Ifugao personal trading pact between members of alien regions into a system of "international" peace pacts. But this is merely one point of significance. The book is pregnant with many others, as the reader will find for himself. It sheds much light on the functions of law as a phase of the system of social control in a society.

Its deepest lesson, however, for this critical age will be found if the system of law that it describes is seen in relation to Kalinga society as international law now stands in relation to world society. International law is primitive law on a world scale. The implications for the future should be plain.

E. Adamson Hoebel

Chicago, Illinois
August 25, 1947

Chapter I

THE KALINGAS

THE subprovince of Kalinga is of somewhat pentagonal shape and lies in the north-central portion of northern Luzon between 120° 56' and 121° 40' east longitude and between 17° 15' and 17° 44' north latitude. Its area is 2,849 square kilometers. Kalinga is bounded on the north by the subprovince of Apayao, on the east by the provinces of Cagayan and Isabela, on the south by the subprovince of Bontok, and on the west by the province of Abra. It is situated in the mountain ranges of the western side of the island; to the south the mountains consist of two principal ranges extending northward from the Benguet Plateau, where the eastern range is the higher, with altitudes up to 2,700 meters. This eastern range begins to moderate in the habitat of the Kalingas, and the slopes, from having been supersteep, become merely steep. The western range, which forms the western boundary of the subprovince, also decreases in height to maximums of 2,200 meters. The subprovince slopes toward the northeast and is drained by tributaries of the Cagayan River. The rainfall is more evenly distributed than in the central and western plains of Luzon, although sometimes the habitat experiences a long drought. The soil is far richer than in Bontok and Benguet; the characteristic plant of the hillsides is the tree fern, which has a predilection for rich soils. Bamboo grows wild or has been planted in and around every settlement. Bananas grow luxuriantly and provide a larger portion of the subsistence of the Kalingas than of any other tribe.

6

They are planted, along with betel palms, even on the walls of the terraced rice fields.

The water resources of the habitat are either greater or more available than are those of the other mountain tribes and have not been so nearly utilized up to the limits possible to the tribal technology. The construction of terraces, while not so difficult as elsewhere on account of the more moderate slopes, is still sufficiently arduous. For by "moderate" slopes, I mean slopes of 20 to 50 degrees rather than of 30 to 80. With more land available for field construction, the Kalinga, naturally, has not used as great care in the construction of his fields as the other tribes—he frequently sacrifices space that could be used for cultivation if he made his terrace banks more nearly vertical. He frequently builds a wall to the height of only a meter and lets the rest of the terrace bank slope at a gentle angle, planting on it a kind of grass—not, itself, obnoxious— which holds the soil and keeps down other vegetation. The Bontok, who saves space for cultivation by carefully built, nearly vertical, walls rising to heights of 6 meters or more, sneers at this (to him) shiftless waste of space that a more nearly vertical wall would make available, and so would the Ifugao, who builds walls only slightly less vertical than the Bontok to heights considerably greater, if he ever came to these parts. The Kalinga can afford the waste because he has a greater area per capita terraced than any other tribe except possibly the Ifugao and because he raises two crops a year, as well as dry rice on clearings. The Ifugao taboos planting dry rice if he plants the irrigated kind, believing that its magical effect on the latter crop is bad; the Kalinga is not nearly so magic-ridden.

The Kalinga's two crops a year give him a great advantage in subsistence over the other mountain tribes. One crop, of the same variety that is planted by the other

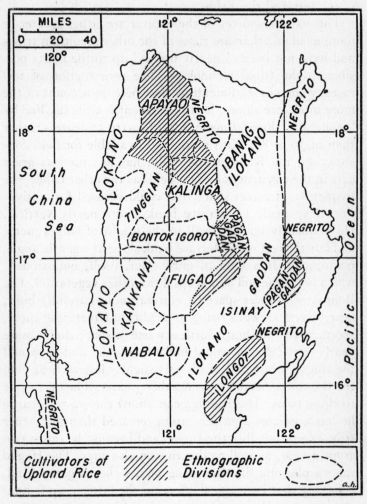

FIG. 1.—Ethnographic map of northern Luzon. (After Barton, *Philippine Pagans* [London, 1938].)

tribes, is a large-grained and very savory kind—the best rice in the Islands, possibly the best in the world; it is planted in January and harvested in June, the period of the lengthening day and does not produce if planted in the other half-year. The other crop, a small-grained, less savory sort, is planted in July and harvested in December. The heads of the former sort contain twice as much rice as the heads of the latter, but the latter puts out twice as many tillers as the other, so that the yield is approximately the same.

The Kalingas have always exported rice and they have no need to depend on the camote, or tropical sweet potato, which is the main item of the other tribes' subsistence. They also raise a great deal of sugar cane, from which they make crude sugar and *basi*[1] for export to the lowlands. They raise many carabaos and a few cattle. They use the carabaos to plow the great majority of the fields, driving from two to six of the animals, their noses strung on a rope so as to keep them abreast, around and around until the soil is trampled into a loblolly. The Kalinga is an expert in getting the animals to the terraces, and if one of them should fall and break a leg—a rare accident, for the beast is an excellent mountaineer despite its seeming awkwardness—why, he simply shares meat with his kinsmen and reckons the loss no great one. A few fields have to be turned with a wooden spade or tramped into condition by persons.

Not only are the Kalingas better supplied with food than the other tribes—they are better housed. There are two forms of houses, the "square" and the octagonal. The average dimensions of the "square-type" house are: height from ground to floor, 1.5 meters; from ground to eaves, 2.9 meters; length, 4.6 meters; width, 4.5 meters. The

1. A drink made by fermenting cane juice. Henceforth the word will not be italicized.

house seems always to be a trifle longer than it is wide. The octagonal house is always a little larger than the other type; it is the aristocratic form and is inhabited by *pangats* (chiefs) and influential men. The floor is of split bamboo. Frequently there are two elevated strips of floor called the *sipi*, about 1.3 meters wide and 10 centimeters high along the side walls, where the people sleep. The low central portion is called *kandauwan*. The fireplace is located a little past the center of the floor to the rear and often to one side or the other, with a floor space between it and the rear wall. Over it is a rack for drying fuel or rice bundles. The roof is either square-pyramidal or octagon-pyramidal and is laid on bowed rafters, so that there is a characteristic doming, but the doming is shorter on the front and rear triangles than on the sides, because there is a long smoke-frame surmounting the roof and extending from the fore backward. Underneath the roof is a ceiling made of parallel runo reeds tied together; it joins the roof at the eaves but lies about a meter beneath its center—like a square or octagonal pyramid without the base. The ceiling is tied to a second set of rafters, on which, beyond the walls of the house, the thatch of the eaves rests; and, since these ceiling rafters are more nearly horizontal than the bowed rafters supporting the roof, there is produced a change of direction of the eaves-thatch so that it assumes a characteristic hump at the eaves. Logs, to be used ultimately for fuel perhaps, are piled along the outer posts that support the house so as to prevent an enemy from going underneath and jabbing his spear through the split bamboo floor. If the walls be of woven bamboo, logs as well are piled high along the walls, with similar protective purpose. On the front side of the house there is usually a narrow veranda, the *kalangan*. The Kalinga house is an admirable one, and the Kalinga

woman keeps it well, taking the bamboo floor to the spring
or brook and washing it two or three times a week.[2]

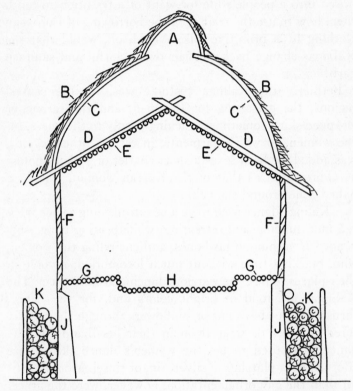

FIG. 2.—Cross-section of a Kalinga house. In the figure, which represents a
cross-section midway between front and back, *A* is the smokehole, a sort of
lengthwise tunnel; *B* is the thatch; *C* is a bowed rafter; *D* is a ceiling rafter; *E*
is the ceiling; *F* is a wall board (sometimes the walls are of split bamboo); *G* and
H are the floor; *J* represents the house posts; and *K* the logs piled around the
house.

The same care does not extend to her family's recently
adopted lowland costume: this is worn until it falls into
tatters, with launderings few and far between. There are

2. See Pls. V, VI, and XII.

few better illustrations of the difficulty of integrating a borrowed trait and of the awkwardness and ugliness introduced into a people's life for want of a tradition to teach them how to use the trait than the borrowing of European clothing by a primitive folk. Would, oh, would that the Kalingas change back to their own colorful and sanitary garb!

Formerly the Kalinga costume was, for the central regions, the gee-string for the men, and the sarong or wrapped skirt, sometimes reaching hardly to the knees, for the women, to which garments, in certain other regions, was added for both sexes a short coatlet or jacket, almost as abbreviated as that of the Korean woman, leaving a naked zone around the belly.

A Kalinga dance used to be a beautiful thing to behold— the men lunging and retreating, while beating gongs suspended from human jawbones, and encircling the women, who, marking time without much locomotion, revolve in their places to face the warriors dancing around them. The Kalingas are fond of bright colors and, for the dance, thrust hibiscus blossoms or sunflowers through their punctured earlobes or wear them in their headbands. In the dance as it used to be, the women's dance skirts were adorned with platelets of silver, tin, or tinsel. More beautiful than the gay ornamentation, however, were the gracefully moving, sinuous, muscular bodies of the dancers and the streaming hair of both women and men, for the men formerly wore their hair banged in front and long behind. But, these days, the grace of movement and the beautiful bodies are concealed under baggy, slovenly khaki trousers and coat or shapeless mother-hubbards. The men's hair is cut European style; the women's hair is bobbed and "permanented" into innumerable curls which approach a shocky ugly frizziness—for the Malay and Chinese hair, it appears, is impossible to wave except with the most highly developed technological appliances which are not yet available in Kalinga.

As Professor Beyer has said, the Kalinga tribe is an ethnological hodgepodge. In part, this must be due to the fact that the region has been populated by streams of immigrants from all directions: from the upper branches of the Abra River across the western range of the Cordilleras; from the lands of Bontoks and Kankanai down the Chico and Tanudan rivers; up the Chico from its lower reaches in the Cagayan Valley. It is said that the Spaniards transported several hundred folk from the Babuyanes and dumped them into the northern part of the Kalinga habitat. In part, also, the somatological variation must be due to regional endogamy, which must have operated to establish local types.

I can give only a tentative somatological description, based on observation without instruments, and limited to the folk of the vicinity of Lubwagan. The Kalinga differs a great deal from the other mountain peoples and has the best build of any. He is taller, larger, and stronger than the Ifugao, not so heavily muscled as the Bontok, taller and lither than the Kankanai and Tinggian—not like them inclined to a dumpiness of the body. He is broad-shouldered, narrow-hipped, graceful, and strong.

His color is surely two full shades darker than that of the other tribes and, together with his features, reveals, I think, a strong infusion of Indian blood. At least 10 per cent of Lubwagan faces would be at home in a crowd in some parts of India. Isolated Indian features are in much higher ratio. The nose is usually straight or convex in profile and high and narrow as compared with that of the other tribes. There is probably a smaller incidence of epicanthus than among the Ifugaos, where the incidence is lower than among the Bontoks, Kankanai, and Tinggian. There is frequent an unusual eye-slit—there would be an epicanthus if the lower lid were straight, but this lid deflects downward and avoids being overlapped by a fold. The skull is dolichocephalic or mesaticephalic.[3]

The Kalinga population according to the 1939 census was 24,452. Former estimates were much too high; for example, Worcester, in 1912, estimated the number at 66,000. In fact, the population of all the non-Christians was overestimated.

The reason was a peculiar one: the Mountain Province formerly consisted of seven subprovinces, each in control of a lieutenant-governor endowed with powers and often ambitious to accomplish great things in his realm. The country was new and poor, and, as the work of administration could not be supported in much measure by local taxation in money, there had to be appropriations from the insular treasury. An annual road and public works tax of ten days' labor was imposed on every male between the ages of eighteen and forty-five. The lieutenant-governors laid out and constructed new trails, kept them clear of slides, even swept them whenever a great men came up from Manila on an inspection trip. They built bridges, constabulary quarters, government buildings, leveled grounds where governors-general, the secretary of the interior, and other secretaries and numerous ranks and conditions of distinguished and important guests might meet the wild men,

3. As this manuscript is being finished in the field, Dr. Henry Field has very kindly made it possible for me to take anthropometric data on the Kalingas by sending me his own personal set of instruments. No great number have been measured yet, but the data are sufficient to make the above description (which I see no reason to change) a little more definite. The average stature is running 1,670 mm., with a range of from 1,572 to 1,734; the cephalic index is running 74.5, with a range, so far, of 72.4 to 79.3; nasal index 80.7, with a range of 66.7 to 89.4. The color range is also great, 18 to 26 (Luschan), with 23 and 24, the darker shades of medium brown, most frequent. Epicanthusi s present, so far, in 15 per cent.

curiously observe them, and tell them what they ought to do. And so, they needed great quantities of free labor. Consequently, they enforced neither end of the age limit. As a result of this "laxity," one saw youths of sixteen, fifteen, fourteen, and even thirteen working out their road tax alongside of oldsters far beyond forty-five. Fairness compels me to add that there was little or no opposition on the part of the boys to enrolling for the tax—they regarded it as an evidence of their maturity—and every boy wants to be a man.

It would have required the righteousness of angels not to have taken advantage of this only statistical toehold—and so advantageous a one—that could be gotten at that time for overestimating the population. For by calculating the population on the basis of males (supposedly between the ages of eighteen and forty-five) rendering road labor, a lieutenant-governor's subprovince could be made to look very important indeed, and this would help in detaching appropriations from the insular treasury. These lieutenant-governors were not angels; they were archangels rather, and it is generally recognized that, while angels cannot be tempted, archangels can, particularly where ambition is involved. The lieutenant-governors of Ifugao and Kalinga were especially archangeloid, each convinced that his job was the most important thing in the world, and it was in those places that the population was most grossly over-estimated. The population of Ifugao was estimated at one time at 130,000 (1939 census, 69,000), and that of Kalinga at 66,000, as we have seen, away back in 1916.

I mention this matter not in any spirit of muckraking or criticism, but solely in order that some well-meaning person, comparing past estimates and present facts, shall not conclude that these tribes are rapidly dying out. I am convinced that, on the contrary, they are now increasing.

The number of new houses and the absence of the many empty ones there used to be bear witness to the fact. There was a setback in 1920 due to the influenza epidemic which hit the mountaineers with especial severity, but it was only temporary. A factor that creates a rapid increase at present is the work in the mines. The high wages paid make possible a better subsistence than formerly. Nearly all the young men and many of the older ones work in the mines. Intensive development of the mines began about ten years ago. The census shows an unusually high percentage of children between the ages of five and nine (namely 3,701) as compared with the age-group ten to fourteen (2,211).[4] Another factor is the stamping-out of rinderpest, which has reduced the price of cattle to one-fourth what it was thirty years ago, and so has made possible an increase in the protein of the ration.

With the exception of possibly one or two very small areas, the tribe speaks one language—that is, there is a lexicographical unity—though the intonation and pronunciation vary greatly from town to town. In Lubwagan these are fantastic in the highest degree—almost impossible for anybody not born to them to acquire. Although there are some Ilokanos who have lived in the town for twenty years, I was informed that only one of them can speak nearly as a Kalinga speaks. And the Reverend Mr. Francisco Billiet, a very fine linguist, who knows Bontok

4. The numerical predominance of age-group five to nine is still higher among the Ifugaos, Bontoks, and Benguets, who work in the mines more than Kalingas do: Ifugao: five to nine, 10,587; ten to fourteen, 5,145. Bontok: five to nine, 11,276; ten to fourteen, 5,965. Benguet: five to nine, 15,460; ten to fourteen, 9,167. Compare with these ratios those found in lowland provinces: La Union (Ilokano): five to nine, 28,581; ten to fourteen, 23,570. Laguna (Tagalog): five to nine, 38,473; ten to fourteen, 31,803. The disproportion is much greater between the two age-groups in Mountain Province than it is in the lowland provinces and, in the main, must reflect an improvement in subsistence beginning about ten years ago, that is, contemporaneously with the boom in mining.

and Ilokano rather better than those born to these languages, complains of his lack of mastery of Kalinga phonetics after more than fifteen years' residence there, although the Kalingas say he is able to correct their mistakes in grammar and in choice of words.

Despite their comparative linguistic unity, the Kalingas differ greatly in physical type according to region. Doubtless this is partly due to the fact that the habitat was settled by diverse types, but I think there has been a good deal of local differentiation since the immigration. There exists among them a strict regional endogamy and more cousin marriage than is found elsewhere among the mountain tribes. Formerly it was almost impossible for persons of other tribes or races to secure wives or mistresses among them. With acculturation, this prejudice is breaking down.

The Kalinga religion is more nearly similar to that of the Tinggian of Abra than to that of any other tribe except it possibly be the Apayao. There is a great difference between these mountain tribes in the respect of their pantheons. The contrast is greatest between the Ifugaos and their immediate neighbors to the north and west, the Bontoks and Kankanai. The Ifugaos probably have the largest pantheon on record, but no deity is supreme; the Bontoks and Kankanai are about as monotheistic as a primitive folk ever are. The Kalingas and Tinggians occupy a middle position, having a supreme deity and several classes of others.

The supreme deity is *Kabunyan*, sometimes called *Kadaklan*, "The Greatest."[5] By derivation Kabunyan means "those to whom offerings are made," "those for whom it is killed." In Ifugao the word designates the Skyworld, the region where the greatest number of deities dwell. Among the Kankanai the supreme deity is some-

---

5. Cf. F.-C. Cole, *The Tinguian* ("Field Museum of National History, Anthropological Series," Vol. XIV, No. 2 [Chicago, 1922]), p. 297.

times called Kabunyan, sometimes Lumauwig, the name of the culture hero. Parts of Kalinga that were settled from Bontok still have Lumauwig as a local god. The stem of this word, *lauwig*, means "field hut" in some Malayan languages; in Tagalog, *lauwigan* means an expanse. The god Lumauwig is a personification of the "miraculous increase" of crops; where he walked he left the "miraculous increase."

Central Kalinga, centering around Lubwagan, has little faith in the "miraculous increase" and does not seek it, thus constituting an outstanding exception among Philippines peoples. After the rice has been planted, husband and wife go out to the fields with a chicken and some rice wine. They offer the chicken to the ancestral souls believed to be lingering about or inhabiting the fields—for the Kalingas bury their dead there. They pray especially to the souls of those who built or improved the fields as follows:

Ancestors of ours who built this field and from whom we inherited it, have pity on us. Do not draw your living from it, do not harvest some of the crop. We are killing a pig (or chicken) to "end" your staying here. Do not come again.

Our god, Kabunian, who is the Greatest ("Kabunian un Kadaklan"), drive those spirits away and make this soil furnish us good crops. Do not permit these spirits to come again, thou who art the greatest and supreme above all others.

Then they put rice, meat, and bananas on the dike and say, "This is the end of you. Eat and depart."

Thus it would appear that the central Kalingas believe in the likelihood of diminishment of the crop rather than in the possibility of its miraculous increase.

Below Kabunian there are various lesser deities:

KiDul is the god of thunder.

KiLat is the god of lightning.

Sun and moon occupy no important position. Some informants say that they are not regarded as gods at all. The moon, however, gives omens.

DumaNig is a demon which possesses the moon (*Bolan*) and causes her to devour her husband, the sun (*Ageo*).

NamBisayunan is the howl or shriek that is heard during a storm.

Libo-o d Ngatu, "Clouds of the Skyworld," cause sickness.

Maman are beings derived from a second death of souls in the Afterworld; they are perceptible in red light, as on a rainy day near sunset. They may cause sickness.

Bungun is the god of the rainbow.

The *mamlindao* are hunting spirits.

The *bulaiyao* live in big rocks, hot springs, and volcanoes. They have a fiery appearance which they can turn on or turn off. They capture or devour souls. *Gulilingob ud Tangob* is the strongest of all the *bulaiyao*. This class is, of course, the same as the Ifugao *tayaban*.

Dumabag is the god of the volcano at Balatok.

Lumawig is the local god of the Mangali-Lubo-Tinglaiyan district.

The *Angako d Ngato* are demons that afflict with sickness.

The *Angtan* are goddesses or demons that depress men, bring worry and bad luck.

The *aLan* are cannibal or ghoul spirits that figure largely in myths and folktales as carrying away or devouring souls and as producing many kinds of transformations in men and in themselves.

The *anitu* are the souls of the dead. In Ifugao the ancestral souls are besought to confer benefits and to support the living, although they are also blamed for death and sickness. On the other hand, the Kalingas appear to expect no good from them and regard them as a bad lot. A Kalinga prayer for relief of sickness is thus reported by Pedro Bingson:

You relatives of this person who died long ago . . . accept this pig, which we have killed to satisfy you for making this person sick. Have mercy on him, for he alone is able to care for his family, and what is your purpose for making him sick, since you, his relatives, have died?

Therefore, I pray you to please stop holding his spirit so that he may recover by tomorrow.

Thou, most gracious Kabunian, I pray thee have mercy on this person, for thou art the greatest person we know on earth who is able to cure sickness. This pig is sacrificed in the name of the relatives—and unto all the persons who have died in this locality.[6]

An informant told me that the following ought to be added to this prayer to make it complete: "Kabunian, who is the greatest, the wisest and strongest of all and who can stop the cruelty of the *anitu*, stop those bad spirits and defend this person."

The *pinading* are extraordinary souls of the dead that have attained a superior power and existence. The Batak of Sumatra have a similar class. They live in the village or its outskirts, some of them in highly prized jars. *Pinading*, derived from ancestral souls, punish their descendants for wrong actions—especially actions against the family interest. Some *pinading* are derived from souls of slain enemies or possibly are spirits that inhabit the boxes containing bits of skulls taken in head-hunting.

In western Kalinga there are guardian stones called *baiyong;* three or more in number stand upright in the ground, sometimes with a stone laid horizontally on the ground in front of them. They remind one of similar stones in Sumatra, the Celebes, and other islands of Indonesia. Each *pangat* has one on his house ground, and so do some other head-hunters. Visitors from other towns on entering the village will not neglect to lay a *runo* tip, its blades tied into a knot, on the first *baiyong* they pass. Heads taken in war are left for a while on the horizontal stone or on a red

6. *Kalinga Herald*, II, Nos. 6 and 7 (1930), 11. Christian influence is obvious in the wording of the prayer.

cloth spread in front of it. Likewise betel nuts must be left
for them whenever anybody in the village makes an important feast. "Spear grass" called *baiyog* is planted around
them.

The Kalingas are confused about whether there is power
in the *baiyong* itself or whether the stones are the habita-
tion of spirits (as the skulls are that hang on the Kayan's
veranda in Borneo). It would appear that we here have
to do again with the village-guardian cult of the Batak and
several other Indonesian groups. The knotted leaves which
a visitor to the town lays on the *baiyong* are probably magic
to tie up the ferocity of the stones or of their indwelling
spirits so that they will not "bite" him. If he should neglect
this, he would be seized with a fearful bellyache when he
returned to his village, and the only cure would be to carry
a chicken or small pig and some basi or rice wine to the
owner of the *baiyong* and to beg the latter to sacrifice for
him so that he might get well. The Ifugao *pili* cult of property guardians operates the same way and may be a
degeneration of the *baiyong*.

The Kalinga cosmos consists of five regions: *Pita*, the
earth; *Ngato*, the skyworld; *Dalum di pita*, the underworld; *Daiya* or *Suyung*, the upstream region; and *Lagod*,
the downstream region. *Ambagdukan* means both "a line at
right angles across the river (at Lubwagan roughly East-
West)" and "on both sides of the river"—figuratively,
"everywhere." *Lagod* and *Daiya* likewise mean in Lubwagan roughly North and South, respectively.

The following is the program, as recorded in my journal,
January 27, 1941, of a ritual I observed in the house of a
bereft family the day after the corpse had been buried;
only those who had been members of the household were
present, namely, the widow (*nabalu*), who sits always un-

der a blanket, the mother, and little daughter of the deceased.

1. About 8:30 A.M. the priestess, wearing a turban, begins walking around inside the house, chanting and ringing a Chinese bowl (*singising*) with a bamboo stick.

2. She takes *tagaipai* vine,[7] wadded into a ball, and sits behind the mother of the deceased; she dips the vine to the floor, then to the back of the mother, chanting the while.

3. Chanting, she gently strokes the mother's back (which is bare—the women are wearing only a sarong) from above downward with the vine.

4. She rings a dish again for a while, then makes circular movements with the vine on the crown of the mother's head.

5. Again she walks about, ringing the dish in front of the widow, who has gone to sit in the space where the death chair holding the corpse stood yesterday.

6. She strokes the back of the widow with the *tagaipai* in the same way as in the case of the mother. All chants close with a jerky "Ha-ih he heh!"

7. She stands near the fireplace, hand uplifted and trembling, and chants.

8. She takes the widow to the corner of the room nearest where the death chair stood, kneels there, face in the corner, and chants.

9. She then repeats Nos. 3 and 6 above.

10. She does something with a tiny wisp of the mother's hair; don't think she pulled any out—seemed to be disentangling it.

11. They bring a chicken. The priestess takes it, boxes its head, and dips it into a coconut shell cup half full of water; transfers water from the head of the chicken to that of the mother several times, always boxing the chicken's head before dipping it into the water. She talks in conversational tone to the chicken as if giving it orders.

12. She takes the chicken to the door, still talking to it, boxes its head several times against the door frame, finally killing it.

13. The chicken is put to cook; the mother gathers all the dishes and pots and takes them to the brook where she scours and washes them. A neighbor woman comes and sweeps the house and all around it outside, gathering up the trash. The rice and cooked chicken are dished out into a food basket, the other child of the family, a boy about seven, is

7. This vine (*Drymaria cordata* [Linn.] Willd) is called *Konupa* in Ifugao and is worn in the hair in order to make the wearer invisible to malicious spirits. It is worn by relatives of a dead person for some time after the funeral. I once saw an Ifugao woman with two small children riding the autobus to Benauwe. Tied in the hair of each child was a sprig of *Konupa*. The plant grows on stone walls, which it very quickly covers and hides.

called from his play, and the household (after inviting me) begins to eat; the priestess detaches a fiber from the breast of the chicken, waves it over the food and pronounces an invocation. The poor widow, already ravenously hungry, no doubt, from two and a half days' abstinence, sits in a corner, under the blanket, stolidly. She may eat only *lugao*, soft-cooked rice, and has about two weeks of that fare ahead of her. Only an ex-Jap-subsisted POW or internee can fully sympathize.

The region of souls is called *Langit* (in some regions *Kakalading*) and is located in *Ngato*, the Skyworld. There, the souls live much as on earth; they own property and live in kinship groups. The soul is ashamed to present itself without property to his kindred: for that reason, the surviving kindred on earth must sacrifice carabaos and pigs for the soul to take with it. Formerly, these were sacrificed on the second day after death—at present on the first day. After the soul has delivered them, it is said that *a part of it* returns to its house and remains until after the rites just described (called *yabyab*) are performed. Then it leaves the house, but remains in the neighborhood until it is dispatched to *Kakalading*. Apparently, there is here an attempt to unify conceptions of multiple souls, or else clashing concepts of the soul carried by separate streams of immigrants into the habitat.

Myths are used in ritual less extensively than in Ifugao and in about the same way as the Kankanai use them; the ritual myths are either formulas made to justify a rite or else they are abbreviated myths having very ancient motifs. They end in a *fiat*, of which the following, from a sickness rite, is an example: *Ofai! Makaan-ka pai, ta anan sapsapu-ak Di sangsangEm; ta pamman Di KabuLiyan intuDtuDu no adi tutuwa? Ofai! Makaan-ka pa amin!* ("*Ofai!* Get thee hence, because I am doing thy *sangsang* rite, and why should Kabunyan have taught it if it be not true? *Ofai!* Get hence, all!"). Myths used ritually are called *abungeL*.

The priesthood is almost entirely in the hands of women. Entry into it is always in answer to a "call" and is, in a sense, compulsory: the woman begins to sleep badly, has many dreams, grows thin, lacks appetite, believes that her soul has married an *anitu* and that she can extricate herself from the condition only by becoming a priestess (*manga-alisig*). Or she may become conscious of the call from getting a stomach upset after she has eaten foods that are taboo to priestesses: eel, dog, certain fish, meat of the cow (but not carabao). She is said to be taught the rituals by the gods themselves, not by the older priestesses. But, of course, she has been watching and hearing these since she was a little girl and wondering whether fate would call her to be a priestess when she grew older.

Priestesses begin their office at from about thirty-five years of age onward. About one out of fifty old women are priestesses.[8] For their officiations they receive the lower jaw and jowls of the pig and half of the liver, or if they have plenty of meat at home already, fifteen bundles of rice, a ganta of mangos, or a peso or two. They never ask for a fee.

Men are much more rarely priests, but there are a few, and some of them have great renown. Priests formerly concerned themselves mainly with head-hunting rites, but, now that there is little or no use for these, there is little use for priests, except the few exceptional ones who undertake to cure sickness. A Christianized young Kalinga told me about a cousin of his who, he said, had "disgraced" him. This cousin was a graduate of a mission high school, but had reverted to the native religion and become a medicine man. He had "gotten into this work" through dreams in

8. My informant was recently a census-taker for Lubwagan and believed that, since he had visited all the households, the number of priestesses, although not, of course, an item of census enumeration, had registered itself in his mind.

which he saw many "true" visions. He plans his rites systematically and writes the program of them out beforehand on a slip of paper. Some of his ceremonies last a day and a half; people come from far to enjoy the privilege of his officiations. "I'm really ashamed for my cousin, but I have to forgive him because he effects many marvelous cures," said my informant.

Corpses sit in a death chair of standard pattern—formerly from three to ten or more days, according to the age and wealth of the deceased, those of old men and of the wealthy being kept the longest. The period is now limited by law to three days. Bundles of rice are placed at the feet. The seat of the chair is wide enough to give a place for the widow or widower, who sits much of the time beside the corpse, facing it, and wailing, bending down and touching the face to the cheek or shoulder of the corpse and sobbing jerkily such phrases as "Uh-uh-uh! uh-uh!" "Pity for you, Spouse. Recall our past, our rice fields, the pleasures of our going on trips, our going and coming together; also our hill farms. Pity our children, bereft—do not throw them away, poor orphans; pity me left alone. . . ." Kindred and neighbors (mostly kindred) come in great numbers; the men sit outside under an improvised shade, the women in the house. The man's mother and father and close relatives, male and female but mostly the latter, also sob and wail, standing in the house in front of the corpse. Rice wine or basi are served the men (Kalinga women do not drink much), and heated arguments occur about genealogies, events, or the custom, ending sometimes in disorder. There is the same reason here for the death wake as in Ifugao— namely, the fear of visitations from ghoul spirits called by the Kalingas *aLan*. In funerals of the aged there is singing, joyful and improvised, and the chanting of epics and stories; the wake bears a festive character. At midnight an animal is slain and served with rice to the people. Why at midnight? "So that the people will stay and notice the dead person." I interpret this answer to imply that even a funeral is a prestige feast. Wailing continues all night sometimes, one woman relieving another. The soul, meantime and until burial, is believed to linger around the house. On the tenth day after interment, the priestess chants a dirge to dispatch it to *Ngato*, the Skyworld, where the region of souls is located.

Burial is ordinarily in a grave, which is covered by a shed of bamboo and thatch roof or sometimes a piece of cloth tied to bamboo posts. The grave is about a meter deep, its sides having an inset (see Pl. XXVII). The body is laid in the grave, then everybody present drops a stone on it. Sections of round bamboo are laid on the ledges of the sides of the grave and are covered with bamboo strips laid across them above the corpse.[9] The earth is shoveled on top of these, a circular wall of stone is built above the grave (sometimes in these latter days only single ring of stones) and filled with earth. Cairn burial is said to be practiced in the western part of the subprovince, but I have not been able to find any cairns around Lubwagan. I incline to believe, however, that this was formerly practiced. Both the form of the present grave, with its circular stone wall, and the fact that those who can afford it build tombs of concrete or stone and mortar argue for such a supposition. One body after another is buried in the concrete tombs. There is

9. Later information indicates that long stones are more frequently laid across the grave ledges above the body than bamboos. In the case I witnessed the body was in a coffin—an innovation; usually it is only wrapped in a blanket.

The more ancient form of burial, which is said to be still practiced to some extent, is to line the grave with flat stones, bottom, sides, ends, and top. This is called *atob*. In Ifugao *atob* means a kind of fish trap made by four stones—two at the sides, one at the rear set edgewise, and one on top. Fish go into this and are caught with the hands. The term is also used to indicate the deities of the four regions of the cosmos.

a sink in the center down which fluids escape and into which bones of former corpses are tossed.

All that I have seen buried with a corpse is tobacco and a Chinese bowl. Cups with basi and cooked rice are placed on the graves for several weeks after a burial. I have also frequently seen a hat lying on a grave. Another form of burial, practiced sometimes by the wealthy and powerful, is scaffold or "air" burial (see pp. 162–63).

Except that there are melodies in common with the Bontoks, Kalinga music, like Kalinga oratory and Kalinga phonetics, is grotesque and singular. It is a great pity that the music of these tribes is one of their culture phases that is quickly vanishing. Some of the musical instruments are not found among other tribes. The *patanggok* is on the same principle as the *anklung*, a Javanese musical instrument; pieces of bamboo varying from 30 to about 45 centimeters in length are tapered on one side from about their middle, and a little hole is made through the rind of the other end. The tapered end is beaten on a bamboo or head ax, and, by closing and unclosing the hole, the tone is varied.

The *balingbing* is a bamboo about 60 centimeters long, split into halves from one end almost to the node, the extremities of the halves being whittled down thin. A hole is made through the rind of the other end near the node. The instrument is beaten on the hand, and the tone is varied by closing the hole.

The *tongali* is a nose flute similar to that found elsewhere in these mountains, having four holes toward the lower end. To play it, one nostril is closed with a wad of leaves or cotton.

The *diudiuas* consists of seven bamboo flutes of different lengths tied together.

The *Kalibit* is a bamboo harp. Either five or seven strings are raised from the body of a four- or five-inch piece of bamboo. The strings are of the same size, but some are lifted by higher bridges than others, so that there is a difference in tension.

The Kalinga, as conditioned by his own culture, is a nervous, vivacious individual, quick and graceful in his movements. He is enterprising and has a quick, keen mind and considerable business sense. His institutions are ingenious, relatively efficient, and are in full operation today despite the superimposition of a colonial government, so that a Kalinga offender, if punished by the government, is usually punished for his offense twice—by the government for a crime and by his own custom for a tort. There is often a ridiculous discrepancy between the degrees of punishment inflicted by the two parallel systems (see Case 102).

Lubwagan has two mission high schools, one Catholic and the other Protestant. Because of these and because of a great influx of lowlanders, and the opening of mines and of roads to automotive traffic, the younger generation is rapidly changing in culture. As must always happen in rapid cultural change, it has neither the morality of the one nor of the other and suffers from a lack of stability and orientation. The Protestant mission publishes a monthly journal, the *Kalinga Herald* (beginning from 1927), which reflects the struggle between new and old. Its pages were open to both sides of the controversy; I quote two curious acculturational documents from them.

A MAN CARRIED AWAY BY A GHOST

One evening in September, a man related the following ghost story to me:

One night about ten o'clock, I felt warm and went outside the house to refresh myself. I stepped behind the house of my neighbor and saw in the distance a pig coming toward me. I started to go back into my house, but my way was blocked by a giant having a raincoat made like the wings of a bat. I held up a part of the raincoat trying to examine his body. With his two hands, he took me by the shoulders and turned me

upside down. I shouted for help. He then drew me inside his raincoat, so
that I couldn't shout. His odor was very bad. He raised me up outside
his raincoat and I shouted again. He was carrying me away; he met
some dogs and held their noses so that they could not bark. He continued on, holding me by the waist, carrying me like a dog. I grasped
hold of a guava tree with both my hands and held on for dear life.

The ghost was pulling me, my companions were coming to my help
with a flashlight. My companions surrounded us and the ghost was
covering me. Being tired, he stopped pulling and gave me the following
advice:

"I will go now. My eyes are blinded by the flashlight used by your
companions. I have taken your heart, already."

Being frightened by these words, I let loose of the guava tree with
my left hand and felt to see if there was a hole through which he had
taken out my heart. There was none. The ghost spoke again with this
advice:

"Go home and make a feast. If I can't get you, I will get others."
Then he ran away like a big carabao. Very soon my companions who
followed me found me. I fell asleep without knowing the time when they
carried me home. The next day, I made a feast, butchering five pigs.
I invited all the people in the neighboring village. Five days after the
feast was over, a young woman in our town was drowned in the river.
Two days later, a woman was drowned.

This is the dream the man told me. The words of the ghost were
fulfilled, and so I also believe that the ghost was real.[10]

SUPERSTITIOUS BELIEF IS A DANGEROUS THING

There is a place by the name of Sayangan which is not very far from
the town of Lubwagan. It contains a spring and a small creek and in the
creek lives a large eel which the people used to see. According to the
people, there is an evil spirit, *ayan* or *anito*, who lives in that place.

One afternoon in the early part of December, 1931, Honorio Baawa
and his companion, Dolongoan, went to fish in this place, taking only
one hook. They were warned before going that an *anito* lived in Sayangan and hesitated about going, but finally decided to carry out their
intention. On arriving, as dusk was falling, they selected a place to set
the hook. While they were engaged in doing this, they heard a slight
noise, like the vibration in the air around them. Immediately they were
frightened and seized with the thought that the *anito* would make them
sick.

They abandoned their hook and hurried home. That very night,
Honorio Baawa began "to have a bad feeling" and did not attend school

10. Honesto Amangao, *Kalinga Herald*, II, No. 3 (1928), 17.

the following day. Then he got sick and went to Lubwagan hospital for treatment, staying there a few days. He felt somewhat better and left the hospital and re-entered school, but it was only a week till Christmas vacation.

At this time I asked him about the cause of his sickness and he related the story as set forth above, asserting his conviction that his soul was left back in Sayangan. He also said that he believed the big eel was an instrument of the *anito* to entice people to go fishing there.

At Christmas vacation, Honorio Baawa went to his home in the Balbalan region. His bad feeling became worse; his body became pale and thin. He had no appetite. His sickness became worse and worse until he died.

I have the thought in mind that the strong influence of the *anito* was inculcated in his mind and his belief became stronger and stronger that would lead him to his death.

Dear friends who believe in *anitos*, I urge you to eradicate at once your belief in this dangerous thing.

The late Honorio Baawa was a young student in the Kalinga Academy. He was a boy of good standing and reputation among his schoolmates. He was humble and meek according to my observations during his stay with us in our house.

On Sunday, January 24, 1932, we had a special offering for the deceased. We collected the amount of three pesos. This money will be given to his parents as a symbol of Christian relation to the deceased and his parents.[11]

The mind of one of the youngest *pangats* (i.e., men of the highest rank) manifests a high degree of selectiveness and droll reinterpretation in its acceptance of Christianity. He told me:

I believe the Bible, yes, but I do not agree that only white men can interpret it. I believe that Kalingas have a part of the truth and that that truth is embodied in the Bible. For example, take the subject of omens. The god *has* to assume a material form when he appears to men—therefore, as we Kalingas know, he assumes the form of some animal—usually a bird or a snake when he wishes to warn men of danger. Thus, when Pastor Witmer held the first services in his new chapel, an *idu* [omen bird] flew into it, remained until the end of the services, then followed the people out. I warned the pastor that it surely betokened a serious misfortune. And it did happen so: the next day, without previous illness, a pupil of his school died. A bird hovered

11. Francisco Viloria, *Kalinga Herald*, IV, No. 8, 4.

over Christ when he was baptized—that foretold his cruel death which came a year later. A snake appeared to our first parents and foretold their being driven from the Garden of Eden.

Likewise the Christian opposition to the *dagdagas* system of legalized mistresses is contrary to the Bible. Not long ago, a Catholic Kalinga was reproved by the priest for having taken a *dagdagas*. He answered "What does it say in the Bible? 'Increase and multiply.' My wife cannot bear children—therefore I have taken a *dagdagas* as Jacob did. I should be disobeying the Bible if I did otherwise. You who do not marry break the command—not I who take *dagdagas* and fulfil it."

The *pangat*'s views on the situation that led to the birth, as he understood it, of the second member of the Trinity will not bear repeating. His conception of sin is almost a straight carry-over from concepts of tribal wrong, vengeance, collective responsibility, the feud, and so on:

Then, too, they tell us that we have sinned against God. What sin have *we* committed against *Him?* The Bontok man was right who, when the priest told him he had sinned against God, answered: "The holy pictures that you give us show that they who killed God's son were bearded men. You yourself have a beard. Maybe your ancestors killed God's son. But we Igorots have no beards. Therefore, those slayers of God's son were not our ancestors. Therefore, we Igorots have not sinned against God."

Chapter II

THE HOUSEHOLD AND KINSHIP GROUP
AND THEIR CUSTOM LAW

KALINGA society is based primarily on the bilateral kinship group, a development of the tribal principle of social organization (the "blood tie"), and secondarily on a territorial unit, hereafter called the "region," which consists of certain villages and their surrounding lands within defined boundaries.

The Kalinga kinship group, like the Ifugao, consists for any individual of the descendants of his eight pairs of great-great-grandparents—that is to say of his brothers and sisters, first cousins, second cousins, third cousins, and of the ascendants and descendants of all these categories with the exception of the descendants of the last one. Normally the adult members of any kinship group are married to members of other kinship groups and live in households for the purposes of reproduction, rearing of children, and subsistence. If children result, parts of the kinship groups of the husband and wife are henceforth united in them and become the kinship group of their children.

The household consists of husband and wife, their children, and servants and other dependents, if any. The Kalingas never had slaves, nor did those of Lubwagan sell human beings—for the reason, possibly, that they were too remote from a market.

The household is the economic unit, and this is true more

strictly than among the Ifugaos, as the following case illustrates:

1. Household a separate economic unit; liability of husband's kindred for wife's property "gambled" by husband (1934).—Kuyuon devoted himself to gambling, to the neglect of his fields and his family. He squandered his own property, then gradually that of his wife. His children, five in number, were said often to be hungry, and three of them died. Finally, Kuyuon sold to his wife's brother her largest field—"the source of their life"—leaving her only a small and utterly insufficient one. He lost the proceeds and then promptly died.

Balungay, the widow, underwent hardships and had to work for wages in order to support her remaining children, all but one of whom died.

"If the remaining child does not die, there will be no trouble, but if it does, then the brother and sister of Balungay are talking about making a demand on the relatives of Kuyuon for the value of the big field her husband sold to her brother."

Q. Why did not the brothers of Balungay help her support her children?

A. Because she did not follow their advice; they advised her not to consent to the sale. She was too much subject to her husband, and this angered her brothers against her.

Q. Then if Balungay had not consented, her property could not have been sold?

A. No, not for gambling. If to supply a family necessity, such as food, sacrifices for sickness or for funerals, then the husband could sell for their joint good in the face even of her opposition.

Q. Well, why didn't Kuyuon's brothers help support his children?

A. They would have helped if the children had come to live in their houses as *puyong* [semiadopted servants]. But it is not the custom to help so long as the children live in another household. *No food will be sent to their house*, lest the uncle's own children, when they grow up, should some day, when angry at their cousins, say to them, "You! Our father fed you in your own house and now you have displeased us. Pay back what our father gave you." Then the orphans would have to pay it back, and there would be bad feelings in the family.

Q. If the remaining child dies and the relatives of Balungay demand indemnity from Kuyuon's brothers, what will the *pangats*[1] say?

A. It seems to me that they will not agree, because Kuyuon's

1. *Pangats:* aristocrats who settle or help settle disputes and controversies and interpret the custom (see p. 147). The word will henceforth not be italicized and will be pluralized as if an English word.

brothers received no benefit from the selling of the fields. It is hard to say because gambling is a new thing to us: it came from the lowlanders who followed the Americans up here. There is no question about the validity of the sale—it is the squandering of the proceeds they are complaining about and for which they want to hold his relatives responsible. But the relatives of Kuyuon will retort with the questions, "Why did not your sister prohibit the sale? Why did you, yourselves, buy?"

Gifts of food, in Kalinga society, are either ritual, such as the distribution of meat, or else they are a simple neighborly sharing of vegetables with the expectation always of receiving favors in return.

Marriage.—A household is usually but *not always* instituted through marriage. Polygamy is not practiced, but concubinage not infrequently is.

A Kalinga is prohibited from marrying: (1) lateral relatives nearer than second cousins; (2) any direct ascendant or descendant, including step-relationships; (3) any member of his household (he may not marry a *puyong* or a stepsister who is living in another household); (4) in-law relatives except that, with some degree of social censure, he or she may marry the widow or widower of a brother, sister, or cousin[2] if the marriage with the deceased relative left no children. The reason given for this prohibition is that "the relationship is too close if a child was left." The prohibition also extends conversely to marrying a sister or brother of the dead spouse. The Kalingas cannot explain the prohibition; but I think the reason given by the Ifugaos for one of their practices fits the Kalinga case equally well. Asked why they do not allow brothers to marry sisters or a brother and sister to marry a brother and sister, they explained: "Why waste a marriage? The other family would be ours with only one marriage!"

2. While such marriages are permitted when there are no children, they are in bad favor and called by a contemptuous term, *palunok*.

Until recently there was strict endogamy[3] within the region (the political and geographic units of the society) over an area almost coextensive with the area in which the peace treaty and citizenship have reached a high development. I could not obtain satisfactory information as to whether endogamy extends into the area of the simpler form of pact. But sometimes a region has overflowed its natural bounds as in the case of Lubwagan's settlement at Uma (the name means "hill farm"). The Lubwagan people found rich land on the other side of the mountain that forms the western boundary of their region and dry-farmed it intermittently for many years. Finally, a few generations ago, some Lubwagan families made terraced rice fields and settled there permanently. Uma now has a population of over eight hundred; it is included in all Lubwagan's peace pacts except the one with Balbalasang, with which it has a separate pact, and its people continue to intermarry with Lubwagan folk. There are several other endogamous couples of this sort having a similar history. In some the former colony has become an independent region, having its own peace pacts, but it continues to be an endogamous unit with the parent-region, as, for example, Bugnao and Butbut, Bangad and Sumadel, Lubo and Gaang. Dalupa was settled from Ginaang and Ableg and intermarries with both parent-regions, but the parent-regions do not intermarry with each other to any appreciable extent.

3. Data taken from anthropometric cards of individuals measured in Kalinga:

Region	No. of Individuals Measured	No. of Instances in Which One Parent Was a Foreigner
Lubwagan............	40	0
Magnao-Naneng......	23	1
Balensiagao..........	22	3

Balensiagao is at the margin of the endogamous area.

The Kalinga attitude toward marrying abroad is shown by the following remark of an informant:

We don't reckon a man a man if he goes to another town to marry—we insult and despise such people. The only relatives we have in other regions are the children of the *dagdagas*[4] of our fathers and grandfathers. [This is too broad a statement.—R. F. B.] Men can have these mistresses there because it involves no change of residence—they go and stay with them a while just for pleasure and then come back. But now the young people begin to look on the matter differently, what with schools and work in the mines and passenger trucks running clear to Bontok and Baguio. They are willing to marry even Ilokanos. The old men, though, despise such a thing.

Investigation of genealogies showed that many people in Lubwagan are descended from a Talgao woman who fled with her son from a feud about six generations ago, came to Lubwagan, and threw herself on the mercy of the pangat:

2. *"Theft" of a bundle of rice; subsequent troubles and flight (six generations ago).*—Amai of Talgao and her female cousin, Lakulá, spread out stores of rice in the same place to sun. Lakulá gathered up her rice first and appropriated some of Amai's—said to have been only one bundle [worth today 1 centavo if a second-harvest bundle or 2 centavos if a first-harvest one]. Amai and her husband demanded Lakulá's field as an indemnity. In trying to seize the field, the husband was slain by Lakulá's husband. Amai's relatives avenged her husband's death, as was their obligation [see p. 52]. It appeared certain that Lakulá's kindred would retaliate.

Thereupon Amai fled to Lubwagan, carrying with her her infant son, Baluyok, a valuable jar, and some precious beads. She took service as *puyong*[5] in the house of a rich man. The infant son lived and married. Others of her relatives fled to Balatok. Most of the people of Lubwagan reckon her as an ancestress.

A few such refugees have been received from other towns. One pangat has relatives in Talgao because his father, being the pact-holder for that town, secured a *dagdagas* there who bore him a daughter. The daughter now has

4. *Dagdagas*, mistress.

5. *Puyong*, household servants temporarily or permanently adopted (see pp. 64–65).

eight children. One of the wealthiest of Lubwagan's pangats is descended from a grandfather who came from Dalupa, a town about eight kilometers away, to work for a rich man.

The regions nearest to Lubwagan and not isolated by geographical barriers, that is, the regions with which inter-marriage would naturally be most frequent, are Tanglag, at the mouth of Lubwagan Valley, and Mabungtut, just across the river. Mr. Dakauwag, a Lubwagan man teaching in Tanglag, states that there are no Lubwagan women married in Tanglag and only two Lubwagan men. These are: OtaL, who married there about seventeen years ago, and MagaLun, who about six years ago married the widow of Kaddu, another Lubwagan man who married in Tanglag about thirty years ago. Both these men are from Dugnak, the barrio of Lubwagan that is nearest to Tanglag. Since the beginning of my field work, a young Lubwagan man who was living with a mistress in Tanglag died from being crushed by a boulder while clearing a hill farm. This is the extent of the intermarriage of Lubwagan and Tanglag. Lubwagan women of the upper and middle classes almost never marry in other towns and only a little less rarely do women from the poor class (see Case 64). Exceedingly rarely Lubwagan men of property marry in other towns on condition that their wives transfer their residence to Lubwagan. Only one such intermarriage has occurred with Tanglag. Several servants from Tanglag are working as *puyong* in Lubwagan, and there have always been such, but nobody ever marries them.

I asked another informant whether any Lubwagan man had married outside his town during the last three years. He said: "No, but four years ago a Lubwagan man married a Bangad girl in Baguio, while working in the mines. He lives in Bangad now. And seventeen years ago, a Ginaang man, while serving here in the constabulary, took a Lubwagan girl as mistress and kept her during the term of his enlistment."

As this work proceeds, it will become increasingly evident that endogamy has been a powerful adjuvant to the local, community, tie in the maintenance of peace between kinship groups. Here we will mention only the fact that endogamy has brought it about that there is always a large number of individuals who are mutually related to the principals in any controversy that may arise. This means that the number of kindred who will take sides and back one or the other principal in the quarrel are correspondingly few. Hence, mediation is much easier to effect.

Almost every Kalinga child is engaged to be married when quite small. The boy must always be the elder, if only by a day or two. Conditional engagements are often made before the girl is born. I recently asked the mother of a two-month-old girl baby whether the child was engaged yet.

"No," she answered. "We received a proposal when she was two days old, but *she* wouldn't consider it."

"I don't like the old custom," explained the father, a former schoolteacher. "Besides, why should I go to all that expense?"

Kalingas have hyperaemic prides and conduct engagement negotiations with due caution not to wound or be wounded. If A, father of the boy, be sure his proposal will not be rejected, he may make it directly to B, father of the girl. If less sure of his ground, he may send gifts of meat for a while and then send the *banat* gift—soon to be explained. If B keeps the latter, A will send a messenger to make a formal proposal.

Not infrequently A will open the subject in a general way at a feast or other occasion, boasting of what a fine baby boy he has—one quite worthy of being the husband of

B's girl—taking care that his remarks be overheard by some of B's close relatives. The relatives will report his overture to B; if B looks upon it favorably, they will see that the news is carried back to A. A then sends two messengers called *mambaga* to B, and these will ask when B will be able to see them on an important matter. Neither messenger may be or may have been a widower, because his having lost his wife might exercise a bad magical influence on the prospects of life of the young bride-to-be. The two messengers will carry with them a gift of beads (possibly very valuable ancient ones) or a gold earring or two—a gift, at any rate, consonant with the wealth of the families—called *banat*. They will go to B's house at night or late in the evening, because that is a "quiet" time. If neither sneezes on the way or hears an animal sneeze (and they hasten so as to lessen the probability of such a bad omen), they enter B's house. But if there be a bad omen, they turn back, and the project is either dropped altogether or renewed only after a wait of about a year.

On entering the house, one of the messengers goes directly to the water jar and takes a drink, thus indicating that their arrival is "clean"—that no bad omen has been heard on the way. Then, for a while, there is talk about other topics than the one uppermost in the minds of all present. After a decent interval, the messengers deliver the *banat* with the statement that it is sent on behalf of A's son. B's wife then washes some rice, takes a cooking pot and begins lining it with *apin*, runo blades, laying the blades in one by one and audibly counting them as she does so, up to about ten blades. If nobody sneezes while she is counting, the engagement proceeds; she puts the rice on to cook, and B sends some men to catch a pig. The pig is killed and its bile sac examined for an omen. A well-filled bile sac is a prognostication of prosperity and long life.

It is said that there is no quibbling about how much property each family will allot its child, as this is pretty well
known already. Basi (fermented sugar-cane juice) is
passed around; rice and meat, when cooked, are dished out,
the two messengers being served first, and "their share is
more." When the messengers leave, each is presented with
a blanket and a Chinese bowl, and they carry the upper
half of the pig, called *longos*, to A as a token that the engagement, called *baga*, is accomplished. The two young-
sters, the principals of the occasion, are called *aBeLyan*;
their parents are *mangaBeLyan*[6] to each other.

Henceforth, so long as the engagement lasts, each household sends the other gifts of meat, *pias*, vegetables from
their hill farms, dainties such as *dauwai* and *diket*, rice
cakes.[7] At all feasts and occasions when a large animal is
slaughtered, the one household sends the other a leg of the
animal. Meat-sharing, a powerful group-unifying institution among all these mountain peoples, reaches farther
than the households immediately concerned and involves
their kinship groups, for the leg of a carabao (water buffalo) will be shared with the brothers and sisters, and sometimes with the first cousins, on both sides of the house.
Likewise, when the brothers and sisters of the parents of
the betrothed slaughter a large animal, they send a large
hunk of the choicest meat to the household of the betrothed of their niece or nephew.

Let us pay some attention to the growth, education and
status in the custom of the two betrothed infants. The
stages of growth are called:

1. *MaLnos* or *ka-i-anak*, "newborn."
2. *Ma-imis*, "beginning to smile."

6. *aBeLyan*: cf. *berian*, a designation widespread in Borneo for "bride price."
7. Sticky mixtures made of glutinous rice and symbolizing constancy and
loyalty.

3. *Manlukbub*, "he creeps."
4. *Umamoi*, "he sits alone."
5. *Mansiksikad*, "he stands up."
6. *Manadadalan*, "he begins to walk."
7. *Manoddak*, "he runs around."
8. *Maba-on*, "he can be sent on errands."
9. *Mamangaikaiyu*, "he can be sent to the forest for fuel."
10. *Bibiyu*, "companion." Full majority in all respects. This time of life is marked by his "beginning to court girls or his marriage and setting up a household, and he can fight."

There is, of course, no formal education of the child, but the very spontaneity and unconstrainedness of the process probably make it the more efficient in molding the young individual to conformity with his group's social patterns. I have been able to find extremely few temperamental misfits among these mountain tribes and have known still fewer cases in which maladjustments might be considered as responsible for a condition approaching psychopathia.[8] The child becomes a Kalinga by an easy, mainly imitative process. The grandparents, notoriously more lenient than the parents, care for the child who is still more or less helpless while the parents work in the field, or else they supervise the older brother or sister who cares for it.

It is noteworthy that children are never taught to walk

8. Speaking generally, it would seem that, where the ethos of a culture is an unyielding, extreme one, such misfits must inevitably be numerous. But it is to be doubted that cultures are often so extreme or unmitigated as they seem. Thus, the Ifugaos appear to be extremely individualistic, aggressive, and quarrelsome, but, on the other hand, they are consummate diplomats and appeasers and, within the kinship group, the most co-operative of all the mountain folk. On the other hand, the Sagada Kankanai, with their large town and ward organization, emphasize ideals of co-operation and harmony, and their prayers express these with a sentimentality comparable to those heard in any little Church around the Corner. But they steal from each other and enjoy suffering from each other almost as much as Quakers do. It would seem that a cultural ethos which proceeds toward extremes must necessarily, as soon as it excludes great numbers of individuals from its successes, also develop its mitigations. Ill adaptations in our own culture can best be attributed to the high degree of specialization it demands and to the fact that it must drive education far beyond that which is spontaneous and imitative.

or talk or to be careful not to hurt themselves. I have taken awls or sharp knives away from children or jerked them back from steep places, and the action has always provoked rage in the child—used to having its own uncontrolled way—and surprise in the elders, who regarded my solicitude as supererogatory.

That part of the child's education that is purposefully imparted relates to the kinship group's history, its troubles with other groups, its vengeances, enmities, its fields and their history, and the debts owed by or to the household. These things he will learn from his father and mother and grandparents. The father will also try to inculcate industry in his sons by precept, but, since he does not often supply a very good example of it, this attempt is usually a failure. Haphazardly, from everyone, the child learns the geography of the habitat, hundreds of names of places, the relations between and within kinship groups, between towns and regions, the pact-holders of these, the names of fields in his own and neighboring regions, folktales, legends, myths, chants. He will know every heirloom of his own and neighboring households, every bead, jar, and gong. He will learn the processes of all the arts generally practiced by his sex through participating and helping in them. Most important of all, he will learn the custom law and the operation of the society's institutions.

There was formerly a feature of the education of boys that deserves specific mention. In order to teach boys how to kill, they were allowed to hack and spear corpses of enemies that were carried home for the purpose. For sons of the pangats, there was sometimes a lesson on the living subject called *lobloba*. If the pangat were an especially doting father, he would take his little son, sneak up behind some co-citizen, and help the boy jab a spear into one of the citizen's buttocks. Then the pangat would pick up his young hopeful and hurry into his house. He would later on pay weregilds. The boy would immediately attain great prestige in his own age group and would be entitled to his tattoo as soon as he came of age. Sometimes these affairs were carefully planned.

3. Didactic wounding—lobloba (ca. *1895*).—Pangat B—when his son was very small—called a woman from Tanglag to work in his fields. One day the pangat took his little son and, helping the child hold the head ax, hacked her shoulder with it. He kept the woman in his house until she was cured; after that he paid weregilds and sent her home.

At about the age of ten—much later than Ifugao, Bontok, or Kankanai children—boys and girls "get ashamed" to sleep in their parents' houses and go to sleep in the houses of others along with their chums. A houseowner probably *could* refuse to be bothered with them but he doesn't. A house so used as a dormitory is called *obóg*. At a somewhat older age, the boy may be attracted to a girl. He visits her and sings stories, *dai-ing* and *unLaLim*. The master of the house will probably succeed in preventing anything improper: he is in honor bound to.

If an engaged girl should fall in love with boy other than her fiancé, her father will observe the fact and will really give a good deal of weight to her feelings in the matter—far more consideration than she would get in any other mountain tribe. If her suitor be not very poor or otherwise objectionable, the father may break her engagement. He will do this by refusing to accept *pias*, the share of meat sent by the boy's family, and by not sending any more himself. If an engagement is broken, the father of the jilted child will wait a few months and then will speak to one of the *mambaga* of the case and tell him he would like the expense of the engagement rites returned to him. This is usually done without any trouble or quibbling. However—

4. Broken engagement; dispute about settlement (ca. *1927*).—Diwag, at the age of about fourteen, was contracted to the daughter of Bangibang, aged about ten. After three years, Diwag manifested dislike for his fiancée. On realizing this attitude, Bangibang sent one of the messengers to Idoba, father of the boy, and asked payment for the pig he had slaughtered in the engagement rites and the return of his presents to the messengers. Idoba returned word that he had a pregnant sow in the care of a man who was feeding it for a share of the litter and that, when the pigs were large enough to be weaned, the sow would be given to Bangibang.

Bangibang was descended from a poor family, had suffered impositions, and didn't relish them. He came for the sow five months later and claimed two of the pigs as interest for having waited so long. A fist fight broke out which passed into a fight with clubs. The relatives of each assembled and joined in. Owing to this fight and further troubles, Bangibang's turbulent life ended in prison. His relatives fled, so that the case is—well, not *ended*, for a case never outlaws in Kalinga, but "unsettled," as the Kalingas say.

Among the Kalingas who really matter, a broken engagement takes the following genteel course:

5. Broken engagement; genteel procedure (1939).—"Mr. A's son [five months old] was contracted to Mr. B's daughter [three months old]. The families exchanged meat and food for fifteen years. Then Mr. and Mrs. B killed a carabao at a *palanos* and did not 'send' to Mr. and Mrs. A. Because of this attitude, Mr. and Mrs. A sent word to the B's that the contract between their son and the daughter of the B's was discontinued.

"Mr. B waited two months after receiving this notification and then he summed up his expenses for the engagement rites and sent his claim through one of the 'messengers.' After that Mr. and Mrs. A, with one companion, carried the pig and blankets to Mr. and Mrs. B. They were invited to partake of food and drink wine. After Mr. and Mrs. A finished eating, Mr. and Mrs. B gave them presents of tobacco and Chinese eating ware, and then they returned to their house."— GASATAN.

If a boy believes that his feeling for the fiancée of another is reciprocated, he tells his father, and, if the latter approves, they may send *banat* in order to encourage the girl and her family to break her engagement. If the girl keeps the *banat*, that signifies that she will do so. The boy's family will not make a formal proposal, however, until the engagement has been announced broken, lest the jilted fiancé spitefully declare *apa* (see p. 90), in which case it would be necessary to delay marriage until the termination of the *apa*, pay what was demanded, or have a fight on their hands.

If an engagement continues in force, the boy will one day tell his father that he would like to marry, or perhaps the father will tell the boy that it is time for him to marry. The father then calls one of the messengers and sends him to notify the girl's father that his son is ready to "unite" with his fiancée. If the girl's family agree, they set a day for the marriage feast, *tugtugao*. The boy now makes daily trips to the mountains and cuts a bundle of firewood each day for about ten days.

On the appointed day all the relatives of the girl will assemble at her house. Each will have brought a contribution to the wedding feast, a parcel of cakes made of glutinous rice (*diket*), a chicken, a jar of basi, a small pig, a load of unthreshed rice—these contributions are called *bunong*. About mid-forenoon, the groom and his cousins of about the same age come, carrying the bundles of wood and followed by the rest of his relatives. Everybody drinks basi and talks affably.

The father of the girl slaughters pigs and chickens, a carabao or, if very rich, possibly five carabaos. Cooking of these and of rice follows. The groom and his relatives are served first and are honored by larger portions than other guests. Toward evening, the groom and his party, bearing the upper halves, the *longos*, of the animals slaughtered, return home. There, the meat is cut into many pieces and distributed among the boy's kin so far as it will reach—to the nearer relationships first, of course. Some of it is sent also to influential people and to the pangats of the barrio.

The two spouses are now called *ka-asauwa* ("newlyweds"), and their parents continue to be called *mangaBeLyan*, just as right after the engagement.

Two or three days later the boy goes to the girl's house and lives with her there for two or three weeks. The two are now called *mandapat*, "uniters." After that he brings her to his house, where his parents give another wedding feast, also called *tugtugao*, similar to that given by the girl's parents. The meat carried home by the girl's relatives is the lower half of the animals slain (*diom*). A few days later the couple go to the girl's house to live.

After three or four months the father of the girl will (unless, by chance, the boy's family has an empty house) have built a house for his daughter, or else he and his household will move into another house and leave the young couple his present one. Their setting-up of a household is called *sumina*, "going separate." At this time, each of the spouses receives possession of his allotment of fields from his parents. This property is called his *tawid*, and, with respect to it, he is called *katotokon*.

After the couple have a child, or after they have lived a year or two without one (and in expectation that the gifts soon to be described will lead to their having one), the girl will invite her kindred, including second cousins and nearer relatives to the house of her father-in-law. There they are feasted and given presents, called *atod*, of gee-strings, blankets, skirts, bolos, spears, head axes, beads, and the like. These gifts clearly correspond to the *hakba* gifts of the Kiangan Ifugao, but their value in the case of the wealthy totals only some seventy pesos, whereas the *hakba* gifts run to a value sometimes of near a thousand pesos in the case of wealthy Ifugaos.

Atod is always paid after a woman's first marriage, sometimes after a second, but never, probably, after a third.

If the couple divorce before *atod* is paid, it must be paid soon after the divorce, and this is true even though the woman shall have demanded the divorce.

Girls are not so frequently forced into marriage among the Kalingas as among the Ifugaos and Kankanai, and, when they are, property considerations are not always the reason. The older generation does not approve of the acculturated modern youth, its working in the mines instead of building rice fields, its gambling, lack of industry, and abandonment of old customs, and this consideration appears to have been uppermost in the following case:

6. *Forced marriage* (*1935*).—Martina, a girl of fifteen, was advised by her parents to marry Baliwag, a widower, "because of his age." They pointed to the fact that Baliwag was an industrious man, experienced, much wiser and of better habits than the young men of today. His only child had married and been allotted Baliwag's field, but, "Never mind," said the parents, "he will acquire." And all the relatives agreed with the parents.

Martina refused "on account of Baliwag's gray hairs" but was whipped and whipped by her mother and advised to obey by her relatives. So finally "she was convinced" and married the man. Now they have three children and are becoming rich. The parents and relatives congratulate themselves on their judgment.

A man is never forced into marriage—even if he has gotten a girl pregnant—except, sometimes, in case of incest (see Cases 98 and 99).

As has been said, nearly always and except when special considerations prevail, the father of the bride builds a house for the young couple or abandons his own in their favor. If he builds, it is the natural thing for him to build alongside his own house. The result is that residence is usually matrilocal within the town and that each barrio is divided into quarters inhabited predominatingly by kindred related through the female line.

Possibly one reason for this matrilocal residence is to be found in the fact that, until a child blesses the union, the safety of the spouses from the kindred of the other in case of a row between their kinship groups does not attain even that relative, comparative "safety" which, it should be kept in mind, must always be meant when that word is used in connection with Kalinga social conditions. For example, if a cousin of the one should kill a cousin of the other, one of the newlyweds might be killed by the victim's kinship group, in accordance with the principle of collective responsibility. "Of course," as one informant put it, *"for courtesy's sake*, they ought to kill some other relative." But, when thoroughly aroused, they might kill the first one they came to, which most likely would be the alien in their midst. Thus the motive of safeguarding the daughters may have contributed to the custom of the father's providing the house and in this way to matrilocal quarters within the region.

If the children die, the spouses are likely to change residence by moving to the husband's quarters and then elsewhere "if their luck should be no better there." Thus Auwiyao, aged thirty-four, has had nine children born to him, of whom only one (aged ten) is living. He and his wife lived first in the quarters of her people in Mabileng, in a fine house built by her father. When the first two children died, their relatives advised them to transfer their residence. Then they went to Kimatan, where Auwiyao's people live. Two more children died, and the relatives advised a transfer to a different barrio. But the children died there, too, so they came back to Kimatan.

HUSBAND AND WIFE

Kalinga marriage may be defined as an alliance entered into by a man and his kinship group, on the one part, and a woman and her kinship group, on the other part, having as its purpose the production and rearing of children. This contract is regarded as a tentative one until children are born to the union; consequently, until a child is born: (1) The household's share in indemnities, weregilds, and *so-ol* (see p. 108) levied and collected by the kinship group of either will remain the separate property of the related spouse. As a matter of courtesy, the share of the wife is given to the husband, but if there be a divorce, it will be reckoned as the wife's property. Conversely, levies by the kinship group will be drawn from the separate property of the related spouse. (2) The property that each spouse brings to the marriage is regarded as strictly his or her separate property.

7. *"Theft" by husband of separate property of wife* (ca. *1907*).— Palikás, a man from Gaang barrio, married a woman of Mabileng, both barrios being in Lubwagan. Both principals were of the *baknang* [well-to-do] class. At the end of three years, they remained childless. One day the man took a chicken belonging to the woman in order to use it as a sacrifice for his mother, who was sick. The woman reported this to her relatives; they assembled, accused the man of theft, and demanded an indemnity. The man's relatives, hearing about the trouble, also assembled, and the two groups were about to fight, but a female relative of Palikás rushed between them with a *gusi*[9] and offered it to the woman's kindred as indemnity.

Palikás was advised by his kinship group to divorce the woman— and did.

Comment: This case is probably extraordinary in that such a trivial cause originated a potentially dangerous situation. Still, it appears that the women of this part of the country regard the most innocent move of the husband to appropriate or dispose of their separate property as about the worst possible insult. H. O. Beyer told me of an incident in the subprovince of Apayao, just to the north: he offered a high price for a woman's tiny knife, which her husband was carrying. The price tempted the husband; he sold it and took the money to his wife, apparently thinking she would be pleased. But she raised a fearful row, called

---

9. *Gusi* are valuable jars of Chinese or sometimes Japanese origin, some of them quite old. They serve to brew and contain rice wine and also have a highly important economic function as means of accumulation of wealth and as high denominations of payment or exchange. Henceforth the word will not be italicized.

her kindred, and it required all the white man's authority to prevent real trouble. On the following day, the wife sold Beyer the knife for the same price her husband had received for it the day before.

If there be no children, a mild degree of incompatibility may lead to divorce. If there are children, the kindred will advise against divorce except for more serious reasons.

If fighting breaks out between the kinship groups of husband and wife, the couple will be "ordered" to divorce. Whether they do so or not will depend on their feelings toward each other. If they do not wish to divorce, they may think best for the sake of safety to quit their own house and go to live in the house of a "good, kind" relative—meaning one who is broadminded and has perspective or who is sufficiently remotely related to the principals in the controversy not to feel deeply about the affair—and live with him until the trouble calms down, giving out that they will be neutral in the affair. Neither kinship group will like this very well.

Violence of a spouse against another probably always requires divorce if there are no living children.

8. *Husband and wife; assault (1940)*.—Tornino and Malkaboy had a child but did not get along well. The child died, and then the situation grew worse, and, besides, Tornino took to drink. One day he was alleged to have choked his wife. The neighbors heard her cries and shouted the news to her kindred. A cousin wanted to attack Tornino, but the people would not let him go into the house. The woman's relatives forced her to divorce her husband.

If a near-relative of one spouse kills or wounds any relative of the other except a third cousin, however, divorce is almost inevitable when there are no children, and very probable when there are.

Kalinga marriage, then, may safely be said to be tentative until a child is born. This event is followed by a series of feasts called *gabok* given by the nearer relatives of the two kinship groups—that is, by the first cousins and brothers and sisters of the child's father and mother—to which the whole kindred of the other side will be invited. Small gifts are made to all who attend, and there is a distribution of meat. These feasts are not merely symbolic—not mere gestures of adoption of the newborn child into the two groups—they go far toward really cementing a union of the two groups thus united in the child. They also mark an entirely new phase of the marriage:

1. The property of the two spouses becomes vested in the child. If the parents subsequently divorce, they must leave all their property for the child or children by this marriage. If they contract a new marriage, they go into it stripped of all their property. Henceforth, so long as the child lives, there can be no such situation as that of poor Palikás, accused of "stealing" his wife's chicken.[10] It may be that now the kinship group of the wife becomes to some extent that of the husband or it may be conceived—and this seems more likely—that, since the property of both parents is vested ultimately in the child, it is the *child's* obligation to furnish sacrifices for his grandmother and that it makes no difference which property is drawn upon to provide them.

But if the only child or all the children of the couple die, then the properties of the spouses revert to their original separate status.

9. Death of only child; reversion of property to separate status (1939).—Sumaal and Ma-aiyao had one child. They decided to build themselves a lowland-style house and, in order to raise the required money, sold property from the inheritances of each of them. Unluckily, the child died and no more children were born to them. Finally Sumaal died. His relatives demanded and received 500 pesos as the part of his inheritance that had gone into the house.

10. According to information more recently gleaned, that case would not have gone so far except that there was bad blood between two kinship groups; consequently, we must regard the action in this instance as extraordinary, although correctly illustrating a point in the custom.

2. With the birth of a child, the husband becomes the manager of both properties, and, to a certain extent, the wife goes into a state of coverture. The husband may sell his wife's property without her consent, though he may be held responsible if he sells it for frivolous reasons. And we must remember that there is a tendency to hold him responsible if he sells it without good reason even with her consent.

10. Husband and wife; "theft" of wife's beads (1940).—Washington married the daughter of Baliwag, by whom he had one child. Seven months ago, he pawned the beads of his wife, worth 300 pesos, for 100 pesos and gambled away the money. His father-in-law and grandmother-in-law (from whom the beads were inherited) complained to the pangats about it, although there was no bad feeling between the husband and wife about the matter. The pangats decided that Washington must repurchase the beads and return them to his wife. It was agreed that the interest should be 50 pesos per year on this amount. Washington is working in the mines to get the money.

Another case, that of Dalpis, is similar to this one in all respects. Dalpis's father, a baknang, deliberated the settlement along with the pangats. Dalpis is working as a policeman.

3. If either spouse be killed after the birth of a child to them, the primary duty of avenging rests on the kinship group of the widowed spouse. If relatives of the slain care to join them, they will naturally be welcomed, but the kindred of the living spouse will initiate and lead the expedition. The vengeance so secured is called *piyokyas* (Ifugao: *numbaluan-na* "for widowing him [her]"). Some informants say that this obligation exists even before the birth of a child, but this is doubtful.

11. Relatives of widow avenge husband's death (ca. 1927).—Saga-ok of Goggotong, a barrio of Lubwagan, was slain in a drunken brawl at the funeral feast of Atumpa by Lintu and Gasatan. These two were arrested and sentenced to eight years' imprisonment. Longao, a brother of Saga-ok's wife, received weregild from the relatives of the two murderers, nevertheless he slew one of them, a woman. He then persuaded his younger brother, Paldao, to take the blame before the court so that he might, while in prison, get a chance to kill or wound Lintu or Gasatan. Longao said that meanwhile he, being the better earner, would earn money for attorneys' fees during the trial-to-be. The younger brother "was convinced" and received a six months' sentence. To his great disappointment, however, Lintu and Gasatan had been moved from Bontok prison by the time he got there and sent to Manila, so he could not kill them.

Remarriage of the widowed.—The widowed spouse must observe mourning, *dinongan*, for half a year—formerly, it is said, for a year. Primary mourning lasts for about half a a month: the widowed spouse must wear old, undyed clothing, stay the whole time in the house, abstain from bathing, eat only soft-cooked rice, and put on no jewelry. During secondary mourning, *langdo*, the same clothes must continue to be worn, the hair must not be cut or oiled, the interdiction on bathing and jewelry continues, and no trips may be made to other regions. The widowed person must conduct himself "timidly" and abstain from dancing and flirtatious conduct.

Infraction of mourning was formerly punished by a fine inflicted by the kindred of the dead spouse. But by paying an indemnity, which was only a carabao for the rich, a person could buy off from the obligation to observe mourning.

The widowed spouse may not remarry for half a year (formerly a year) except upon payment of an indemnity to the kindred of the deceased, called *baiyad*. "The younger generation of Lubwagan, however, do not observe the mourning; they say, 'To hell with those customs! We'll marry within a month if we want to.' "

12. Remarriage of widow (1939).—Baiyugao and Soldao of Lubwagan had been married two years and were without children when Baiyugao died. Soldao, the widow, received a proposal of marriage within two months. She asked permission of her dead spouse's relatives to remarry soon, giving her reasons, which were that she was an orphan and all alone and wanted to have children as soon as possible in order to have somebody to leave her property to. The relatives demanded four blankets, one each for the mother, two brothers, and sister of Baiyugao. She paid and remarried within three months.

The Kalinga custom is thus very lenient in this respect. In one part of Ifugao, the widowed may not remarry within three years and then must pay a *gibu* to the relatives of the dead spouse amounting, for the rich, to about a thousand pesos.

Divorce (*idang*) is less frequent among the Kalingas than among the Ifugaos. There is some advantage on the Kalinga side, no doubt, in this respect, from the almost universal betrothal of infants and the custom of early marriage. The epoch of promiscuity before marriage in the *unsupervised* dormitory (*agamang*, *olag*, and *ebgan* of the Ifugaos, Bontoks, and Kankanai, respectively) has thus, to a considerable extent, been eliminated in Kalinga. This period of promiscuity among the other tribes probably develops a habit that at least makes for discontent "with the one" and leads often to adultery, which among them is a frequent cause of divorce.

Another factor that is not negligible is the greater affluence and amount of property owned by the Kalingas. The Kalingas are able in the sale of property to distribute gifts to their wife's kindred as well as to their own; they are also able, more often than men of other tribes, to exercise that strong tie of alliance, the sharing of meat. In payments of indemnities and weregilds, and in the purchase of fields, the Kalinga calls on his wife's kindred for help just as on his own. Diplomatically he will see that they get a little more than his own kindred when anything is to be divided and will ask a little less from them when a collection is being taken up; whereupon they are likely to insist on giving as much or more than his own people. These relations bring it about that Kalinga marriage allies two kinship groups more firmly than in Ifugaoland. Another factor contributing to the stability of Kalinga marriage, no doubt, is the semi-legalization of mistresses, the *dagdagas* system, and the fact that the Kalinga woman does not divorce her husband very frequently for adultery.

Among any of the mountain peoples, it is possible for almost any cause of disagreement to lead to divorce. The Kalinga division of labor between man and wife is fairly definite: the wife does the greater part of the drudgery of supporting the household. The man shares only in the heaviest part of this such as the "plowing" of the fields by driving carabaos around and around, the harder work of clearing the hill farms and turning their soil, the getting of fuel and the like. His activities lie predominantly in the field of inter- and intra-kinship-group relations, the advancing of the interests of his own and his wife's group, trading, buying and selling, the politics of the community, offense, defense, and the like. An ineptness or sluggishness in the performance of the duties incumbent on either spouse may give rise to rows and nagging which may easily lead to a divorce. If the one insists on divorce, the other has to yield to it. The most frequent cause of divorce is childlessness.

13. Divorce: division of the acquired property (1933).[11]—A married B in 1918; the two lived harmoniously for fifteen years until "one day A thought of separating from B because they have no children." He suggested to her that they had better divorce because possibly by each marrying somebody else one or the other or both of them might have children. Reluctantly the wife consented. A then left B's house. A and B were well-to-do commoners—*baknang*.

A month later, B proposed that they have a division called *bubuwa*, of the acquired property, the *gatang* [each, of course, would keep his own inherited property]. They agreed on a date, and at the time appointed A, with two "influential" relatives, went to the woman's house where she, with two of her "influential" relatives, awaited them.

The influential men first requested A to enumerate the acquired property. He did so. Then they asked B if she had any additions to make or if anything had been included that was her separate inherited prop-

11. This is an especially interesting case because it shows the accumulation of an average household (except that it was childless) for a period of fifteen years.

erty. After a little talk, it was decided that the following property would be divided: 4 rice fields; 2 valuable wine jars; 2 gongs; 1 pair of gold earrings; a string of valuable beads; 5 carabaos; and 30 Chinese bowls. The division was as follows:

> *A's share:*
> 1 rice field in Tokpao, producing 4 *uyon*[12] of rice annually and worth 6 carabaos[13]
> 1 rice field in Pudpud, producing 3 *uyon* and worth 4 carabaos
> 1 gusi worth 7 carabaos
> 1 gong worth 3 carabaos
> 3 carabaos
> 4 pigs
>
> *B's share:*
> 1 rice field in Gapio, producing 4 *uyon* and worth 6 carabaos
> 1 rice field in Benao, producing 2 *uyon* and worth 2 carabaos
> 1 string of beads worth 10 carabaos
> 1 gusi worth 5 carabaos
> 1 pair of gold earrings worth 3 carabaos
> 2 carabaos
> 4 pigs
> 30 Chinese bowls

In this instance, the husband received a value of about twenty-four carabaos and the wife a value of at least thirty, for the thirty Chinese bowls would probably be worth a carabao and might be worth two. That is to say, the total accumulation of husband and wife during fifteen years was equal to fifty-four carabaos or about 1,600 pesos, a little over 100 pesos a year. This husband was generous and gave his wife the larger share; it often happens that the husband receives a little more than the wife on the ground that his work is more effective in "acquiring." Dividers of the property between divorcing spouses receive no fee as they do in Ifugao.

12. *Uyon*—for definition and table of rice currency see p. 92, n. 3.

13. A discrepancy will be noted between this pricing of the fields in carabaos and the modern pricing set forth on p. 110, n. 8. The discrepancy arises from the fact that carabaos were worth three or four times as much in 1918 as now.

14. Divorce; rudeness to husband's relatives.—So long as D and E had no children, E was respectful to D's parents, but when two children had been born to the spouses, E became rude to D's whole kinship group. D warned her that such conduct must cease, else he would divorce her, but E did not mend her ways. Finally, D's relatives advised him to divorce her, and he did.

15. Divorce; rudeness to guests.—It seemed that F and H enjoyed all that is embraced in the Kalinga's concept of good fortune: they had many children and great wealth, and F was on the highway to pangathood, the goal of Kalinga ambition. He was already the holder of two peace pacts, he had *abuyog* or trading partners in several other towns. Consequently, his house was nearly always full of guests; their carousing and drunken babble irritated H, and she was often rude and discourteous to them. Two or three times when F was not at home, she refused the door to guests from other towns.

F divorced her, went forth from her house stripped of all his property, for he had to leave that to their children.[14] He went to live with one of his sisters, who treated his visitors cordially. Having divorced a woman on their account, he was acclaimed by his trading partners and by the people of the towns with which he held the pacts. His brothers and sisters loaned him the things necessary for maintaining his prestige. He took a young and pretty *dagdagas* and became wealthy a second time. He attained pangathood and was able to provide well for the children he had by the *dagdagas*.

During the first year of married life bad omens are not a cause for divorce as they frequently are among the Ifugaos.

Adultery on the part of the husband is never a cause for divorce by the wife unless it should amount to keeping a *dagdagas* while the wife is young and before she may be presumed to be barren. An adulterous wife is not punished otherwise than by being divorced—execution or indemnity falls only on her paramour.

Children always stay with the mother while small, but the boys sometimes go to live with their father when eight or nine years old. There is never any quarrel about custody of children, because both parents always live in the same town.

14. See p. 51.

16. Divorce not recognized (ca. *1928*).—Tupyak and his wife had a child, but they didn't agree well together. They were probably both committing adultery—at least Tupyak asserted that his wife was. However, he did not kill the paramour for fear of being imprisoned, for he was a constabulary soldier and knew the danger of that better than most Kalingas. Also, because he was a constabulary soldier and had regular pay, he was regarded by the women as a good catch; his wife didn't want to lose him and if she was really committing adultery, it was only in order to get even.

Tupyak, however, divorced the woman and married another wife, doing a simple *palanos* sacrifice without much ceremony or formality. Bana, his first wife, did not "recognize" the divorce, "because there was a child," but went to the house of the new wife and stabbed her. Maybe she would not have done this if Tupyak had been living there, but of course he was living in the barracks. "Fortunately, the woman's intestines were not injured," so she recovered.

Taking Tupyak's disposition and employment into consideration and the fact that the primary obligation was on him to avenge his new wife, Bana's relatives, being poor and unable to pay weregilds, considered that they would probably be safe if Bana skipped the country, so they advised her to go to Bontok with her child and try to get employment. She went to a sawmill, and the foreman there, a lowlander, favored her and through his influence with the officials got her a job as gatekeeper on the public highway.[15] Later she married a lowlander and is living in Bontok. There has been no further trouble.

Comment: Non-"recognition" of the divorce may have been based on the consideration that the second marriage, because of its informality, appeared somewhat like a *dagdagas* relation.

THE DAGDAGAS

The root *daga* means "to tarry," "stop on a journey to rest." *Dagdagas*,[16] by derivation, then, may mean one with whom one tarries for a casual relationship while presumably journeying toward marriage or through marriage—in other words, it means a mistress or concubine. It is said that most blood kinships of Lubwagan people with other

15. The roads are so narrow in these mountains that only one-way traffic is possible as a rule. This is governed by gates connected with each other by telephone.

16. The word will not be italicized henceforth.

towns come from this relationship. A Lubwagan pangat or trader who constantly goes to a town with which Lubwagan has a peace pact is likely to contract such an alliance with a girl of the people, contributing secretly in a small way to her support, and her children are recognized as relatives by his legitimate kindred, though they are outside the scope of kinship obligations save only that of blood vengeance.

The dagdagas relationship is condemned for poor men, but for the wealthy it has a semilegitimate, semirespectable status. Wealthy unmarried young men with sometimes only mild censure have a dagdagas in their home town for a few years before settling down to marriage. Sometimes they never marry, but recognize the first dagdagas with whom they have had children as the wife. Thus Maddalum, oldest of Lubwagan pangats, has never married. He had a son by his first dagdagas, and this son was recognized as his heir. He then secured another dagdagas in Ableg, then one in Biga, then one in Balatok, and finally one in his present residence, the Lubwagan barrio of Agsian. He has had one child by each of these. The whole of his great inherited property was allotted to his son by the first dagdagas, who has squandered much of it in unsuccessful campaigns for the office of mayor and is now working in the mines. If Maddalum had, at any time, married and had legitimate children, then the child of the dagdagas would have received only a field or two. If Maddalum had not allotted nearly all his property to the child of the first dagdagas, that is, if he had tried to divide it among his other children by dagdagas, the mother of the first child would have complained. She would have said: "If you marry, I can say nothing, but since the other women are only dagdagas like myself, you cannot give your property to anybody except to my child." And he would not have done so, even if he had wanted to give the other children something, because it would have meant great trouble when the children grew up.

Thus, if there be no marriage later of one of the principals, a dagdagas relationship enjoys the same priority with respect to subsequent relationships of the kind that a first marriage enjoys with respect to subsequent ones. That is to say, all of a man's property goes to the offspring of the first relationship whether that be one of marriage or of dagdagas. The custom discountenances inheritance of two or more households of whatever kind from the same estate.

A man may recognize his dagdagas as his wife, and for this no rites of any sort are necessary or ever performed. Possibly the reason is that the kinship group of the dagdagas are always poor folk and would be unable to celebrate with the pomp that would befit the other spouse.

17. Dagdagas acknowledged as wife (ca. *1932*).—Adung, a rich man or *Kadangyan*, but not reckoned as a pangat because he has never shown qualities of leadership, was not engaged while a child because his mother was reputed to be hard to get along with. He took a dagdagas by whom he had three children. The dagdagas died, and he married the daughter of a pangat. But he acknowledged his dagdagas as his wife and left all his property to the children. He was advised to do this by his kinship group. Had he wished, he might have kept the bulk of his property and given the children of the dagdagas only a little of it.

A young man ought to have the consent of his parents to contract a dagdagas relationship. A gift called *banat*, some beads, perhaps, or cloth or a new sarong, is sent to the girl desired, and if she keeps them, the acceptance of the proposal is indicated. So long as the relationship endures, the boy ought to help his dagdagas economically. If she be killed, he ought to help her kindred avenge her;[17] if she

17. But he is not obligated to do so and, in any case, merely assists her kindred. In the case of a slain wife, there is a primary obligation to avenge (p. 52, Case 11).

becomes ill, he supplies animals for her *posipos* (recovery feast); if she dies, he provides her *utong* (funeral sacrifice).

Mention has been made of the custom followed by Kalinga children of sleeping with children of the same sex and age group in other people's houses, a practice called *maki-obog*. The word *obog* is plainly cognate with *ebgan*, the Kankanai word for the girls' dormitory (Ifugao *agamang;* Bontok *olag*). The Kalinga practice may be regarded as a degeneration of the practice in Bontok and northern Kankanai towns where special dormitories are provided for children of both sexes, in which unengaged children are sexually free. The Kalinga girl, even when not engaged, has no such freedom, since the master and mistress of the house where she sleeps are in honor bound to keep an eye on her. The youths may come, however, to visit her and her companions and banter talk, sing songs, and chant folktales (*unLaLim*). If an attachment begins to form, the master of the house will ask the boy what his intentions are and inform the girl's father. Sometimes commoner parents will consent to a girl's becoming a dagdagas of a commoner, if they are convinced that the boy truly wants the girl for his wife but is temporarily unable for some reason to marry her. Only poor folk will, as a rule, permit their daughters to become dagdagas of the rich, for the rich man will nearly always cast aside his dagdagas and marry a wealthy girl—though *not* always, as we have seen. Sometimes wealthy youths engaged to little girls keep dagdagas until the fiancée grows up.

When that happens, the man may quit his dagdagas entirely, he may break his engagement and cling to the dagdagas, or he may marry and surreptitiously continue to visit the dagdagas. The last course is likely to lead to the stabbing of the dagdagas by the wife. Quite rarely it will happen that the wife will tolerate the union with the dagdagas, in which case the latter becomes a sort of servant and helper of the wife, carrying water, pounding rice, and helping in the fields, but she lives in her own house. If the wife bears no children while the dagdagas does, the man may give a part of his property to the child, but not all. The forms of dagdagas union so far enumerated are more or less condemned by the tribal ethics.

If a man's wife proves barren, however, he will not be censured for taking a dagdagas, rather the contrary. Likewise, the Kalinga has solved another problem by means of the dagdagas institution. An injustice of nature that half the human race suffers under and bitterly resents is the aging of women more rapidly than of men. This creates problems in any society, and they are especially acute among the Kalingas for two reasons: (1) Kalinga spouses are usually of about the same age; (2) Kalinga women work very hard. In addition to all the work done by the other mountain women—patient drudges!—they are excellent housekeepers, wash and scour like Aunt Mary. Together with childbearing, this work ages a woman prematurely at a time when the man, who never hurts himself with hard work, still feels like a gander.

One day the man will state the situation diplomatically: his wife needs a helper and whom would she prefer that he take as dagdagas? There are women divorced because of barrenness, still youngish; there are widows; there are comely wenches of the poor a plenty. The wife will prefer a woman drawn from the first or second class. She will have known that this day was coming, and she will usually grant the youngish old man what he wishes, attaching a string to her consent, namely, either that she shall herself choose the dagdagas or must approve of her. For she will want to choose an agreeable person and a good worker—herself, she can't work like she used to! Even if the husband should insist on choosing from the third class, there is at least the consideration that the brood he is likely to beget cannot lessen the inheritance of her own and will help them in their fighting and avenging.

The dagdagas will henceforth help the wife in her work; the husband will live most of the time with the dagdagas and occasionally with his wife. If the wife dies, the dagdagas, whether she has borne him children or not and without any ceremonializing, *automatically acquires the status of legal wife*. If there are children, they will inherit all that he henceforth acquires; his children by the first have no right to any part of it.

This sort of dagdagas relationship is not at all censured in the case of the wealthy or of men able to maintain two households. The consent of the wife is not necessary—"it is for courtesy's sake that she is asked."

Infidelity of a dagdagas does not constitute adultery. "Men fight only with their fists over a dagdagas—they fight today and tomorrow are friends again."[18] The Kankanai have the same rule with respect to girls in the *ebgan* (girls' dormitory). And the Ifugaos never fight over a girl unless engagement rites have been performed.

If either of the principals in a dagdagas relationship dies, the other will observe the same primary mourning as for a wife—or did until recently. Men incline to cut the period short. If the deceased had both a wife and a dagdagas, both of them mourn for him.

A man may not make his second cousin his dagdagas; if he wants her, he must marry her.

The obligations existing between lover and dagdagas are

18. Except when *apa* has been declared (see p. 90). Furthermore, it is likely that a pangat or influential man would regard seduction of his mistress as a good excuse for adding to his reputation as a killer.

indefinite, and the dagdagas is controlled by her kindred to a greater extent than the wife.

18. Treachery of dagdagas by order of her brothers (pre-American).— A wealthy Ableg man fell in love with a woman of Lubwagan, also wealthy. They would meet wherever they might: sometimes he would come to Lubwagan, sometimes she would go to Ableg. The brothers objected to the union because there was an unsettled feud between the two families. They commanded their sister to appoint a rendezvous with her lover in a field on the Ableg side. The man came, and they slew him.

ADOPTED RELATIVES; SERVANTS; SLAVES

There are no rites or formalities connected with adoption, hence there is no definite line between an adopted child (*inanak*) and a servant (*puyong*) who has served long and faithfully.

Adopted children are preferably related to both spouses and receive a factual recognition of adoption through the words and behavior of the adopters. The length of time a child shall have lived with his adopters and the extent to which he shall have fulfilled the obligations incumbent on a natural son or daughter helps determine the extent to which he shall participate in inheritance of their property. Other factors are the degree of his relationship to his adopters and the amount of the property in question. The adopted child rarely entirely displaces near-relatives in the inheritance—he receives more or less than one-half, which may be taken as the norm.

Lubwagan is a wealthier region than most others surrounding it, so that a good many boys and girls come in from other regions to become *puyong*. *These are safer than any citizen of Lubwagan.* First of all, they are protected by Lubwagan's peace pact with their region. Second, they are protected by their master; he is in honor bound to avenge them should they be wounded or killed, or he will pay *lotok* to whomsoever avenges them. Fornication with the *puyong* is strictly prohibited as regards the master, any member of his household or his relatives, including his first cousins. If the *puyong* should become pregnant by any of these, the master will seize the offender's field and give it to the *puyong* to be her child's. Thus the same prohibitions exist with respect to a *puyong* as between blood relatives. It is a matter of pride with the Kalinga to clothe a *puyong* well. *Puyong* are not overworked and are said to be treated rather better, sometimes, than the children of the family.

If the adopting household be childless, the *puyong* taken will most likely be a relative of one or both of the spouses, and may receive recognition as an adopted child, but it is not always so.

The master is obliged to furnish animals for sacrifices when the *puyong* falls ill or for sacrifice at the funeral should he die.

If the *puyong* acts the part of a natural child toward his adopter, providing sacrifices in sickness or at death, he will, if a relative, receive up to one-half of a childless master's large estate or all of a small one. Nonrelated *puyong* receive less. If the child be too small to be able to attend to these duties, he will not receive much, if anything, unless an older relative performs them for him. The performance of such duties toward a childless person is called *basigan*, from *basig*, "childless," meaning "to childless him [her]."

The Lubwagan region had no slaves, but I heard of a case in which a Naneng master sold a *puyong* from Tanglag into slavery in Pangol, in the eastern part of Kalinga. The slave, on being denied permission to marry in Pangol, escaped and returned to Tanglag.

PARENT AND CHILD

Kalinga parents punish their children by whipping more than do those of the other tribes; still they do not whip their children very much.

The principal aim of parents, the goal of the custom, is to give the children a good start in life. They turn over their entire property to them and often lead lives of downright poverty thereafter. The obligation of the parents of a girl to furnish her a house at marriage has been mentioned.

The outstanding obligations of children to parents are to furnish animals for sacrifice (*posipos*) when they are ill and, at funeral feasts, to sacrifice animals for the soul to take with it to the other world. Children are also obligated to take the parents into the household when they become old and feeble.

There are the usual obligations to avenge that exist between near-kindred and, in addition, the obligation on the part of the child never to eat with a slayer of his parent. It is believed that if he should do so he would die very soon.

THE KINSHIP GROUP

As has been said, the kinship group embraces all of a man's relatives who are descended from an individual's eight pairs of great-great-grandparents (see Fig. 3). These he calls *mana-agi;* more remote ones he calls *kapo-ón,* "descended from one ancestor." It is true that this word covers the kinship group as well as distant relatives outside it, but it often has this special sense of designating only those outside the kinship group.

The kinship group of any individual consists of the kinship groups of his parents *minus* their third cousins—these become to him *kapo-ón* (Ifugao: *nabaiyat*). Thus the kinship group progresses through time by constantly uniting with another and by molting its periphery at each such uniting. These Kalinga and Ifugao kinship groups are in very many respects similar to the groups of western Europe that resulted from the decay of patrilineal clans, espe-

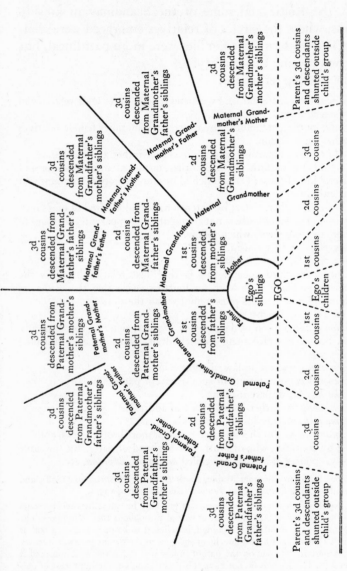

FIG. 3.—Diagram of Kalinga kinship group. Note that if there has been no intermarriage of ancestors, none of the groups of cousins is related to any other group of equal degree, but only to Ego and his brothers and sisters. Dotted lines show how the outer circle of a parent's cousins are shunted outside the child's kinship group in each succeeding generation.

cially the Keltic and some of the Scandinavian kinship groups, where the circles of relatives embraced were similar.[19] The western large families were more patrilineal, but they were losing this quality.

The kinship terms are:

1. *á-ma*, father, stepfather by courtesy; sometimes male relatives of father's generation.

2. *í-na*, mother, stepmother by courtesy; sometimes female relatives of mother's generation.

3. *ul-i-tég*, brothers, sisters, and cousins of father and mother.

4. *á-po*, (1) grandfather, grandmother, or more remote ancestor and the lateral kin of these; (2) grandchild or more remote descendant and the lateral kin of these.

5. *sun-úd*, brother, sister; by extension, lateral kindred of one's own generation. The second use is not frequent; it is apparently yielding to the more definite terms which follow.

6. *ka-pín-san*, first cousin.

7. *ka-pí-du-a*, second cousin.

8. *ka-pit-lu*, third cousin: this is the "last relationship," as the Kalingas say. There is no word for fourth cousin other than *kapo-ón*, which includes all degrees more remote than the third.

9. *an-ák*, son, daughter.

10. *am-o-nák-on*, son or daughter of brother, sister or cousin of any degree. Sometimes also their grandchildren, who may also be called *á-po*.

11. *man-ú-gang*, son-in-law, daughter-in-law.

12. *ku-má-mang*, relatives of spouse except parents-in-law.

13. *ka-tu-gáng-a*, parent-in-law.

14. *ma-lóng-ag*, father-in-law (used in address).[20]

15. *mad-án*, mother-in-law (used in address).[20]

16. *man-sun-úd*, brother and sister, two or more brothers, two or more sisters; by courtesy, wife of brother or husband of sister. By the same courtesy, spouses of cousins are called *kapinsan, kapidua*, etc.

19. See Sir Henry Sumner Maine, *Early History of Institutions* (1878), and W. Gronbech, *The Culture of the Teutons* (English trans., 1931).

20. Neither father-in-law nor mother-in-law may be called by their personal names—a prohibition that is almost universal throughout the Philippines. The infringer of this prohibition, in Kalinga, is believed to be punished by a boil or carbuncle that will not heal unless he or she goes to the parent-in-law, confesses, and asks pardon, whereupon the parent-in-law will touch the affliction, and it will get well. The Ifugaos do not have this prohibition but are in process of borrowing it from the lowlanders. They say they are "just now learning to show respect" to the spouse's parents.

17. *hiú-man*, brothers and sisters born of the same mother whether of the same father or not; hence, sometimes, half-brother or half-sister on the mother's side.

18. *ter-bú-Log*, brothers or sisters on the father's side.

19. *mang-a-Bél-yan*, persons whose children have married.

20. *ag-ga-bák*, bastard; child of dagdagas.

21. *dag-dag-ás*, mistress, concubine.

22. *lo-Lák*, generation; *sinLoLak*, one generation; also *sinpaRsoo*, one generation.

23. *pu-tút*, incest; also *ina-aso-da*—"they did like dogs." I doubt that the first is a Kalinga word. I made repeated inquiries among the Ifugaos, Kankanai, and Bontok without being able to elicit any word for incest.

There are no designations for the step-relationships. Usually the person is called by name; otherwise he is called by the term for the corresponding natural relationship.

The primary duty of members of the kinship group is to support each other in controversies and to avenge in case a kinsman is slain or wounded. If no other factor were operative than the blood tie, then that duty would be strong in proportion to the amount of common blood. It would rest most strongly on brothers and sisters, one-half as strongly on first cousins, one-fourth as strongly on second cousins, and so on. But there are inherent contradictions in kinship organization whereby such factors as personality of the individual, his wealth, prestige, "influence," reputation, co-operativeness and the like modify the loyalty of kinsmen to these obligations. The nearer the kinship, the less are the obligations imposed by the blood tie modified by these other factors; conversely, the more remote the kinship, the greater is their influence.

Only brothers and sisters have the same kinship group, and, after they have married, their affinal allies are different. The members of any individual's kinship group are held together only by their common tie to him and his brothers and sisters and function as a group only when they act in behalf of these. There are cousins on the father's side and cousins on the mother's side who are not related to each other. There are four different groups of second cousins, the descendants from as many groups of great-uncles and great-aunts, and there are eight groups of third cousins, descended from as many groups of lateral ascendants, unrelated to one another except as there may have been inbreeding, as, of course, there always is. Two facts follow from this: (1) a man who backs any relative except his brother in controversy, must act with other persons who are not akin to himself; (2) controversies may arise and killings may occur within a man's kinship group, that is, between persons or groups not themselves related, but both related to him. Both facts constitute an internal contradiction in the kinship principle.

Furthermore, in any crisis, controversy, or necessity of determining the group's policy, there are certain to be all sorts of divided and contrary counsels—hence a situation that favors lending an ear to the wisest, boldest, most influential, and most resourceful among the relatives. Thus a leadership is set up. In the normal probabilities of the case, the leader will rarely be the principal in the situation or even one of his brothers—he will likely be a cousin, possibly a distant one. Thus, the tribal principle of social organization, the principle that loyalty, zeal, and interest in a kinsman's cause are in proportion to amount of blood in common with him is to an extent overleaped. Likewise, in any case of such leadership, many of those who act for a kinsman will be entirely unrelated to the leader, and this amounts to a subversion of the tribal principle.

The second fact tends still more definitely to strengthen the territorial principle of social organization. Suppose two of ego's second cousins who are not related to each other become involved in a controversy. The two principals are related to ego, but each has a host of relatives who are not, some of them anxious to add to their laurels by killing, *and these are likely to kill ego!* Indeed, there would be approximately three times as many kindred of the principals to whom he would be fair game as there would be who would pass him by, since some three-fourths of a second cousin's relatives are not related to ego. And when the vengeance is tossed to the other side, he is in danger from that side, and so on—in danger from whichever side holds the ball in that game of pitch and toss.

Now in such a situation, it can well be imagined that ego is strong for peace. He pleads, threatens, coaxes, wheedles, and runs to the pangat, to anybody, related or not related, who has "influence." He usually does succeed in preventing further bloodshed in his kinship group and in saving his own skin, but for the kinship principle it is a Pyrrhic victory, for he has appealed to the territorial principle of social organization to attain these ends.

We have noted certain contradictions in the kinship principle of social organization which weaken it or betray it into the hands of its rival, the territorial principle. But the society also has complexes of factors and institutions which bolster and maintain it. The more important of these in Kalinga are: (1) blood vengeance; (2) collective procedure and responsibility in controversies, with assessments on kindred for the purpose of raising weregilds, indemnities, purchase price of property, or distribution of these among kindred when they are received; and (3) sharing of meat.

The nature and operation of the first two will appear concretely many times as this work develops, so that there is no need of detailed consideration now. It may, however, be pointed out that the first is quite centripetal in relation to the kinship group. Avenging is a dangerous business, and, since the obligation is strongest on the near kindred, the natural tendency is to leave it to them. This centripetal tendency is compensated in Kalinga society by an institution called the *lotok:* a field must be given by the nearest relatives of the slain to the avenger, and it is a disgrace to the kinship group if this gift goes outside the kinship group.

The second obligation also contains its own compensations for certain centripetal features inherent in it; there might be a tendency to object to contributing to a distant relative's business deals or indemnity, but there is none to sharing with him when there is an intake. Then, too, the collective nature of responsibility makes the distant relatives uneasy in case a relative has slain a man, for any of them, however distant, provided they are within the group, will serve for vengeance. Hence common peril draws them together. Consequently, there is rarely any trouble in inducing the contribution of distant kindred toward buying off—besides, intake and output of weregilds may be expected in the long run to balance each other. In general, the procedure holds that the third cousins of the offender will buy off the third cousins of the offended, second cousins will buy off second cousins, and so on.

As will appear later, rank and influence and wealth—the success Kalinga society offered the individual—were to a very great extent attained through killing people. Killing, consequently, was frequent, so that the kinship group received a constant drill in co-operation through the necessity of retaliation, or collection or paying of weregilds. But, while this strengthened the kinship group as a social unit (and so the kinship principle of social organization in the society), it also strengthened the territorial principle. For killing made everybody afraid of the killer—that is, it increased the killer's control over the people of a locality and promoted an incipient territorial or political organization, whose functionaries were the greatest killers. But this selection of killers for positions of honor and power reacted to incite more killing and so to strengthen the kinship principle. Thus, as between these two principles, there was a deadlock, with each strengthening the other, and with the territorial principle (which, be it said, is the progressive one) unable to achieve a preponderance over its rival so long as its functionaries were so selected. This fact will appear clearly in the section that deals with the territorial unit, the region.

The third obligation is another powerful tie in holding the family together. To a Kalinga a ritual gift arising from family relationship is a far more powerful bid for loyalty and co-operation than one based on kindness of heart or benevolence, which latter two do not exist in his own society and only puzzle him when some soft American manifests them. Meat distribution is mainly on a kinship basis, although, if a buffalo is butchered, a man will include his immediate neighbors, the pangats, and all visitors who come for a share. We shall describe it in some detail, if only to emphasize its importance.

The Kalinga kills a carabao, as a rule, in this way: One man holds up its head by means of a rope passed through its nose and around the horns. Another, with a single stroke, slashes its throat with a bolo. The carcass is usually allowed to lie for an hour or two, then it is rolled on a bedding of palm or banana leaves to be cut up.

Butchering begins with cutting off the legs. If one or more legs are to be sent to a family or families of fiancés of the children of the household, two chicken feathers are stuck into the leg at the place where it was severed from the torso. The legs not so allotted, together with the rest of the carcass, are cut up, and pieces approximately equal in nutritive materials are strung on flexible bamboo spits, *ilang*—four or five men will have prepared them just before the animal is slain. These are about 55 centimeters long. One end is sharp, and below that, for about 10 or 12 centimeters the woody portion is not trimmed off, so that the spit will be stiff and can be thrust through the meat. The woody part is trimmed off all the remainder of the length, however, and the other end is tied into a loop which keeps the meat from falling off. Two men butcher the carcass and throw hunks of as nearly equal desirability as possible to two men who string them each on a spit, after which they pass the end of the spit through the loop at the end. They tie two such pieces together and hang them over a pole. As one of the butchers cuts up the legs, another cuts away the sternum of the animal and opens thorax and belly. In these days the skin is cut off in irregular pieces and thrown to the dogs and hogs, but formerly it was saved to be eaten by the people when they should become meat-hungry. The butcher of the carcass cuts off small hunks of perhaps two kilos of the better meat (to which are added small pieces of liver) for the near-relatives, and these, as has been said, are hung on a pole. Larger weights of joints, pieces of the enormous stomach, intestines, lungs, spleen, and so on, less desirable portions, are also spitted but are left lying on the palm leaves. These shares are for visitors, second and, possibly, third cousins. Occasionally, one of the butchers (these are usually the givers of the feast) will cut off an especially large hunk of first-class meat and hand it to a bystander with directions for its delivery to a pan-

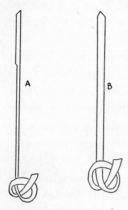

FIG. 4.—The *ilang* spit, used in meat distribution. *A*, Side view; *B*, Front view.

gat or an especially influential man, and if the family of the
fiancé of one of his children is not, in this particular feast,
entitled to a whole leg, then a large hunk of the very choicest meat will certainly be sent them. Aside from these ex-
ceptions, the meat is entirely cut up before it is distributed.
The host takes the head and, if the feast has as its excuse
an illness, the patient receives the brains.[21]

At a *posipos* feast for an old woman, two grandsons
slaughtered two half-grown carabaos. There were eighty-
six spits of first-class meat hung on poles for the brothers,
sister, uncles, and first cousins of the two brothers and their
wives. About forty spits containing heavier pieces of lower
quality were distributed to second cousins and visitors. At
another feast of this nature, where only one carabao was
slaughtered, there were sixty-two spits for the near-relatives of husband and wife.

The host himself distributes the meat, first disposing of
that which lies on the palm leaves, calling the guests to
receive and carry away their portion. Then he calls his
relatives, many of whom will not be present, and gives
meat to those who come forward, with shares for absent
relatives living in their neighborhoods and directions for
their delivery. The meat is received indifferently, without
any expressions of gratitude, sometimes appraisingly as if
the receiver wished, like the small boy, that it were an
orange instead of an apple. Bystanders sometimes protest,
and always they are shouting suggestions or directions.
The host looks at them and at his relatives as if he wished
they were in the Americano's hell, and occasionally responds to a remark with a sneering glance or snort of contempt as if to say, "a lot *you* amount to"; he certainly considers them nuisances to be gotten rid of as soon as possible. The preliminary private rites of an Ifugao about to

21. See Pl. XX for meat distribution.

give a prestige feast frankly express this attitude. The Kalinga doubts, perhaps, the power of even the gods to alleviate the pother.

The Kalingas have no specific prestige feast such as the *bumaiyah* and *uyauwe* of the Ifugaos, the *pachit* of the Nabaloi, or the *bumaiyas* of the Kankanai, nor do they have that form of rivalry in prestige which expresses itself in destruction of property, a form that previously existed among the Kiangan Ifugaos: rivals in prestige there would break precious jars, pulverize precious beads, throw gold earrings into the lake; impoverish themselves in the attempt to outdo each other in destruction. But, with the Kalinga, nearly every feast is, in a sense, a prestige feast.

In these prosperous days since rhinderpest was stamped out by the colonial government and of the consequent multiplication of buffaloes, these days of hitherto undreamed-of wages in the mines and of importation of pigs by truckloads, the distribution of meat is so frequent that nearly every Lubwagan family has meat twenty to thirty times as often as formerly, and "influential men" have more every day than their households can eat. In a sense, distribution of meat is tending to follow the development of the treating custom—you treat because you have to keep your end up, treat so as not to lose prestige rather than to gain it.

Still, as has been said, distribution of meat has always been and still is a powerful institution in holding the kinship group together. It is also a powerful lever for lifting a man to eminence, a way to influence that no ambitious man can neglect. Nothing else perhaps, especially in the old days when the whole population was meat-hungry, could so poignantly demonstrate a man's greatness as his ability to reach the third cousins and the rest of the folk of his barrio in his distribution of meat. Thus, paradoxically but understandably, the more remote the relationship between giver and receiver, the stronger the impression made by the gift. And this situation constitutes yet another slap in the face to the blood tie: it puts the third cousin who is rich on a higher pedestal than the first cousin who is poor.

Meat distribution is, no doubt, a continuation from a necessary institution of hunting life, as is shown by the fact that the ancient hunting terms are still used in it, and it is still made necessary by the lack of any good means of preserving meat. But even the introduction of refrigeration probably would not weaken it much.

It is a mistake not to recognize a powerful, though possibly an unconscious, economic motive in the striving for prestige. Prestige facilitates exploitation, and exploitation is a concomitant of and probably a strong factor in the decay of the tribal or kinship social tie and the development of the territorial one. To the individual in a primitive society, prestige has an economic value relatively as great as monopoly and political power in our own society. Indeed, it contains some of the essential attributes of both of these.

INTRAFAMILY TORTS AND PROCEDURE

Only when an offense is committed by a brother or sister against a brother or sister can there be a true instance of intrafamily tort. If the father wrongs a child, the mother and her kindred are offended and will retaliate not on the father probably, but on his group (see Case 80), or if a cousin wrongs a cousin, half the relatives of the offender are not related to him and will punish him or one of his kindred. When a wrong is committed by a brother against a brother, however, the obligation of the whole kindred, all equally related to the brothers, to defend the offender neutralizes their obligation to act in behalf of the offended. In such a case, in Ifugao, the offense is unpunished. In Kalinga, however, the procedure has risen somewhat above

the kinship principle, and the father (or father's brother if
the father be dead) settles the matter as he deems best.
The brothers and sisters of the principals, however, remain
neutral.

19. Intrafamily tort; wounds (1935).—Siwasiu is an indolent moron
who goes around town looking for Americans. If he sees one, he salutes
and asks for *tanso* [5-centavo coin]. He has two brothers and a sister.
His oldest brother frequently used to admonish him that he ought to
help in the field work, especially in view of the fact that he is a heavy
eater, and threatened him that he should have nothing to eat unless he
helped produce. One day, exasperated at the boy's refusal to help, the
brother whipped him with a stick. Later, when this brother was sitting,
not suspecting danger, Siwasiu slashed him in the arm with a bolo, and
again, when he turned his face, in the mouth, then ran away. The
constabulary was called and arrested Siwasiu; he was sentenced to be a
servant in their barracks for six months—and learned to salute.

Pangat Galamoy, brother of the dead father, consulted with the
other pangats of the barrio and decided that Siwasiu's fields should be
given to his brother and that his share of the family heirlooms should be
sold and used for the purchase of animals for sacrifice in the recovery
rites for his brother's wounds.

Q. What attitude did the brother and the sister of the principals
take?

A. They were neutral—how else could they be?

Q. Why did Galamoy consult the other pangats?

A. He wanted to be sure that his settlement of the case would not be
criticized.

Comment: May we not see in Galamoy's consultation with the pangats
an incipient jurisdiction of the territorial unit even in intrafamily torts?
(See also Case 94.)

Where the offense involves first cousins, the situation is
more complicated. In the following examples, let A and Z
stand for unrelated strains of blood; let L stand for a strain
into which each has married; and let "–" stand for any
strain other than A, L, or Z.

Then the children of A and L are AL . . .'s, and the children of L and Z are LZ . . .'s, and the children of A and Z
are AZ . . .'s. The AL . . .'s, the LZ . . .'s and the AZ . . .'s
are mutually related first cousins.

Now suppose that one of the AL . . .'s kills or wounds his unmarried first cousin LZ.[22] According to an idiosyncrasy of Kalinga viewpoint, killing and wounding are regarded as identical—or at least equivalent. In the ordinary speech, the same word, *patoi*, meaning "kill" is used to cover both offenses, whereas the word which properly means "wound" is a strictly surgical term. And there is no doubt that in the theory and practice of the custom law, both offenses are identical.

Besides the mutually related first cousins mentioned above, four groups, each containing cousins of the first, second and third degrees are involved: (1) the A–'s, A—'s and A——'s; (2) the Z–'s, Z—'s and Z——'s; (3) the L–'s, L—'s and L——'s; and (4) the AZ's, A—Z's and A——Z's. We oversimplify the combinations of blood in the second and third cousins for the sake of brevity.

If the offense should be settled by paying weregilds,[23] then the A–'s would pay the Z–'s. It is true that the AZ's and L–'s would be liable to pay on account of their kinship with the offender AL, but they would be entitled also to receive weregilds on account of their kinship with the LZ's. Kalinga custom commits no such absurdity as to take from Peter in order to pay Peter.

Does this mean that AL, the culprit and the other AL . . .'s, his brothers and sisters, do not have to pay the LZ . . .'s? Yes, the good L-half does not pay, and, no, the accursed A-half does.

But there is another payment that can hardly be avoided

22. We specify that the slain be unmarried, because, if he were married, the primary obligation to avenge him would lie on his wife's people. This rule of custom functions to bolster kinship society by helping it out of just such predicaments as we are about to portray—although sometimes out of the pot into the fire.

23. Kalinga weregilds are multiple and individual—they are not the single, more or less standardized ones, paid or received by kinship groups as units, with which our European ancestors compounded their killings.

where kindred are concerned—the *pakan* (p. 242) for making peace and removing the taboos against eating with enemies. Weregilds diminish with increase of common blood, but *pakan* increases in that direction. The total of a half-weregild plus a half-*pakan* when offender and offended are full cousins is equivalent to just about the full weregild that would be paid between unrelated persons. That equivalent the AL's would have to pay. It is quite logical.

Let us suppose, though, that the case be not settled by paying weregilds. Suppose that the A–'s and AL's consider their kinsman was justified in killing LZ, as they might if LZ had had an adulterous relation with AL's wife. Retaliation is now in order, for the Z–'s will be of a different mind.

In Ifugao, where the kinship principle is overwhelmingly predominant, and where weregilds are accepted only when there are exceptional, alleviating circumstances, the following might occur:

a) A Z– might kill an A–, an L–, or an AL, but not an AZ or LZ.

b) An L– might kill an A–, a Z–, or an AZ; he would not kill another L, so that so far as all L's are concerned, the principal and his brothers and sisters, the AL . . .'s, are safe.

c) An AZ would kill L–'s but not A–'s, Z–'s, LZ's, or AL's; here, too, the principal and his brothers and sisters are safe, as also are the A–'s and in fact all first cousins of the principal except the L–'s.

d) An LZ would kill only A–'s.

But in Kalinga weregilds are usual settlement. Accordingly a man who decides to avenge LZ will reason thus: "The A's and AL's would not pay weregilds, but they will accept them." Unless he acts impulsively (and the very expectation of paying weregild makes this less likely), he selects for his victim some one of AL's kindred who has few near relatives to buy off, for to buy off a brother requires four or five times as much as to buy off a first cousin, and to buy off a first cousin two or three times as much as to buy off a second cousin. The requirements of vengeance are as well satisfied with a second cousin as with a nearer kinsman, and even a third will answer, although not so well. Small wonder that Kalingas want large families!

No man who intends vengeance publishes his identity or his intention to act advisedly; consequently, all who are liable to vengeance are on tenterhooks. And this is especially true of the L's and the AZ's, who are in double peril —likely to be killed on either the pitch or the toss. And so they act as mutual kindred always do—they stimulate the activity of the pangats in every possible way and cooperate with them to bring a peaceable settlement.

Thus we see that an offense involving kindred of any degree beyond that of brothers makes the case one of intergroup rather than of intrafamily procedure.

It is noteworthy that the offender and his brothers and sisters are the safest individuals of all. Only the Z's, not including the AZ's would kill them. That it should be so proves how welded kinship society is to collective justice. It cannot fix individual responsibility. It is therefore a very poor agency of public order.

If one viewed the situation without *almost* fully realizing the strength of intrenched tradition—I believe none of us ever *fully* realizes it—he would wonder that the kinship principle had not long since gone down before the territorial one, so shot through is it with contradictions.

Effective range.—Theoretically, the kinship group includes the third cousins; in practice the tendency is toward a narrowed group. Marriage is antithetical to kinship solidarity, for the reason, partly, that it introduces a different kind of tie into the group, also second cousins may marry, so that in this respect the group is narrowed to the first cousins. Meat distribution except when made by the wealthy, includes only the influential among the second cousins (though in this respect probably it must formerly have been still narrower on account of the limited supply of meat). Collective responsibility for an offense reaches to the third cousins, although it is considered in bad taste to kill a man's third cousins for his offense. Active support and backing to a kinsman involved in controversy hardly reaches beyond second cousins. Forbearance in case of tort hardly reaches the third cousins and is pretty thin when it reaches the second. Distribution of the proceeds from the sale of fields and valuable heirlooms includes the more influential of the second cousins only when the sale is large. Weregilds ought always, theoretically, to include the third cousins, but the payments to them are individually only about one-fiftieth that to the offended principal or to one of his brothers; often they do not receive them. Assessments for raising weregilds have the same range.

Alienship of a kinsman, in Kalinga society, strengthens the kinship tie instead of weakening it, as in Ifugao. Owing to the dagdagas system, to asylum granted occasional fugitives in the past, and to a very few deliberate intermarriages, nearly everybody has "relatives" in foreign regions of so remote degrees that he would consider them utterly unrelated if they lived in his own. When the Talgao woman previously mentioned came to Lubwagan with her infant son six generations ago, some of their relatives fled to Balatok instead. Consequently, the Lubwagan people have "kindred" there. Shortly before the coming of the Americans, Lubwagan broke the pact with Balatok, invaded its territory, and a battle was fought in which Lubwagan got the worst of it and fled. Balatok pursued. Some of the Lubwagan people shouted a plea to their Balatok relatives that they persuade their coregionists to stop the pursuit. The Balatok relatives did so. Ifugaos of so distant degree would not have. The regional endogamy and political organization of the Kalingas throw the accent on any kinship at all in foreign parts.

OBLIGATION OF HOST

A host is obligated to avenge the slaying or wounding of his guest. This obligation holds with respect to citizens of his own region only while they are at his house, but it applies to citizens from foreign parts so long as they are within the bounds of the host's home region. The obligation is probably based on the consideration that the guest is for the time being a member of the household.

20. Obligation of giver of feast (1940).—"Last year a member of A's family died. At the funeral feast, B told C about the great wealth of his own family and especially about their bravery. He mentioned the fact that his [B's] cousin wounded C's brother, and 'they are not afraid, as they are all rich.' C could not endure more of these rough words and stabbed B in the groin. A, at whose house this occurred, has been unable to wound a relative of C so far, as they are very watchful. Most likely, he intends to wound from ambush, by hiring one of his relatives or by coming to them while aimlessly swinging his work bolo and then suddenly springing upon one of them."

Informant explained that he did not give names because he did not want to interfere in a matter that did not concern him. He further considers that the custom is a good one and does not want me to be able to frustrate it.

Q. Did not C pay weregilds?

A. Yes. Weregilds were paid B and his relatives. But A, the host, refused to accept a weregild.

Q. Why was that?

A. The host dishonors himself if he accepts weregild. He must kill or wound.

Comment: The Ifugaos are a little more liberal in this regard. The Ifugao host is obliged either to collect it or to avenge. If he does not, he must himself pay a *tokom* to the aggrieved group. No such payment is due in Kalinga if the host fails to avenge.

Q. What do you mean when you say "hiring one of his relatives"?

A. It is not hiring exactly, but he is rich, and they know the *lotok*[24] will be large.

24. See p. 72; see also Cases 57 and 58.

Chapter III

THE CUSTOM LAW OF THE ECONOMIC RELATIONS

THE UNOWNED

THE game of forest and field, the fish of the streams, wild vegetation, and trees that have not been planted are unowned and ordinarily anybody may take of them or appropriate them as his own property. This is also true of lands that are not held in private ownership and of waters not so held or subject to flowage rights. Whether or not forests fall into this category is not clear; a powerful individual can certainly appropriate them, but a weaker one cannot.

But opposition to an attempted appropriation would certainly come not from the community as a whole but from individuals who had been accustomed to use the forest and who would challenge the attempt to keep others out rather than the power to appropriate. The fact that bounds between regional states are accurately defined is no argument that wild lands are communally owned, for the bounds are set not in the least degree for the purpose of defining territory but in order, for the purposes of the peace pact, to define the inhabitants of the regional state. Nowhere is there any overt assertion of ownership by the community or any move by it to intervene against appropriators. Possibly a faint beginning of community control, and so an assertion of ownership, may be seen in some aspects of *apa*, to be hereafter described. The regulations

of custom regarding appropriation might possibly be regarded as an assertion of a tenuous sort of community
ownership, but in this connection it must be remembered
that an appropriator's claim is never challenged by the
community but only by another individual. Community
ownership has, no doubt, to be developed, just as any other
property conception. Probably there is a vague feeling on
the part of the people that the lands *appertain* to them as a
community, but it has not crystallized into a sense of community *ownership*. Increasing scarcity of tillable and forest
lands may in the future initiate strict rules limiting private
appropriation and simultaneously a sense of community
ownership.

Hunting, fishing, and collection of wild products.—The
hunting grounds of every region are open to every Kalinga.
War between two regions closes the grounds of the one to
hunters from the other only in so far as the latter fear to
hunt near hostile villages. That there is no formal closure is
shown by the fact that treaties renewing a peace pact never
mention renewal of permission to hunt.

Wherever game be brought down, whether in alien or in
domestic territory, the hunters must give a share to any
inhabitants of that place who, having heard the baying of
the dogs and the cries of the hunters, "come out" to participate in the kill—provided they come before the process of
cutting up the carcass has begun. This proviso functions to
avoid the confusion that would result if hunters had to re-
vise their plans of division for every late-comer. By this
limitation and by a taboo against giving away any part of
the upper half of the carcass (thorax, neck, head) the
hunters are protected against having to give away an in-
ordinate portion of the carcass. Infraction of the taboo, it
is believed, would adversely influence the future hunting
spirit of the dogs. The shares given are very small unless

the quarry should have been a large animal. Persons whom the hunters meet on the way home must also be given a "share."

When hunters, whether of the home region or aliens, are pursuing game, any man from anywhere has the right to spear the quarry, but he must not touch the carcass until the pursuers come up.[1] If he should carry it away or begin cutting it up, the hunters would be justified in seizing his rice field or a carabao. The "comer-out" who spears an animal is entitled to its loins.

Division of the carcass between the hunters is on the following basis: (1) each "dog" (understand "dog's master") is given two shares; each dogless hunter is given one share. These shares are called *ilang*, which really means the spit on which a chunk of meat is strung (see p. 74). The dogs really receive the lungs, hide, and bones. If the share of each hunter is very small, as when the animal is small and many gifts are made to "comers-out" or on the way home, the hunters may pool their shares and cook together. If neighbors come to participate in the feast, portions given them are called *bilay*. A share given uncooked to a neighbor or relative in person is called *ilang*, but, if it is sent him by another, it is called *pias*. The same terms are used in connection with the distribution of the meat of slaughtered domestic animals.

21. Hunting quarrel (1915).—Dananao hunters followed their quarry into the region of Sumadél. Folk of the latter region ran out and killed

1. The ancient civil law gave the hunter ownership only when he had actually taken the animal; before that he had no vested interest in it. The common law gave the hunter a vested interest when he should have wounded an animal, provided he remained in pursuit of it. American decisions and statutes incline to follow the civil law, although some follow the common (A. C. Train, *Mr. Tutt's Case Book*).

From the practical standpoint of bringing down the game, especially in the tropical jungle, and of avoiding altercations, the Kalinga law is much the best provision. It probably holds among all the mountain tribes; I know it does among the Ifugao and some of the Bontoks.

the pig. When the Dananao hunters came up, the Sumadél men were already burning off the hair. Dananao protested. The Sumadél people claimed that they were the original hunters. Dananao people pointed to their dogs as evidence that they had been hunting. "But we also have dogs," said the Sumadél folk. This so enraged the Dananao hunters, knowing, as they did, that the dogs had followed their masters from the village, that they attacked the Sumadéls: two Dananao were wounded, one of whom died; two Sumadéls were wounded.

Fishing is not economically important. Men may fish anywhere, even in streams that lie entirely within a foreign region. It is said that sometimes there are objections on the part of the citizens, but that the pact-holder shames them, saying, "Why—did you plant the fish? Was it not the god of nature that planted them? Instead of prohibiting our friends from fishing, better go and help them!" In the same way, there is no restriction on the rights of aliens to collect wild foods. Even lumber and firewood may be taken in any unowned forest of a foreign region. However, the rights of both residents and of aliens are subject to interruption because of the privilege called *apa*.

"*Apa*," *withdrawal from public use.*—The word probably means "prohibition to use," and I suggest that it is a cognate of the Polynesian *tapu* and of Ifugao *paowa*, each of which means essentially that. As applied to unowned lands and localities, it appears to have one root in the concept that the death of a relative establishes a temporary right over the place where he died. It has also become connected with head-hunting.

Apa is declared on that portion of streams that lies within the regional state, on bamboo clumps, forests, fruit trees, unowned lands and, sometimes, on women. Its application is presumptively temporary, but with respect to bamboo clumps, at least, it sometimes becomes permanent and amounts to appropriation. In theory, too, it may be declared by anyone, but failure to enforce it results in making a declarer not only ridiculous but afflicted with enlarged testicles (*mabutu*) besides, so that in practice only powerful men (pangats or near-pangats) do really declare it.

The imposer of *apa* declares the withdrawal from common use either by *purdus* (or *peiLdus*), a runo reed with its blades tied into a loop (which is the usual sign of ownership or prohibition against trespass) or else by *sangi*, the preferred sign, since it is the more permanent. *Sangi* is a bamboo set in the ground with its upper end split and holding a twig crossways or else the jawbone of a pig.[2]

1. *Streams.*—Usually *apa* is declared on fishing in streams between the place where a person was drowned and the place where the body was recovered. Sometimes the declarer proclaims that the stream will be closed until he or a relative takes a certain vengeance.

22. Apa *on stream; infraction; ignorance no excuse; punishment* (ca. *1910*).—The wife of Pangat Dukaiyag of Magnao was drowned in a creek. He declared *apa* on all that portion of the stream that lay in Magnao territory and kept the stream closed for ten years until he himself opened it by going and fishing in it.

Fish multiplied in the stream, and some Ableg travelers, knowing nothing of the *apa* that had been declared, stopped their journey and fished. They were detected, threatened with death unless *dosa* [weregild] be paid, and held captive until their townfolk paid for them.

The ordinary indemnity for *apa* not connected with the death of a person is called *apas* and amounts to a pig of *kaga* size (worth ten pesos) as a rule.

2. *Fruit trees.*—Any man may declare *apa* on a fruit tree, even one privately owned. People pluck fruit anywhere, and the owner may declare the *apa* on his own tree "in order to taste its fruit." The *apa* will endure until the declarer or his relatives makes a head-hunting expedition.

2. The symbolism is said to be: "Do not violate this *apa* or your jaw will be taken and set in a stake like this pig's."

When that has been accomplished, the declarer, followed by a crowd of his co-regionists, goes to the tree, announces the *apa* opened, is the first to pluck the fruit, and is followed by the others who vie with each other in seeing who can pluck and eat the most.

23. Apa *on mango tree and bamboo clumps* (ca. *1900*).—Ogas, of Malbong, "prohibited" a certain mango tree. When its fruit was ripe, he led his followers to a barrio of Balensiagao in order to kill and so to open the *apa*. But the Balensiagao people rushed out, pursued and drove them home. After that his town sent a spear as *sipat* [see p. 175].

Shamed by this failure, Ogas renounced his *apa* on the fruit tree, but declared another on some bamboo clumps. A distant cousin, Ballud, disregarded this *apa* and cut bamboo several times. Ogas, being angered, menaced Ballud with his head-ax, but refrained from attacking him on account of their kinship. Then Ballud, in order to embarrass Ogas [who was pact-holder of Malbong for Mangali], killed a Mangali man, believing that Ogas was a coward, would not retaliate, and so would lose his "honor." But Ogas killed Alingan, a second cousin of Ballud, preserved the pact, and in turn embarrassed Ballud.

3. Bamboo clumps.—The first man to stake a bamboo clump not privately owned is recognized as having control over and prior rights to the bamboo so long as he keeps up his rights by cleaning around the clump and caring for it. Such an *apa*, unlike all others, may become permanent and make the declarer, in effect, almost the owner—at least he may sell bamboo from the clump. Still he is expected to give permission to his neighbors to cut bamboo within reason.

24. Right of apa *upheld* (ca. *1910*).—Baligud of Magnao staked a great number of bamboo clumps between Magnao and the barrio of Nanabadan. People respected his rights as prior staker and would always ask his permission before cutting bamboo. About ten years later a man who had previously cut bamboo with permission, but wastefully and harmfully, fearing perhaps that permission would be refused him, went without permission and cut a number of bamboos.

Baligud discovered him and refused to let him take the bamboos home. The man appealed to the pangats, but they sustained Baligud's *apa*, so the bamboos had to be left lying on the ground.

4. *Forests.*—*Apa* declared on a forest resembles that declared on a stream.

25. Apa *on forest* (ca. *1885*).—Daowangan was killed in a certain forest in the Balbalan region. His son declared *apa* on the forest. Nobody stepped in that forest or gathered fuel there. The son did not avenge the father's death. The third generation needed lumber, so the forest was opened by the grandson, Kabanag. He did not kill anybody to open the *apa* "because the Americans had come in the meantime." The first trees were cut by the descendants of Daowangan in a body.

5. *Women.*—*Apa* sometimes assumes a form of spitefulness which men may exercise toward women with whom they have had a disagreement, and on whom they have some claim, as in the following cases: (1) when a man has had a row with a woman with whom he has had the dagdagas relationship; (2) when a woman has broken an engagement to marry; (3) when a woman has divorced a man. The *apa* prohibits any man from courting the woman for a definite period, usually from two months to a year, unless the permission of the declarer has been secured to do so. The declarer may or may not exact a payment for his permission. He must kill or wound any man (or the man's relative) who, without his permission, has amorous relations with the woman before expiration of the term declared, else he will suffer great loss of prestige and, it is believed, enlarged testicles.

26. Apa *declared on dagdagas; settlement* (ca. *1922*).—Lukya, of Lubwagan, had a girl named Kimadan, in Ableg, as dagdagas. After about a year, Kimadan requested that the relationship be terminated, as it was interfering with her chances of marriage, and she wanted to marry. Lukya, however, rejected the request and kept going to her house. When the girl refused him her favors, he declared her his *apa* and, after announcing the fact to the people of Ableg, returned to Lubwagan. A few months later, Kimadan came to Lukya and wanted to know his demands for remitting the *apa*. Lukya demanded three blankets. The girl got these from her suitor and paid them, after which she married.

6. *Hill lands.*—All cases of *apa* on hill lands that I have been able to learn about have originated in connection with the death of a relative. The following is a typical one:

27. Apa *on hill land (pre-American).*—The wife of Manao, in Balensiagao, bore a child on a certain hillside. After some years the child died. Manao "wanted not to remember that tract of land," so he gave a feast for the people and declared *apa* on it.

After several years, Manao opened the *apa* by giving another feast and making a *koipa* [see p. 98] there himself. All the people who made clearings on the land during the year following the removal of *apa* paid Manao a *dalan* of unthreshed rice.

In another case of *apa* on a hill site; a fire spread from an adjacent site and burned over the region of *apa*. Although this was accidental, the starter of the fire was mulcted for a weregild.

At present *apa* is rapidly becoming dissociated from head-hunting and killing and is becoming a means of reserving for private consumption what has hitherto been more or less shared with the community, as, for example, fruit or sugar cane, or of asserting ownership over portions of the unowned.

WEALTH

The Kalinga's classification of wealth is as follows: *tawid*, inherited property; *ginatang*, acquired property; *odon*, any property except animals; *aiyaiyam* (literally "pets"), property in animals.

Cultivated lands are either *paiyao*, irrigated rice fields, or *uma*, hill farms—clearings on the mountainsides that are cultivated for a year or two and then abandoned to revert to jungle and regain their fertility.

Rice lands.—The greater part of the Kalinga's wealth and that which gives the highest prestige is his irrigation systems and rice lands. Lubwagan is a wealthy region; it is said that every household has at least one rice field. Most rice fields—all the old ones—bear individual names. The fields are very productive under the two-crops-a-year cultivation practiced in Kalinga. The prestige value of rice lands is so great a factor in boosting their price that the return is very low as compared with interest rates on money, but prestige is not nearly so great a factor in the value as in Bontok, Ifugao, or among the Kankanai. A field called "Bulan" in the flat between Lubwagan and the school site was offered for sale not very long ago in order to raise money to send one of Galamoy's children by his second wife to school in Manila, but the boy changed his mind, and so it was withdrawn from sale. Gasatan, one of my informants, considers that the price, 1,000 pesos, was high as compared with other property but that the offer might have been accepted on account of the prestige value of the field, for it is one of the oldest in the region. It produces 6–7 *uyon* the first harvest and 12–13 *uyon* in the second. In Ableg, I was shown a field priced just the same which produces 8 *uyon* in the first harvest, and 15 *uyon* in the second.

The yield of the first harvest (planted in January and called *unoi*) is almost equal to that of the second (planted in July–August and called *uyak*), so that 2 *uyon* of the *uyak* are worth 10 pesos and 1 *uyon* 2 *dalan* of the *unoi* harvest are worth 10 pesos, or, in other words, ten heads of the second harvest give the same amount of rice on an average as six heads of the first.[3]

3. The Kalinga's table of rice currency is as follows:

1 *bUtok* is a small tie of rice as big around where tied just below the heads as a man's thumb

6 *bUtok* (tied together) make 1 *iting*, or bundle

2 *iting* equal 1 *lakom*

5 *lakom* equal 1 *dalan* (which gives approximately 4 *gantas*, first harvest; 2.4 *gantas*, second harvest)

5 *dalan* equal 1 *puwak*

2 *puwak* equal 1 *uyon* = 100 *iting* bundles

Good informants have told me that the Ableg field was correctly priced—that is, that a field which produces 8 *uyon* in the first harvest is worth 1,000 pesos. A very large part of this value is prestige value.

I got the figures on cultivation expense for only the first field, "Bulan." They are as follows:

EXPENSE OF BRINGING IN CROPS

"Plowing": 1 man at ₱1.00 a day for 2 days.....	₱2.00	
5 carabaos at ₱1.00 a day for 2 days..	2.00	₱4.00
Transplanting: 12 women at 50 centavos a day......		6.00
Weeding: 6 women at 50 centavos a day—twice during the season..		6.00
Cleaning dikes and terrace walls—same expense...........		6.00
		₱22.00
Expense for second crop—same, so far...................		22.00
		₱44.00
First harvest: 10 women at 50 centavos..........	₱5.00	
2 carriers at ₱1.00..............	2.00	7.00
Second harvest: 15 women at 50 centavos........	₱7.50	
3 carriers at ₱1.00.............	3.00	10.50
Workers must be fed twice a day with meat at one meal: 108 meals at, say, 6 centavos...........................		6.48
Grand total of computable expenses.....................		₱67.98

VALUE OF THE CROPS

First harvest:	$\dfrac{6\ uyan}{1\ uyon,\ 2\ dalan} \times$ ₱10.00.....	₱50.00
Second harvest:	$\dfrac{13\ uyon}{2} \times$ ₱10.00.....	65.00
		₱115.00

Certain expenses are not computable; for example, the fields have to be watched against theft of the water at night; they have to be visited almost every day in order to irrigate them; the seed bed has to be planted, the rice must be spread out in the sun to dry, then has to be stacked in the granary. Deducting, however, only the computable expense from the gross value of the crop, we have 47.02 pesos—certainly a modest interest on 1,000 pesos, the investment. And, as Pangat Dugyang asks, "How would you like to get up at midnight in order to take your turn at the irrigational canal—even when the weather is fine?"

To a certain extent, the low profit from this field is due to its unusually high prestige value. But even computing in the same way the yield from the other field, we find the profit to be only $6\frac{1}{4}$ per cent. The usual rate on money loaned on heirloom security (see Case 10) is 50 per cent. Perhaps, a good part of the value of rice lands is due to safety of investment, but a large part is certainly prestige value.

Even so, Lubwagan, with its two crops a year, is a less striking example than Sagada and Bagnen (Kankanai Igorot), where fields are regularly valued at twenty times the value of their average crop—with no deductions for expense of cultivation—or Ifugao, where the gross return is about 6 per cent.

As has been stated in chapter i, the Kalingas usually wall their terraces to a height of only about a meter, letting the rest of the bank slope at the angle of repose. A great part of the value of the wall is that it serves to maintain a boundary between properties, although the wall serves another purpose as well, that of keeping vegetation from hindering the growth of rice planted at the edge of the field. Another way of marking boundaries is to plant stones as landmarks (*pagek, padak*). The partial walling of terraces brings it about that there are fewer boundary disputes than in such regions as Kiangan and those of Ifugao farther south, where the terraces are frequently unwalled. The

Kalingas never settle a boundary dispute by a wrestling match with champions, as is done in Ifugao; the settlement is by fighting or by reference to "influential men," especially those having fields in the vicinity. A case that happened not long ago in Lubwagan was as follows:

28. Boundary dispute (1930).—Konay, a very old woman, childless, has a big field in Pudpud where the most aristocratic fields of Lubwagan lie. A, a first cousin, wanted some of this field, but he had no inheritance rights, since there were brothers of Konay. Konay's field adjoins that of A and is on the same level, so A changed the dike so as to include some of her field in his own. Bina-ay, a brother of Konay, noticed that this had been done and protested to A. The latter insisted that he had not touched the boundary, that it remained where it had always been. Bina-ay challenged him to come to the field and fight it out with spears. A did not answer. Mutually related kin, sensing danger in the situation, called Pangat Galamoy, whose field lies near by [the field, "Bulan," heretofore mentioned]. Galamoy went to the field and felt with his feet for the hard uncultivated strip on which the dike had formerly stood and restored the line. "A great pangat you are—trying to work such wonders!" Galamoy said to him, in effect, and A lost prestige.

At that time A was about to become a pangat, but, partly because of loss of popular confidence owing to this incident, he never attained that rank.

Tenure of irrigated fields is perpetual. There are many restrictions, however, on ownership that reinforce the principle of Kalinga custom that inherited fields shall pass down the ages to a stream of an owner's descendants. The custom permits sale only in certain designated crises. As concerns bequeathal, an owner having children may dispose of the land to none except them and to them only within rigid customary rules.[4] And his very possession and right of disposal automatically terminate when the child who ought by custom to receive them sets up a household. If childless, a person has little latitude in bequeathing his

4. For the purpose of rewarding an avenger, the custom allows a little deviation (see p. 238).

inherited property to any except lateral relatives, next of kin.

Rights of aliens.—Aliens do not convert a region's wild lands into rice fields because, if the pact of their own region with the other should be broken, they would lose their crop and access to their fields for many years. They may use them for hill farms, but, if owned, they must secure the consent of the owner; this is almost never sought or obtained.

Aliens may acquire rice lands by purchase or in payment of debt or indemnity. They never purchase as a matter of fact, and they usually sell lands acquired by the latter route.

House grounds.—The probabilities are that, following the pattern of Bontok and Kankanai villages, the first settlers in Kalinga left a good deal of space between houses and cultivated the land about the house as a garden. Now, however, in Lubwagan the houses are often very crowded owing to the custom of building houses for daughters near the household from which they sprang. The result is that building space sufficient for a house has a value up to 600 pesos. Where building space is unoccupied, it is regarded as property to be allotted to the children like other inherited property, and the two elder children have a superior right to it subject to the following modifications: the tendency is to give house grounds to the daughters "because they can't go out and look for them," and if the aged and dependent parents are living at their death with a younger son or daughter, as is usual, that one gets their house and house ground.

29. *Dispute about a house ground (1939).*—G's father received a share of a town lot. One of his brothers wanted to build there and was given permission to do so. He lived there in a Kalinga house for ten years, never claiming the property as his own in any way while G's father

lived. But after the death of the latter, he claimed it as his own and began to build a lowland-style house there. G forbade this, and the uncle threatened to take the case to court. G consulted a lawyer, who told him that, according to Philippine law, ten years' possession was prima facie evidence of ownership. G, therefore, consented to give his uncle half the lot.

Hill farms.—The Kalinga practices the *kaiyingan* system of cultivation of hill lands; that is, he clears away the forest, cultivates a plot two or three years, and then abandons it to revert to jungle when its fertility diminishes and the grass becomes troublesome. As has been said, the Kalingas are little dependent on the tropical sweet potato or *camote*, which is usually the staple food of Ifugaos, Bontoks, and Kankanai. From this standpoint, then, the hill farm is of little value to them. On the other hand, the hill farm is the source of two export crops, sugar and mongo peas, especially since the establishment of peace by the Americans. A further value is that it can sometimes be converted into rice field. For that reason and because there has been a rapid increase in Lubwagan's population due to its rise as a political and trading center, hill land around Lubwagan has a higher value than among the Ifugaos.

It is safe to conclude that to the first settlers hill lands had no value, for they were as free as air. Yet these settlers brought with them a tradition, a principle of ownership widespread among primitive folk—the principle that "the land belongs to the first cultivator"—so that both the greater safety in a head-hunting culture of the plots near the village and their greater convenience must have led, with increase of cultivation, to occasional assertion of ownership against newcomers when a previous cultivator wanted to recultivate a plot himself. The difference between that time and the present is not so very great from the standpoint of a Kalinga who wants to clear and cultivate a plot, for he will rarely be refused permission by the present owner, and no rental is charged him, though it is coming to be the proper thing for him to take the owner a basket of camotes or a ganta of mongo peas as a gift when the crop is harvested. Today, a man must go far (3–4 km.) to find unowned cultivable land.

A man establishes his claim to cultivate a parcel of land by *koipa*, that is, by beginning to clear it and by sticking up runo stalks as *purdus* (ownership symbols). Having eyes on a plot of land to cultivate, he goes to do this title-establishing bit of clearing early in the morning before the omen bird has awakened so as not to be cheated out of his choice by bad omens. On subsequent trips he may disregard bad omens, but on this first one, where the Ifugao observes them meticulously, he circumvents them. This illustrates how the Kalinga is most commendably losing his religion.

Formerly a number of households, four to seven or eight, all or nearly all related, would select a large enough patch of land, clear it working together or individually, and apportion plots which each household would cultivate for itself. Their numbers lessened the danger from head-hunters. Today, when more peaceful conditions prevail and hill land is rising in estimation, there are often lone cultivators, and people go several kilometers and select fertile plots in order that they may claim them ever after.

The size of the cultivated plots is not often over 1,000 square meters, yet sometimes plots of up to 3,000 or 4,000 square meters or even a hectare are claimed. Sometimes only a single owner of those who cultivate a place asserts his ownership, and he includes what his companions have cultivated in his claim. On the contrary, sometimes a number of others do assert ownership, and it is quite possible for all of them to do so. Considering the facts that the Kalinga cultivates a plot only two or three years, and that every

household always has one, the number of plots that must
have been cultivated even during a single past generation
must have been enormously greater than the number
claimed. There is said never to have been a serious dispute
between nonrelated persons over hill land, and, while there
are some times differences of opinion within a kinship
group about who is or ought to be the owner of a hill plot,
these hardly rise to the dignity of being quarrels and altercations and are easily settled by reference to kinsmen of
influence. Hill land as yet, it would seem, is considered
hardly worth the exertion of a determined stand.

Pasture lands.—The idiosyncratic meandering of custom
law and the wide range of forms that ownership can assume
are illustrated by the usage with respect to pasture lands.
A man secures ownership of such land by being the first to
pasture his stock on it. Grazing a single carabao is sufficient for the purpose. But his ownership does not exclude
others from pasturing their stock on it also—it continues
to be, for this purpose, "for all the people." Nor need a man
ask his permission to clear a patch of it and use it for a hill
farm: a man may fence it and use it. But, in this instance,
he cannot claim the land he has cultivated afterward. Furthermore, no one may build a rice field on pasture land
without asking the owner's permission, because a rice field
is a permanent one; only the owner of the pasture land may
build rice fields on it.

Alunday, the most important pangat in Lubwagan during my stay there in 1916, claimed the hill back of Goggotong and Tabangao barrios as grazing land. The hill is
now practically a commons for hill farms; it is so much
used for that purpose that people have ceased grazing their
stock there so that the hill farms do not need to be fenced.
But his descendants are the only ones who have the right

to build rice fields on the land—which is practically all that ownership of pasture lands really amounts to.[5]

Forest lands.—Around Lubwagan, the natural forest is free and common. The only owned forests are those near the town which have been cared for for generations or which have been planted on former clearings. A man may, with the owner's consent, plant trees on the clearing of another when he sees the owner abandon cultivation of the plot. He must clear the brush from around the trees thereafter, and if the owner sees that he is not doing this, he may, thinking, perhaps, or well knowing that the planter is a lazy man, warn the latter that, unless the undergrowth be cleared from around the trees, claim to the forest will be lost. Sometimes the planter of the forest will not heed the warning, and the owner will do the work himself and thus establish a claim on the forest. It does not appear that any serious controversies ever rise in this way—possibly because permission to plant is usually given to relatives.

Ownership of forest lands is about the same as that of rice fields, except that the owner has more freedom in allotting them among his children.

Ownership of forest planted on another man's land is a different case. When the trees are large enough to use, the landowner may order them cut off if he wishes to use the land.

Q. Does the owner have the right to order trees cut before they are large enough to use?

A. Maybe he might, but that would not be kind.

This answer, I think, means, "A man would be foolish to make his neighbor or kinsman hate him on such a trivial account, so the question is never raised," and it illustrates an essential difference between our legalistic concept of a

5. Priority of ownership has a value with respect to fencing obligations (see p. 135).

right and the conception of primitive folk. Our right is
described and inflexible, and we have a state to enforce it
for us, so that we do not need to take personalities, circumstances, or procedure into much account. The Kalinga has
a body of rights that are just as described and inflexible,
namely, his familial rights—the domestic concerns of his
primary social unit, the kinship group. But in his relations
with outsiders, his rights are so dependent on personalities
and circumstances as to be little more than feasibilities.
The reason is that his little state is not sufficiently developed to occupy itself with private rights and wrongs of this
kind. Nations from lack of an effective suprastate are in a
similar situation—they have only feasibilities.

Heirlooms.—Like all Luzon mountaineers, the Kalinga
is an antiquarian, and almost any old object, such as a
bead, gong, jar, or plate, has, in addition to its use value
and exchange value, an antiquarian value. And if the article has been in the possession of a family for several generations, it will have acquired for that family a fourth kind
of value, an heirloom value—which, however, does not
enter into its exchange value. If the owner of such an heirloom has to part with it in order to make payments, he will
take it to a kinsman and exchange it for an article of somewhere near equal value that is less precious to the family,
so that the heirloom may remain in the kindred, and he will
sell or use the article received in exchange.

A large part of the exchange value of objects such as may
become heirlooms derives from the fact that they are not
consumable and hence can be media of accumulation of
wealth, always ready to use in case a field is to be bought or
weregilds to be paid. Indeed, these antiques form the high
denominations among the Kalinga's media of exchange. In
these days when the Kalingas have become somewhat
sophisticated, heirloom value is not so high as formerly.

Gold earrings having an intrinsic value of 20 to 40 pesos are usually worth four to five times as much if old. Heirloom value might raise the price to ten times in the eyes of a particular family. It would be futile for anyone to cast a new earring or bead, however closely the color and form of the old ones might be imitated in it, and try to get a high price for it, for every Kalinga knows all the old beads in his community or neighboring ones. He values ancient Chinese and Japanese jars (gusi) at considerably above their prices as antiques in the world market; they vary in price from 100 to 500 pesos or perhaps more, while ordinary new jars bring from 2 to 10 pesos. Gongs are valued at from 25 to 125 pesos. Chinese bowls run from 25 centavos to 20 pesos. I counted sixty-six of them on the shelf for antiques (every house has one) in the house of Kanao, five of which were worth 20 pesos each, the rest being worth 1–3 pesos. The most valued heirloom gusi, together with some old plates or bowls, are kept on a shelf called *pagud*, and a guest is supposed to notice its position and not sit with his back toward it or spit toward it. Beads of carnelian or agate, even old glass beads, are valuable in proportion to their age, as also are Chinese imitations of ancient Greek beads. I looked in vain for the genuine Greek beads.

The Kalingas have spears and headaxes coming down from the days when spears were hammered out of broken Chinese kettles (cast iron), but do not prize them so highly as do the Ifugaos, nor, strangely enough, do they prize ancient shields.

Other property.—Textiles, blankets, gee-strings, girdles, and sarongs are made and accumulated largely for gifts on ceremonial occasions (birth, marriage, death, etc.), or in cases of exchange. Other articles such as spears, bolos, and looms are used for gifts in exchange but not often as ritual gifts.

OWNERSHIP OF WATER

He who builds the first rice field irrigated by a spring owns the spring, whether it gurgle up inside the field or not. A man who builds a field just below his must pay him for the water that passes from his field, the usual price being one pig, although it might be that he would not exact this payment if the second builder were a kinsman of himself or his wife. In like manner, the second builder might demand from a third the payment of a small pig or a chicken. Having received this payment, or having waived it by silence, no owner may divert the water from his field to another field; for example, he must not pipe it away in a conduit, but must permit it to flow its natural course.

Neighbors and relatives pool their labor to build irrigation ditches, but it appears that there is no name for such an association of owners, as there is among Ilokanos. The subprovince of Kalinga sometimes has a well-marked dry season when a ditch will supply too little water for the fields of the builders. In order that there be a fair distribution in such a contingency, a system called *tobtobwak* is practiced. This is illustrated in Figure 5.

The lands of the owners along an irrigation canal are divided into groupings designated in the figure as *A*, *B*, *C*, and so on (*E* being unreclaimed land). The grouping is such that the fields in each group or section lie in an ascending-descending relationship. Each group receives water in proportion to its area. Thus in our diagram, *A* will receive it, say, from noon till dawn (three-fourths of a day); *B* from dawn till noon on the succeeding day (one and one-quarter days); *C* will receive it half a day; and *D* will receive it two days. This arrangement is to protect the lower fields, for if the ditch were allowed to run into all the fields, the water would be insufficient to reach the lower fields.

Now, suppose an outsider wants to build a field and draw water from the canal. He may not build a field on the same level as that of any owner. He may build a field below their lowest fields if he secures permission. And he will probably secure that permission in this way: he will give a bribe to the most influential of the canal owners, and when this man puts in a word for him with the other owners,

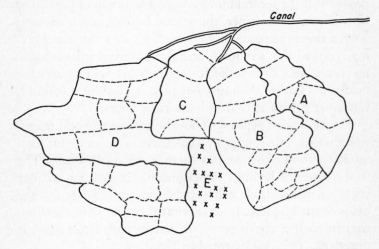

FIG. 5.—Diagram illustrating ownership of water rights. See text for details

"everybody will follow—what else can they do?" Sometimes a man is granted permission simply in order that the owners may have another helper in cleaning the canal or on his promise, with his relatives, to clean the canal once or twice.

An owner of the canal is in the same position as an outsider when it comes to building a new field on land acquired after beginning the project. A canal owner may make fields only on land owned and declared before the building of the canal began.

Flowage rights exist among Kalinga users of water. The first users of water from a stream have the right to prohibit any diversion of water upstream from them. Enforcement within the bounds of a single town is accomplished without trouble. It is said that much of the land above the town of Lubwagan could be irrigated without endangering, except in periods of exceptional drought, the supply to present fields lower down, but that the owners of these fields prohibit more fields. Flowage rights often cause great troubles and perpetual feuds between towns. One such feud is that between Dananao and Sumadél. The Dananao folk keep building new fields, and this lessens the water in a stream that flows through Sumadél territory, with the result that Sumadél's fields suffer. A murder case I was appointed to defend in Lubwagan in 1916 was an incident in the long feud between these two towns which occasionally flares anew.

Sale of a field carries with it the sale of the water right of the field and an interest in the canal supplying it.

30. Irrigation; wounds; responsibility of canal owner (1930).—Bagíon's father had an excellent large rice field with a stone wall. He permitted his second cousin, the father of Sabado to build a canal along the base of the wall. When Bagíon inherited the field, he feared that the ditch would undermine the terrace wall and "also it seemed to him that his relationship with Sabado was very far." He told Sabado several times to replace the canal with an aqueduct [*tolalok*] of palm trunk, bamboo, or tree fern. Sabado refused, so Bagíon took the case to the pangats, who decided that the ditch was not injuring the wall nor likely to do so.

However, Bagíon worried about the wall, and one day, perceiving Sabado at his canal, he threw a spear at him but fortunately the wound was slight. A go-between [*mangi-ugud*] was selected for each side, and after three months the following weregilds were arranged:

Weregilds	Contributed by—	Distributed to—
2 fields	{ 1 field, Bagíon { 1 field, his brothers	Sabado
3 gusi	Bagíon's uncles and aunts	Sabado's uncles and aunts
14 carabaos	Bagíon's first cousins	Sabado's first cousins
Numerous small articles, blankets, etc.	Bagíon's second cousins	Sabado's second cousins

The question of the canal is unsettled, as the field that caused the trouble was not one of those that was ceded. The case probably will not be settled except by intermarriage. But the two principals do not have children suitable for marriage. Therefore, the only way to make intermarriage possible will be to trade the field around some way so as to get it into possession of one of Bagíon's relatives who has a son or daughter of the right age and sex to marry one of Sabado's children.

Q. Might the son rightfully revoke the father's permission given for the canal?

A. The rice field was there before the canal. If the son saw that the canal was really damaging the terrace wall, he was right in warning the canal owner to take steps to make the damage impossible, and if the canal owner did not act, he could revoke the permission. But in this case the pangats viewed the field and decided that as a matter of fact there was no damage nor likely to be.

31. Murder; ownership of water (pre-American).—Men from Ableg killed Abuli, a naturalized citizen of Balensiagao who had fled from Lubwagan. The Balensiagao people immediately shut off the water from an Ableg irrigation canal that lay partly within their territory. The Ableg people paid weregilds, but Balensiagao did not permit the re-opening of the canal until Ableg purchased the water by paying a very large pig worth 40 pesos and by building an irrigation canal for the Balensiagao people. It cost the Ableg people the equivalent of two carabaos for the sustenance of their men who worked on the canal.

After the canal was finished, the pact between the two regions was renewed. A number of Balensiagao people built fields under the new canal.

Comment: This case appears to me to sustain rather than controvert my contention that unexpropriated lands, waters, etc., are unowned rather than communally owned. Note that the Ableg people had been permitted to build a canal in Balensiagao territory and draw water from its streams without making any payment. Balensiagao asserted ownership only as a device of retaliation.

LANDLORD AND TENANT

There are two kinds of tenants: the inside tenant, *tagabu*, who lives in his master's household and works a certain field for his keep, and the outside tenant, *tubyao*, who lives in his own house. The latter kind pays a rental, *binglai* of one-half or one-third the crop, the master furnishing the seed. A tenant, either inside or outside, was formerly expected to help avenge his master's death, to help his master in roofing his house, etc. The master was expected to help avenge the tenant and to assist him in time of sickness, marriage, or death in his family.

TRANSFERS OF PROPERTY FOR CONSIDERATION

Even today money enters but little into the purchase price of a field. The price is reckoned in water buffaloes—indeed all large values are reckoned in terms of that animal—and is paid in buffaloes, pigs, heirlooms, and minor articles.

Gifts to the seller's kindred must be made by the purchaser and should amount to from 25 to 50 per cent of the value received by the seller; they are not so minutely named and divided into categories and subcategories as in Ifugao, but they are likely to be more numerous, for the seller's spouse's kindred are included with his own even when it is his inherited property that is sold.

These gifts are obligatory when the following kinds of property are transferred by sale: rice fields, town lots, gongs, valuable jars, gold earrings, old beads, houses whether sold with or without the house ground, carabaos, and pigs unless small.

The same circles of kindred who participate in the gifts in case of sale are assessed to provide them in case of purchase, excepting, however, the aged ascendants. The circles that participate in the gifts are, when the sale is a large one: (1) the parents, uncles, and aunts of the seller and his spouse; (2) the brothers and sisters of each spouse; (3) the first cousins of each spouse; and (4) the second cousins of each spouse. It was formerly the rule that each of these circles of kindred ought to receive approximately equal amounts; the third and fourth circles grow in numbers of included individuals—therefore, each individual of these subsequent circles received a smaller share. Nowadays, there is a marked tendency to give the third circle less than the second and to omit the fourth one. As the values exchanged diminish in scale, the second cousins, first cousins, and some of the brothers and uncles drop out. Two rules governing the distribution of the gifts are: (1) Kindred of husband and wife share equally, but the husband, who is the manager and the seller of his wife's property as well as his own, ought tactfully to insist on more in the way of presents for giving his wife's people a little more than he does to his own, if he is selling. Likewise, he will demand a little less contribution from them if he is buying. (2) In circles of equal kinship the senior lineage and the firstborn of each lineage will receive a more valuable present than the rest "as a mark of respect." The Kalinga distribution differs from that of the Ifugao in that it embraces the nearer ascendants as well as the lateral kindred. In Ifugao the distribution is almost entirely to the lateral kindred; even the nearest vertical kin get only token presents.

The purchase price may be regarded as consisting of the following major groups: (1) the *gatad*,[6] which is the seller's share; (2) the *so-ol*,[7] also called *paiyak di mamlak* ("wings of the seller"), consisting of two divisions called *pangat di so-ol* ("chiefs of the so-ol") and *biyu n di so-ol* ("companions of the so-ol") go to the relatives; and (3) certain ritual payments.

The payments to the kindred may conceivably be descended from a former communal ownership. It is quite apparent that they serve the following functions: (1) they

6. The corresponding payment in Ifugao is called the *pu-u*, meaning "base"; I do not know whether the Kalinga word has any figurative meaning—but Kalingas readily accepted "base" as a good English term for the payment.

7. The *so-ol* is not given in the Balbalasang district or in any regions north of Magnao and Naneng. In these two regions it is said to be a new thing. It reaches as far south, at least, as Tinglaiyan—informant did not know about Bontok or about the regions of eastern Kalinga. Henceforth this term will not be italicized except in compounds.

clear the title—no relative of the seller can claim the field as his after being feasted and given a present; (2) a Kalinga who sells a field has qualms of conscience; he is doing a dangerous thing, and his relatives may reproach him afterward, for he is lowering his own prestige and that of his kinship group—but the edge of any reproaches they might make is taken off by the fact that they have shared in the proceeds; (3) the presents give the buyer a chance to splurge, to elevate his prestige, and to ingratiate himself with the seller's whole kinship group.

A sale is effected in the following way: Two agents are selected, called *mantauwag* or *umoi mamlak*, one an influential kinsman of the wife, the other an influential kinsman of the husband. Sometimes there are more, but always half are drawn from the kindred of each spouse. When these have found a buyer, they appoint a day for the formalities of the exchange. When that time comes, the seller and his kindred proceed to the house of the buyer. One of the go-betweens formally asks the buyer if he wishes to buy and is willing to pay the price asked as "base." Nothing is said about the so-ol or other payments. When the buyer answers affirmatively, the go-between takes a Chinese bowl from the shelf and puts it on the floor, leaving it there for several minutes, during which silence reigns.

If somebody sneezes, the agent leaves the bowl on the floor, the seller and party go home, and the deal is off. If there is no such bad omen, the agent picks the dish up and hands it to the seller. The dish constitutes a ceremonial payment, called *patay*, that begins the whole series of subsequent payments, although as a matter of fact it does not stay with the seller—it becomes part of the agent's commission.

The relatives ask for their so-ol one by one, and it is said that a man who is a "good talker" will get more than one who is not. However, the buyer has on hand an influential relative, called *mangiwatwat* ("distributor"), also a good talker, who takes charge and tactfully beats down the demands of the greedy ones, keeping them "regular." So-ol are more numerous, of course, if the seller has many relatives.

Saklag was thinking about buying the field, "Bulan," of Galamoy when it was offered for sale. If it had not been withdrawn, the following are the payments that would have been appropriate if he had bought it; consideration is taken of the actual number of kindred the sellers have.

I. The Gatad or "Base"—to Galamoy and his wife, Gamiloy:
   20 carabaos[8]
   1 gusi, valued at 6 carabaos
   1 gong, valued at 3 carabaos
   1 pair of gold earrings, valued at 6 carabaos

II. The So-ol or "Paiyak di mamlak" ("Wings of the Seller")— to seller's kindred

A. *Pangat di so-ol* ("chiefs of the so-ol")—to the agents and elder kindred[9]

2 big pigs to the agents drawn from Galamoy's kindred	2 big pigs to the agents drawn from Gamiloy's kindred
1 big pig, given to his uncle (his father and mother are dead)	1 big pig, given to her aunt (her father and mother are dead)

B. *Biyu n di so-ol* ("companions of the so-ol")—to the remaining kindred

4 medium pigs, given to Galamoy's brothers and senior first cousin	4 medium pigs, given to Gamiloy's brother and senior first cousin
3 dogs and 6 blankets, given to the senior first cousins of junior lineages	3 dogs and 6 blankets, given to the senior first cousins of junior lineages
5 sarongs, 4 chickens, 2 bolos, given to his junior first cousins and senior second cousins	8 sarongs, 2 head axes, 5 chickens, given to her junior first cousins and senior second cousins

8. The average value of carabaos changing hands in exchanges is probably around 25 pesos, because young animals will be accepted along with older ones worth 30 or 35 pesos.

9. Receivers of *pangat di so-ol* must make a return gift of less value.

2 gee-strings, 12 Chinese bowls, given to his junior second cousins	3 gee-strings, 8 Chinese bowls, given to her second cousins

III. RITUAL PAYMENTS:

Pa-inum: basi and/or rice wine given the seller's and buyer's kin to drink during the occasion

Palanos: a large pig is slaughtered; the lower half (*díom*) is cooked to feed the guests

Longos: the upper half of the pig is presented to the seller and his kindred and by them carried home and shared

Palnok: a present given the seller and his wife:
1 small pig
2 blankets
3 Chinese bowls

Gaiyauwa: gift sent to a relative of pangat rank even though he be absent—"because they are afraid of him"

On the following day the agents will go to the house of the buyer and receive the six gusi, the gong, and the pair of gold earrings that are part of the "base" payment. The seller and his kindred would have been too drunk the day before to carry them away safely. The buyer will also take the agents to his pasture and deliver the twenty carabaos. These may often be left grazing in their accustomed pasture if desired.

Under the Kalinga's two-crop system, the field is almost certain to be under crop at the time of the sale. In that case, the buyer will receive actual possession only after the crop is harvested.[10]

A kinsman cannot stop a sale by refusing to accept so-ol.

The *pangat di so-ol* must be divided equally between the kinship groups of the spouses; in the case of the *biyu n di so-ol*, however, there is some leeway. If there were five relatives of the husband and seven of the wife in a certain category, the division would probably be equal, the relatives of the wife getting each five-sevenths as much as those of the man. But if there were only three or four relatives of the man and seven of the wife, then something

10. See "Invalid Sales," p. 113.

would be taken from the husband's side and given to the wife's, although individually the man's relatives would still receive more than the wife's.

Relatives must appear and solicit so-ol. Gifts are not sent or reserved for absent ones, except the *gaiyauwa*—for those of pangat rank. In sales in distant towns, as of gusi, gongs, or gold earrings, a townmate may ask so-ol when not many relatives have come along to solicit it. He does not have to claim kinship.

If a portable object be sold in a foreign town, there are added payments, and the distribution of the so-ol is different from that above. Since dealing is with outlanders who may have different ideas of what is proper, the so-ol is fairly definitely agreed on beforehand. Let us suppose that a very valuable jar is being sold. The seller, accompanied by the agents and probably, but not necessarily, the pact-holder of the region for his own region, together with up to thirty men, his relatives on both sides, proceeds with the gusi to the buyer's house. The gusi, we will suppose, is to be sold for six carabaos. The payments then will follow this pattern:

> GATAD, six carabaos (to seller)[11]
> PATAY, two Chinese bowls (to the go-betweens)
> PA-INUM, basi and/or rice wine
> PALANOS, lower half of pig or dog cooked for the guests
> LONGOS, upper half of the animal, presented to the seller's party
> PALNOK, gift of blankets, gee-strings, tapis, small pig, or other
> articles to equal about 10 pesos in value (to the seller)
> SO-OL: *Paiyak di mamlak* ("wings of the seller")
>> *Pangat di so-ol*, two large pigs, two small ones; one-half goes to the pact-holders, if present; one-half to the agents, who are usually kindred of the seller
>> *Biyu n di so-ol*, blankets, gee-strings, sarongs, small pigs, bolos, spears, head axes, china plates, etc. (to the seller's companions)

11. For a list of the payments among the Ifugaos in such cases see R. F. Barton, *Philippine Pagans*, p. 126. Some of the payments have the same symbolism as in Kalinga. Many of these payments are becoming obsolete.

APON, two or three textiles (to seller and his kindred). The payment is symbolic of something given the party in which to wrap up the articles received and carry them home. This payment might consist of a blanket and a sarong or gee-string.

PA-ANAO, about the same as the above, but symbolic of an *anao* rain cape, used to protect the articles from rain on the trip back home.

PADALKOT, glutinous rice made into cakes (*diket*), for a snack for the seller's party on the road home.

KALPAIYAN or PATALI, one or two gee-strings, symbolic of ropes given for leading home animals received in exchange.

So-ol is given even in sales of carabaos (average price 25 pesos) or large pigs, but it is not large and includes only the seller's brothers and sisters and perhaps the senior first cousin. The effect of so-ol on native trade is bad. The payments make animals so dear that there is almost no domestic trading in them; if animals are needed, they are borrowed. Great numbers of pigs and carabaos were formerly bought in the lowlands and driven up into the mountains. Today, lowland merchants bring them up by double-decked truckloads.

Agents get no fee for affecting a sale of animals between relatives; they get only their share as kinsmen (for they are always kinsmen of the seller or his spouse). If they effect a sale for a nonrelated person in the same town or village, they get a small fee; if to a person in another town, they get a large fee—half the *pangat di so-ol*.

Invalid sales.—In sales of carabaos, the present practice is for buyer and seller to agree on a point on the homeward route of the buyer at which the sale becomes irrevocable— that is to say, a point beyond which, should the animal fall over a cliff, the buyer will bear the loss and inside of which the purchase price will be refunded. If the two are of different regions, this point will usually be the boundary line between the regions.[12]

12. In the Magnao region death by accident is not taken into consideration but there is sometimes a provision against death by pest for a number of days

At the time of my first stay in Kalinga (1916) there was a rule of custom that if landslides or other forces of nature badly damaged a field before its delivery to a purchaser, that is, while it remained in possession of the seller owing to its being under crop, then the purchaser might refuse to accept it and require repayment of its price. That rule is far more liberal to the seller today. The rule is, "There must be a field to deliver." If it should have been entirely washed away or otherwise destroyed, the purchaser is entitled to refund—otherwise not.

"*Coverture*."—Until a child is born to a married couple, the husband, as we have said, may not dispose of his wife's property. After that event, he may do so for reasonable purposes, even against his wife's will. It will probably be correct to say, then, (1) that the properties of the parents become vested in the children from their very birth and (2) that the father, rather than the mother, holds the properties in trust.

This form of what in some respects resembles coverture is absent from Ifugao, Kankanai, and Bontok custom.

TRANSFERS OF OWNERSHIP BY ALLOTMENT
OR INHERITANCE

Transfers within the household.—Inherited property (*tawid*) always passes into the hands of the child to whom the custom law allots it on that child's setting up a household. He does not receive it, although he be married, until he and his wife leave the household of the parents of one or the other and "go separate" (*sumina*).

The oldest son and daughter, in particular, have known which would be their property almost from the time they were able to talk. The Kalinga custom is a peculiar combination of primogeniture and homoparental inheritance; the oldest son inherits the best fields of his father, the oldest daughter the best fields of the mother. If the parents were only middle-class folk, these two children formerly took the lion's share of the inherited fields, although the tendency now is toward more equal division. The children know their rights, and the force of custom, public opinion, and the influence of the kinship groups are so strong that even if the parent wanted to deprive the child of his rights, he could not. But the parent doesn't want to, of course— at least, if he does, he drives the desire back into his unconscious mind. But probably he really doesn't, for with getting his children married off and getting relieved from his property, there begins a new epoch for a man still comparatively young, experienced, and endowed with the prestige of having reared a family—an epoch of freedom from the drudgery of looking after fields and their irrigation, from the necessity of upholding his prestige (surely a great relief!), from the strict requirements of ritual gifts, for these are connected with the property—a period in which he can turn his knowledge of local "politics" to his advantage, live by his wits, scheme and acquire. Many a man acquires rapidly and *ipiduan na'n mangkadangyan*, "repeats becoming a rich man."

It is considered that the eldest child ought to inherit the largest estate, and this consideration sometimes conflicts with and overwhelms the custom of homoparental inheritance. Thus, if the firstborn be a daughter and if the mother (from whom the daughter ought to inherit) has considerably less wealth in fields and heirlooms than the father, then the daughter is often given the father's fields, or, if such a situation be reversed, the son is given the mother's fields.

32. Inheritance; conflict of customs (1933).—Seven years ago a man named Rafael had four children, two boys and two girls, the girls being the elder born. When the elder girl married, she was allotted Rafael's

property as if she had been a son. All the children married. So long as
the parents lived, the children got along together harmoniously, but
after their death the oldest sister became stingy to her brothers. The
elder of the boys laid claim to the rice fields his sister had been allotted
from the father's inherited property. She claimed the field as having
been given her on her marriage by her father of his own free will. There
was almost a fight between this boy and his sister's husband. The uncles
and cousins intervened; there was a family council, and the case was
decided in favor of the boy.

In this case the sister's unpopularity probably influenced
the decision.

The younger children get the tail-end of the parents'
inherited rice fields, the acquired rice fields, if there be any,
and a large share of the heirlooms, hill farms, forest and
pasture lands. The parents do not even hold back for themselves, as do Kankanai parents, a small field called by the
latter *manganán* ("field to eat from"), although, if the oldest child has many fields, he may leave one with them, receiving it back after the death of the father. But the parents do hold to their hill lands or most of them, acquire
new ones, perhaps, and if the father can somehow circum-
vent the law of riparian rights or discover a water source,
he will convert some of the hill plots into rice fields for the
younger children. One day, when the father is old, he will
take his children to his hill plots scattered over the mountainsides and will give each child his share. Girls are ordinarily given preference in the inheritance of the house
and house ground.

Although Kalingas speak of the father more often than
of the mother as allotting property to the children, they do
not mean that the mother has necessarily less voice in the
matter than he but only that he is the active member in
carrying out the joint decision of the two.

The parents have greater discretion in apportioning or
willing such property as town lots, hill lands, and heirlooms
than they have with respect to the inherited rice fields.

33. Inheritance of house ground (ca. *1920*).—HaLa had three children. He allotted a house ground to Sumita, a son, and Sumita built a house and lived on it. After that, Sumita permitted his brother, Mata, also to build on the ground. Ten years later, Sumita became seriously sick. Before he died, he allotted the lot to Lonay, his eldest son.

Lonay did not build on the lot, because he married in Dongoy barrio and lived in his wife's house. His sister, however, continued to live in her father's house. Five years later, Mata asserted his part ownership of the lot. Probably the reason that he did so was that lots had risen tremendously in value and lowlanders were buying them. There was a great quarrel and family row which was ended only by the intervention of the influential men of the town. They induced Lonay to give Mata one-third of the lot on the ground that he was also the son of HaLa.

Lonay's ownership of the lot was beyond question. This case shows that the influential men of the town sometimes override the custom and justice in order to secure peace and quiet in the town.

The shares of the children grow successively smaller after the second. The youngest child, however, usually lives with the parents, who may keep on "acquiring." The youngest will inherit the property acquired by the whole household since the date of his marriage. This is said to be because the household acquires as a whole so that it is impossible to separate the parents' share from that of the youngest child and his spouse. A married pair, one of whom is a youngest son or daughter, practically always goes to live in the house of the parents of that one.

The rights of adopted children to allotment or inheritance of property have already been discussed (see "Adopted Children").

When a married person who has children dies, there is no inheritance of property by the surviving spouse, since the property, as we have seen, is vested in the children of the union. The surviving spouse, on marrying again, has precisely nothing, except that possession of the property of unmarried children for the purpose of management is vested in him or her.

Married person who dies childless.—The inherited property in this case reverts in its entirety to the deceased's father and mother for reallotment to his brothers and sisters or, failing these, to the parents themselves. The acquired property is divided between his relatives and the surviving spouse; sometimes the division is equal, but sometimes the husband or his relatives receive a little more than the widow or hers, on the ground that "the man was the more important in acquiring."

Unmarried persons who die during the lifetime of their parents will not have come into possession of any part from their parents' property.

An unmarried orphan will have received his share of his dead parents' estate. If he dies, that share will be inherited by his brothers and sisters or, failing them, by his uncles and aunts on both sides or his cousins.

In the inheritance of estates of unmarried orphans or childless married persons, three circumstances may apply:

1. Normally the property or the greater part of it will go to the oldest and nearest relative.

2. But the dead person's wishes in the matter, if they have been definitely expressed on his deathbed, will be taken into consideration. He has some right, though a vague one, to will his property, especially if it be a small one, to a favorite brother or sister, or an adopted child, but not to a more remote relative.

3. The estate, if not very large, may pass in its entirety to the brother, sister, nephew, niece, or cousin who slaughtered animals (or considerably the greatest number of animals) at the feast for the deceased's recovery (*posipos*) and for his funeral feast (*utong*).

Q. Suppose a married man, dying childless and having four fields, his inherited property, leaves his widow, his father, and a brother and sister. How will the fields be inherited?

A. Divided between his brother and sister.

Q. What about his acquired property (*ginatang*)?

A. Equal division between his widow and the brother and sister, or maybe the last two will get a little more than the widow.

Q. Suppose a man dies, leaving two fields worth sixteen carabaos, his parents and three brothers being his nearest of kin. One brother sacrifices four carabaos for the funeral feast, the second and third brother none. What will be the division?

A. The brother who furnished the sacrifices will receive both fields. But the case is an impossible one, because, with such a valuable inheritance in sight, the second and third brothers will not fail to do their kinship duties.

Children by a dagdagas have no inheritance rights but may be given something by the heirs, especially if these be wealthy. During his lifetime the father will have given the eldest child by the dagdagas a field. His right to do this, at least if he be wealthy, is well established in the custom, but his right to give anything to succeeding children of a dagdagas is not. He will probably have managed to give them heirlooms secretly.

34. Dispute over inheritance; rights of primogeniture; homicide (1918).
—Lambaiyong was the elder of two sons, there being no sisters, and was given the lion's share of the estate of both parents, which, all told, was about enough to make him a *baknang* [moderately wealthy]. When Masadao, the younger brother, married, he brought his wife to live with his parents. He and his father working together improved a field allotted him from his father's inheritance, enlarging it until it was greater than the inheritance of Lambaiyong.

The years passed, and Lambaiyong's son, Palngipang, became a lusty, aggressive fellow, feared by the people and possessed of the ambition to become a pangat. He expressed dissatisfaction that his father, being the elder, had received the smaller estate, and he demanded a revision of the allotment of the grandfather's estate.

The grandfather was long since dead, and Lambaiyong did not support his son's claim. Nevertheless, the son seized the field of Masadao, which would become the property of the latter's son, Dauwaton, and began to "plow" it. Dauwaton, emboldened by his uncle on his mother's side, lay in ambush as Palngipang came back from the field and beheaded him with a single stroke of his head ax.

Dauwaton was sentenced to twenty years' imprisonment. Masadao paid weregilds[13] so that the other side would sign a petition for the boy's pardon or parole, but the boy died after two years' imprisonment.

Q. May a reallotment be demanded by a child who has already received his property from his parents' estates?

A. After a father has given the eldest child the latter's allotment, if he is an industrious man and shrewd so that he acquires property rapidly and it appears that he will leave the second and third sons more

13. Or, perhaps, *pakan* (see p. 242).

than the first received, then the eldest may ask the father for an additional allotment, and the father will probably grant the request because it is the custom to give the eldest child the most.

Q. Then, in this case, was Palngipang's claim good?

A. No. His father, Lambaiyong, ought to have advanced it during the lifetime of his own father—that is, before Masadao, the brother, inherited.

35. Irregular allotment.—My uncle has three big parcels of rice fields; his wife has three small ones, not worth much. They have three children. The oldest, a son of twenty-four years, was engaged when small but did not like his fiancée and ran after many dagdagas. He has finally married and received his allotment. The sister next to him was married when fourteen. The youngest of the family, a girl, is still in school. The allotment made among the children was: the two older children divide the father's fields, the son taking the greater share. The youngest child will take the mother's fields when she goes to live with her husband.

36. Improvement of hill lands gives no title.—Talog, a widower, left his two minor sons with his married daughter and remarried, leaving his entire property, acquired and inherited, to the children of the first marriage.

He had children by his second wife, and the two converted a piece of hill land that his first wife had inherited into rice fields, which he gave the children of the second marriage. A cousin of the first wife, however, informed the children of the first marriage that the hill land had been their mother's, so these demanded the fields. Relatives of the mother came forward and testified that the land had been hers, and a bitter dispute arose. The pangats convinced the father that the only way to prevent serious trouble was to yield the field to the children of the first marriage.

TRANSFER OF PROPERTY BY GIFT TO THE AVENGER
OF A NEAR-RELATIVE

This form of transfer is explained under the heading "Rewards of the Avenger" (p. 238).

TRANSFER OF POSSESSION OF PROPERTY
BUT NOT OF OWNERSHIP

Transfer of possession of a field as security for a loan and of the use of it as compensation to the lender in lieu of interest is the most ancient form of hypothecation to be found surviving with little change in modern legal systems, where it is called antichresis. It dates back at least to ancient Babylonia and is widespread in both Near and Far East. Except that they contain a few modernisms, the following articles from the Philippines Civil Code (Napoleonic) describe it as Ifugaos and Kalingas are practicing it today and have practiced it for ages. The modernisms are: (1) Ifugao and Kalinga loans have no strictly defined term; (2) the reference to the "Law of Civil Procedure"; (3) the kind of interest mentioned as being substituted by the usufruct of the property is not the kind of interest that is practiced by these two tribes.

ART. 1881. By antichresis a creditor acquires a right to receive the fruits of real property of his debtor, with the obligation to apply them to the payment of interest if due and afterward to the principal of his credit.

ART. 1883. The debtor cannot recover the enjoyment of his property without previously paying in full what he owes to his creditor. . . .

ART. 1884. The creditor does not acquire the ownership of the real property by nonpayment of the debt within the term agreed upon.

Any stipulation to the contrary shall be void. But in this case the creditor may demand, in the form prescribed by the law of civil procedure, the payment of the debt or the sale of the realty.

In Ifugao the provision of Article 1884 regarding the creditor's demand for a sale works out in this way: If the creditor wants to recover his loan, he tries to wheedle the debtor into paying. If unsuccessful in this, he demands that the debtor sell the hypothecated field and tries to find him a good bargain. If the debtor refuses all offers, there is nothing the creditor can do—there is no such thing as foreclosure.

Throughout this mountain country no rule is so strongly intrenched as that "he who plants shall reap." It holds both in sales and in *banat*, a form of "mortgage" with an indefinite time limit. An owner cannot get a field that is in crop back from the creditor to whom it has been given in *banat* until the creditor has reaped the crop.

In Kalinga most instances of *banat* result from seizure to cover debt: the seized field acquired the status of *banat* automatically. This is not the case in Ifugao. For that reason, seizures in Kalinga, it is said, never lead to bloodshed or even to much irritation. The lowland form of pawning, *salDa*, is a much more lucrative method of exploitation, so that wealthy Kalingas are fast adopting it.

The "salDa."—This form of possession differs from the foregoing in that there is a time limit for repayment of the loan, after which, in case of nonpayment, ownership passes to the creditor. It is said that Lubwagan is the only region of Kalinga that has as yet adopted the *salDa*.

INTEREST ("PA-ANAK")[14]

If a young animal is loaned, the debt must be repaid by an animal of the size of the loaned animal would have attained by the date on which repayment is made. To determine that size, reference is made to some animal of approximately equal age. The interest in such a case is (1) care of the animal for the period and (2) insurance against extinction of its value through death. If an adult animal be loaned, a sum of money or palay is collected as interest when the loan is made—usually 10 pesos a year for a carabao or 5 pesos for a large pig. Formerly, when carabaos were dearer, the interest was larger.

If interest is not agreed on in advance, how much will be collected from a nonrelative will depend largely on the personalities of the principals and the strength and loyalty of

14. In olden times Kalingas did not practice interest on debts or loans. *Pa-anak*, or interest, is of foreign origin. Kalingas formerly loaned only within the kinship group or to outsiders whose fields or other property they wished to secure possession of. Regardless of time, whether it were ten years or more or less, a carabao two years old was payable by one of the same age.—CAMILO LAMMAWIN.

their respective kinship groups. From a related debtor, a man will not usually demand high interest.

Under the *salDa*[15] method, a man will give his carabao as security for a loan of 10 pesos, say, agreeing to repay within a month with interest at 2.50 pesos per month. If the animal dies, both creditor and debtor will lose, since the animal is worth much more than the debt, and so the debt is considered as extinguished. The creditor will not be strict in enforcing the time limit because Kalingas are not used to strict reckoning of time and are accustomed to the old form of "mortgage," the *banat*, under which the pledge could be redeemed at any time. However, the spread of the gambling habit has been a godsend to loan sharks: gamblers will agree to almost any interest when the craze is on them, and, in a case like the above, the creditor has only to let the debt run on for two or three months and then, after two or three notifications that the animal will become his if the debt be not repaid, take the animal, giving the debtor possibly a peso or two to gamble with, so that his feelings will not be hurt.

Interest is not presumed unless a loan was made; if there was no loan, interest will not be levied as damages for breaking contractual obligations.

37. Sit-down collection; interest not collected (ca. 1931).—Palanyao of Lubwagan went to Butbut, a barrio of Tinglaiyan, and there sold a carabao for 40 pesos. He had not brought the animal with him, and it was agreed that the purchaser should come to Lubwagan to get it. Before this happened, however, the carabao fell down a steep hill and died from the injuries, and Palanyao had spent the money for building materials for a house and could not return it. There was this sad news to break when the Butbut man came for his carabao. Palanyao, of course, promised to get one but didn't, and the Butbut purchaser came in vain for his animal several times. Finally, he came and slept in

15. *SalDa* is practiced only in southern Kalinga in the vicinity of Lubwagan. It is a form of usury that has been taken over recently from the lowlanders.— CAMILO LAMMAWIN.

Palanyao's house for three nights. By this time, the case was a public scandal, and news of it came to the pact-holder for Tinglaiyan. He forced Palanyao to borrow a carabao and fulfil his obligations.

Q. Was interest paid on the debt?

A. No—there is no interest unless there was a loan.

Q. Why did not the Butbut man inform the pact-holder about the case immediately on his arrival?

A. That is hard to say. Maybe he thought he would have to give the pact-holder a present. But the pact-holder didn't ask any present; he took action solely in order to prevent trouble and because he is obligated to help collect debts.

Gambling debts.—Gambling is a new thing in Kalinga; informants state emphatically that they had no form of it until after the Americans came. According to Camilo Lammawin, it is practiced only in the Lubwagan Region. It is said to have been introduced by a Sagada Igorot, Lucas Galpo, who became friends with a Kalinga named Piwik, whom he knew in Bontok. Galpo came to visit his friend, expecting to find gamblers, but no Kalingas knew the game or cared to play. Then Galpo took Piwik with him to Abra, where they found gamblers a-plenty. The game played was *biling.* Two coins are used, which are spun and then covered with a coco-shell cup. One man spins, the other covers. If two heads fall or two tails, then the spinner wins; if head and tail fall, the coverer wins.

The two companions soon lost all their money—or claimed to have done so. Then Lucas "gambled his companion"—that is, he borrowed a fairly large sum of money on condition that, if he lost it, his companion would remain as hostage until redeemed. He staked the whole sum borrowed on one cast and used a prepared pair of centavos that had no tails. He spun these, they were covered, everybody saw them, saw that he won, then he picked them up quickly and next time used genuine centavos. They gambled a long time; occasionally Galpo would use the fake centavos. They won 2,000 pesos. Something made the

Abra people suspicious, and they searched the two, found the mutilated coins, and imprisoned them. At midnight an Abra man came and offered to put up a ladder for 200 pesos. They agreed, obtained their freedom, and returned to Lubwagan, where their exploit gave the game a lot of publicity and led to the adoption of *biling* by the Kalingas there. More sophisticated now, Kalingas gamble with cards.

The custom has not had time to crystallize, but it is plain that it is tending to crystallize into the rule that gambling debts are frivolous and void. Note, for example, the following case:

38. Theft of gong; gambling debt not recognized by heirs (1939).— Palikás, the husband of my father's sister, came to my house asking for drinks. I went out and bought a frasco of gin and a bottle of beer. During my absence, he must have taken one of my gongs and hid it outside the house. I gave him three drinks of gin washed down with beer, after which he was drunk and asked permission to go home.[16] Soon I looked up the road and noticed that he was carrying something under his blanket. I then noticed that one of my gongs was missing, but I did not stop him, as he was drunk.

After sleeping all afternoon, as I was later told by my aunt, Palikás went at night to gamble and gambled my gong.

Next morning, I went to his house for my property. On hearing that the gong was gambled, I went to some habitual gamblers, and they told me who had won the gong. I went to that man's house, and, finding him not at home, I entered and took the gong. The gambler never approached me about the matter, but he went to my uncle and made him promise to pay 20 pesos. Unfortunately, my uncle died without having paid the debt. Then the gambler went to my uncle's sons and dunned them.

My uncle's sons told him, "Go for that debt to our father who is in Langit [the Skyworld]."

Comment: The sons would not and could not have denied any other form of debt.

16. The Philippine custom is for the guest to ask permission to leave. The mountain people drink gin as if it were as mild as their own brewed beverages. Three slugs of gin such as a Kalinga would pour would inebriate anybody.

COLLECTION OF SECURED DEBTS

Ownership of a pledged property can pass to the creditor only when the pledge was given as *salDa*, never in cases of *banat*. The custom is not definite with respect to whether so-ol, gifts to the kindred, are required when property passes under *salDa*, the reason probably being that the custom has not had time to crystallize since introduction of this form of mortgage. Some foreclosers give so-ol on taking possession; some do not. There is no period during which lands may be redeemed.

COLLECTION OF UNSECURED DEBTS

Any obligation is inherited—it never outlaws. During the old days, when lieutenant-governors had justice-of-the-peace powers, cases were not infrequently brought before them that went back to the grandfathers' days or even the great-grandfathers'.

Debts run long for various reasons: sometimes the creditor is afraid of the debtor and prefers to wait until the debt is inherited by a less dangerous individual. Collection of foreign debts may be rendered impossible for years by a rupture of a peace pact. I feel pretty sure that the most frequent reasons for noncollection are just plain procrastination, lack of energy, and weakness in facing unpleasant situations.

The Kalingas have three methods of collecting debts: (1) direct dunning by the creditor; (2) seizure, or distress (*taliwan*); and (3) sit-down collection.

Go-betweens, so important to the Ifugaos, are not used in debt collection, but sometimes the creditor will go to an "influential man" of the debtor's kindred and bespeak his good offices in influencing the debtor to pay up. The influential man receives no pay for his services—at least so my informant, himself an influential man, insisted. I suggested to him that his class might be overlooking a source of income. Rather sadly he admitted this, but said it would be a fearfully risky one, because the creditor might tell how he managed to get the debt out of the fellow, and, if this happened, the influential man's influence would be gone forever.

Property seizures.—To cover debt or tort, the Kalinga seizes only property—he never kidnaps human beings as the Ifugao does. The seizure, too, is always made in contemplation of return to the debtor when payment is made —which is not always the case in Ifugao—and usually it does not greatly arouse the wrath of the debtor.

Nearly every man has a rice field, and loans are not made to men who do not have; it follows that, within the region, rice fields, not heirlooms or movable objects, are seized. The seizure, as has been said, has the effect only of initiating a *banat* possession of the field—when the debt is paid, the field will be held until harvested, if under crop, and then returned to the owner. Seizures are made by planting *purdus* (Ifugao, *pudung*), runo reeds with the blades tied in a knot—the symbol of ownership. The Kalinga's system of seizure is a truly admirable custom policy and reveals his genius in social arrangements.

The same peaceableness extends to seizures in foreign regions. The approved procedure in making such a seizure is for the creditor, with or without a companion from his home town, to go to the foreign region and consult the pact-holder there for his own region about whose property he had better seize. With this advice, he goes to the house of the man suggested, and, if this man be absent in his fields, he may, "as a courtesy," send for him so that the seizure may be made in his presence. It is not at all necessary that he do this. Indeed, it is not even necessary that he consult the pact-holder—that is only a comity. It is the creditor's right to enter any man's house and seize an article worth two or three times the debt owed. If the owner is not present, he will proclaim as he passes through the barrio, *Tinaliwan-ak naya'n gusi* [*gansa*] *tai si utang* [name] *ken sakon* ("I have seized this gusi [or gong] because of So-and-so's debt to me"). He will seize only a gong or a gusi; he will not seize beads because these are multiple, and he might be accused, if they should be redeemed, of having detached some of them. He carries his seizure to his town.

The owner of the seized thing will say in effect to the debtor and his kindred, "If you pay your debt within such and such time (usually about a month), I shall accept my gong back, but if you do not, I shall seize your property. My gong is worth twice the amount of your debt." The debtor always, it is said, raises the amount. The owner may seize from any of his near-relatives, so that it makes no difference whether the debtor be poor or not. The pangats uphold this procedure. No present to the owner of the thing seized is due from the creditor except in one case, namely, if a carabao be seized. In that case the creditor must give him a gee-string or head ax or something of equivalent value, called *ma-ongaiyan*, for the "tiredness" of the animal due to its being led away from its accustomed pasture. It is said that long ago, however (probably before the peace pact by treaty confirmed the procedure of distress), a gratuity (*pasoksok*) was given the owner in all cases.

The seizer of the property is responsible for its delivery to the debtor in perfect condition if the debt be paid, while the debtor is responsible for it while bringing it on the return road home.

39. Seizure (*pre-American times*).—My uncle, Pasunglao, left a sow in Ginaang in charge of a certain man [a *namakan;* see p. 133]. Another Ginaang man took it as *daiyag* [for this privilege see p. 132]—that is, he wounded it a little because he needed it for sacrifice in sickness-recovery rites. A long time passed and the debt was unpaid. After a year, my uncle went to dun the man, but in vain. He dunned several times, and, getting tired of going so far, he seized a carabao from another Ginaang man. At that time, a carabao was worth five large pigs. The pact-holder in Ginaang for Lubwagan ruled that my uncle might keep the carabao because the sow, if not taken as *daiyag*, would have borne many litters of pigs. My uncle gave a pig to the caretaker.

40. Seizure (1920).—Kamaton called as his companion his kinsman Kaldingon and went to sell a string of valuable beads in the town of Ginaang. They stopped at the house of the pact-holder there for Lubwagan, whose name was Bagsao. Bagsao, on being informed what base price [*gatad*] was demanded, went to sell the beads. Diwaiyan agreed to buy them, so the pact-holder called Kamaton to Diwaiyan's house to effect the sale. The purchase price was:

Gatad ["base"]: 3 carabaos—to Kamaton
Pangat di so-ol: 2 pigs and 5 blankets—to the pact-holder, who acted as agent
Biyu n di so-ol: 1 small pig—to Kalingon, Kamaton's companion

Diwaiyan asked for and received credit on one of the carabaos, promising to deliver it after three months. Kamaton took two carabaos and went home. After three months, he went for the other, but there was none. A year later he went, "and there was none again." Three years passed and the debt was unpaid. Kamaton went to the pact-holder and informed him that he had come to make a seizure from a wealthy man called Gaddauwan. Then he went to the house of the latter, took a gong worth three carabaos, and carried it to Lubwagan.

Gaddauwan, from whom the gong was seized, told Diwaiyan that if the latter did not pay his debt and bring the gong back within a month, he "would not care for his gong anymore." "So Diwaiyan was scared that his debt will become more." He sold a field, paid his debt to Kamaton, redeemed the gong, and brought it back to its owner.

41. Seizure (ca. *1916*).—Ga-ot of Tanglag came to Lubwagan to buy rice. He had no money, but Pataotao let him have 1 *uyon* 4 *dalan* on his promise to bring a pig. But he did not do so, and Pataotao, on going to Tanglag, found that he had no pig.

Pataotao went to dun several times, but the years passed and never did he find Ga-ot with any pig. So he followed Sokong, a relative of Ga-ot to his house, saw a gong worth a carabao, took it, and carried it home. Sokong offered no objection

Sokong then went to Ga-ot's house, informed him what had happened, and told him that if he did not redeem the gong within a month or if the gong should be cracked, he would not care to receive it. Ga-ot did not relish the idea of paying a carabao when the debt was only a pig, so he paid up and got Sokong's gong back.

Questions asked of two good informants separately; their answers were in substantial agreement:

Q. If the debtor and his kindred really cannot pay the debt, can the "influential" men get his gong or gusi back from the seizer?

A. It is hard to conceive that neither the debtor nor his kindred would have fields. That is not the case around Lubwagan. But if such a case should happen, it is impossible to say whether the seizer would give the heirloom back; there are no cases.

Q. Can that influential man refuse to permit the seizure?

A. No; it is the creditor's right.

Q. May a seizure of an heirloom be made directly from the debtor himself?

A. Yes, but there might be trouble.

Q. In case the gusi is broken or the carbao falls over a cliff while in possession of the creditor, who is responsible for the loss?

A. The creditor, of course. But the debtor is responsible if the accident happen while the seized thing is being returned to its owner. The debtor is responsible for bringing it back from the seizer.

Sit-down collection.—We are told by Sir Henry Sumner Maine that among the Persians, a creditor, as an extreme debt-collection measure, used to go to his debtor's house and scatter barley over the house ground as an indication that he intended to stay until the seed grew up to provide him food. After this symbolic act, he would sit on the doorstep day after day until paid. This form of debt collection is widespread in the Far East. Both Ifugaos[17] and Kalingas employ it—I do not know about the other mountain tribes.

Despite the efficiency and smoothness of their system of distress, the Kalingas still use the sit-down quite extensively when the debtor lives in a foreign region. It nearly always gets results within less than six days and has the advantage that the creditor does not incur the risk con-

17. See R. F. Barton, *Ifugao Law*, p. 103; *Philippine Pagans*, p. 184.

nected with responsibility for an oftentimes very valuable heirloom after he has seized it. It can be carried out without danger, since a creditor is protected against his involuntary host both by the sacredness of his status as guest and by the local pact-holder for his region. The lot of the Kalinga or Ifugao sit-down collector is most enviable, surely, as compared with that of the Persian crouching on a doorstep in the dust and heat of a mid-Asian village.

The Kalinga sit-down is called *adugan*, meaning "watching over" or, perhaps figuratively, "sitting by." Its operation is shown in the following examples:

42. Sit-down in band (ca. *1930*).—Pedro, of Lubwagan, sold his gong to Tobagon, of Mabungtut, for a base payment of three carabaos, but credit was given on one of them on Tobagon's promise to have the animal within two months. On the elapse of this time, Pedro went to collect, but Tobagon had no carabao. Another month passed, and again he had no carabao. Two years later, the debt was still unpaid, so one day Pedro called five companions and went to Mabungtut. They stopped at Tobagon's house and informed him that they intended to stay until they led that carabao away.

After a day or two, Tobagon's wife told him that he would better borrow from his relatives and pay because she never saw anybody eat like Pedro and his companions, and if they should stay much longer all their rice would have been used up, since they had only 3 *uyons* left for the rest of the year. Accordingly, Tobagon went to his eldest brother, Andomang, and explained the situation saying that, unless Andomang should lend him his carabao, he, Tobagon and family, would be doomed to starvation soon, because their rice was vanishing fast. So Andomang "was convinced."

On the fourth day of their stay, Pedro and his companions led away their carabao, praising their host's hospitality highly. Tobagon paid Andomang later.

Comment by informant (PANGAT GASATAN): "But the best method of sit-down collection is to stop at the house of an influential man among the debtor's relatives, so that you will be helped by him. In such cases the debtor is ashamed before his influential kinsman, so he is obliged to borrow from his brothers and sisters."

43. Sit-down in band (ca. *1930*).—Madarang, of Tulgao, gave Carlos, of Linas, Lubwagan, 30 pesos with which to go and purchase a carabao for him in Isabela. Carlos spent the money on personal matters and could not find a job so as to pay it back. During the following five years, Madarang made many fruitless dunning trips. One day, he came with six companions and stopped at the house of Kosme, an influential cousin of Carlos. They told him they intended to be his guests until Carlos paid his debt. Kosme went to the house of Carlos and, summoning the latter's nearer relatives, invited them to contribute. On the third day, Madarang and his companions left with the money in their pockets. Carlos reimbursed his relatives later on.

44. Solitary sit-down collection (1934).—Dangay, a man of Lubwagan, loaned 10 pesos to YangaR of Ginaang on the promise of being repaid with a pig. YangaR promised to bring the pig after a month. A year later the debt was not paid. Dangay went to Ginaang ten times to dun in vain. Tired of this, he slept in the debtor's house two nights, continually talking to the latter about his debt. Dangay grew more and more angry as he did this and seemed to be trying to pick a quarrel. Pangats and baknang heard the rough language and assembled to prevent anything that might break the peace pact with Lubwagan. One of the baknang who was related to YangaR gave a cow to Dangay in the presence of the pangats with the understanding that, if the cow was not paid back next harvest, YangaR's field would be seized.

Comment: Kalingas are extremely sensitive to a threat to a peace pact—especially a pact with a stronger region.

A SPECIAL RIGHT OF SEIZURE UNDER URGENT NECESSITY: THE "DAIYAG"

To the Kalinga the necessity of sacrificing for recovery from wounds or sickness appears as urgent as medical attention does to us. The need for animals to sacrifice in funeral rites is no less urgent. Any man confronted by either of these necessities and lacking animals may slightly wound an animal belonging to anyone and take it to be sacrificed. He is obliged to pay it back, of course; "if the owner is kind, he will take a pig of the same size in repayment, if unkind, he will demand a bigger pig or even a carabao." This method of seizure is called *daiyag*.[18]

45. Seizure by daiyag; *seizure to cover debt thereby incurred (1927).*—Palaiyok of Lubwagan region left a cow with Imang to be cared for with

18. *Daiyag* means "forced loan," and the borrower must repay it at whatever price the owner demands, which is usually much more than the value of the animal taken.—CAMILO LAMMAWIN.

the agreement that the third calf to be born should be Imang's. When the cow had been with Imang for two years, she had borne two calves. At this time, Langag, brother of Imang, having suffered the loss of a child and urgently needing a sacrifice for its funeral, slashed the oldest calf and took it as *daiyag*.

When this debt was unpaid at the end of three years, Palaiyok went to Tanglag, seized a field of the debtor worth three carabaos, and sold it immediately to a Tanglag man for two carabaos plus so-ol.

SPECIAL DUTIES AND LIABILITIES OF
CARETAKERS AND AGENTS

Caretakers.—Caretakers called *mamakan* feed pigs for a share in the increase (two or three pigs from each litter); the owner who gives the pig out to care is called *impaka-kan*. Those who care for cattle receive every third calf. If the owner is dissatisfied with the feeding or care the animal is receiving, he may take it away from the caretaker, but must compensate him for the period the animal was under care.

If an animal under care dies, the caretaker must carry the carcass to the owner; if he desires, he will receive a share of it. If the animal be stolen, the caretaker must bring witnesses and prove the fact. If the animal be seized by *daiyag*, then the seizer must settle with the owner, and the owner, with the caretaker.

Agents.—All sales and purchases in foreign regions and all of importance within the home region are conducted through agents. There are two methods of buying and selling: *tokdai* and *angkat*. When giving an object to be sold on the *tokdai* basis, the owner tells the agent (*mantokdai*) for what price it is to be sold and the agent receives part of the so-ol as his fee. Under *angkat*, the owner states what price he wants for himself, and the agent keeps all he can get above that for himself. Both systems of sale are used within the home region.

The *tokdai* method is used when an owner himself takes

an article, say a gusi or string of valuable beads or a carabao, to another region and sells it through an agent. It
may be that he has a trading partner in the town, one who
regularly sells for him and for whom he sells if his partner
comes to his own town. If not, then the pact-holder for his
region will undertake the sale for him or will find him an
agent.

When, however, a man selects his agent from his own
region and sends him forth with the article to sell in foreign
parts, the transaction is on the *angkat* basis. *Angkat* is also
used in buying abroad. For example, if a man wants to buy
a carabao, he will give his agent a sum of money, say 30
pesos, and will specify what length of horn the animal must
have. The agent, *manangkat*, will go where he pleases. In
order to have a good profit for himself out of the 30 pesos,
he will probably go to a far place where carabaos are cheap.
On returning home he will receive:

> *Pabaal*—1 gee-string
> *So-ol*—1 small pig, worth 3 or 4 pesos
> *Palanos*—1 small pig or chicken killed to feast him
> *Pa-inum*—a good drink or else one-half a peso

Agents are responsible for the property that is intrusted
to them and must make it good if it be broken by accident
or taken away from them by robbers or enemies. Formerly
even though a man resisted and had a wound to show, he
had to make good a loss, but now, in such a case, he must
make good only one-half the loss. Charging him in full was
justified on the ground that his greed for profit had led him
to venture beyond the region of safety to regions with which
Lubwagan had no pact, so that the fault was his.

It was not the pangats who backed the buyers (the
mampa-angkat) in demanding full compensation and in-
sisting on the rule of absolute responsibility of agents—it
was the pact-holders, the college of pact-holders, we might

say, seeing that Lubwagan, for example, normally has over forty of them.

Q. Why did the pact-holders make the agents pay the full amount regardless?

A. There were several reasons: (1) the pact-holders did not want their people taking risks and going into danger, because that meant trouble; (2) the pact-holders did not want the buyers of animals, the *mampa-angkat*, to be afraid to give their money to agents, because this would make it impossible for enterprising men to secure opportunities for gaining money; (3) the pact-holders wanted to encourage the importation of animals.

The pact-holders, it must be remembered, derive a good deal of their compensation from foreign trade. It was to their interest to keep agents from going to the lowlands so that animals would be sold from town to town. In this way there would more often be so-ol for the pact-holders.

Q. Well, why did owners begin to ask only half, provided the agent could show a wound or prove superior force?

A. Sapao [Governor Hale] adjudged a case or two that way, and the agents began to stipulate beforehand that they should be charged only half in such cases, else they would not go, as there were lots of opportunities to earn wages after the Americans came.

RESPONSIBILITY OF OWNERS FOR ACTS OF ANIMALS

Custom law on fencing.—If a pasture is first utilized after fields in the vicinity already exist, it is the duty of the cattle owner to fence his pasture land. If, however, a field be constructed subsequent to the pasturage of adjacent lands, then it is the duty of the field owner to fence his field.

Responsibility for damages by animals.—The owner must pay if a carabao breaks through a fence that is its owner's obligation to build. If the field owner is responsible for the fence, the latter must be a good fence, otherwise the owner of the animal is not liable for damages it does. Unless the case is clearly one of negligence on the part of the field owner, however, damages will always be paid, because the owner of the animal will fear that the field owner will slash or spear his carabao as a revenge. It is about the same with pigs. If the owner does not pay damages, the field owner will watch and when the pig goes to the field again, he will plant sharpened bamboo stakes (*suga*) along his dike, then frighten the pig into them. If the owner of the latter complains, the field owner will say, "All right, pay for the damages to the rice and I'll pay the damage to the pig." There is no obligation on the part of field owners to fence against pigs; that work is done by the villages. If a pig in Ifugao habitually breaks fence, the owner must blind it; this he does by inserting a piece of guava leaf under each eyelid.

Responsibility for dogbite.—If a dog bites a man, the man may kill it if he wants to.

If a mad dog bites a person and the person dies, the owner of the dog must contribute to the *utong* (funeral sacrifices) of the deceased. The *utong* will be a little less if the deceased were a child.

46. Mad-dog bite; settlement (1930).—The dog of Songag in Gungugung [Lubwagan] went mad and bit the child of Kinal. The child became mad and died. The pangats agreed that Songag ought to furnish two carabaos for the child's *utong*, and this was done. Had it not been done, Kinal or one of his relatives would have killed Songag, one of his children, or one of his relatives.

Chapter IV

THE REGIONAL UNIT: ITS INSTITUTIONS AND CUSTOM LAW

ALTHOUGH the territorial principle of social organization is much weaker, much less often in the people's
consciousness, than the tribal or kinship principle, it is of
almost unexaggerable importance, since it is the progressive principle, the one from which the state arises. The
generalization is sound that human society develops by
forming ever larger units, based on new principles and
loyalties, which engulf and unify the older, smaller, and
contending units. Thus, in both Kalinga and Ifugao, territorial units are dominating the kinship groups. The process
is considerably more advanced among the Kalingas than
among the Ifugaos.

The territorial unit in both cases is the region. But it is
vague in Ifugao, where, although in an indefinite way a
valley does constitute a territorial social unit,[1] still the unit
is a shifting one, to a considerable extent a different one for
every barrio. For example, the village of Haliap is somewhat doubtfully spoken of as belonging to the Kiangan
region, and geographically it does belong, but it is a some-

1. I call this unit the "home region" for convenience and because the term
seems to me to be psychologically correct, although neither Ifugao nor Kalinga
has a designation for it. The Ifugao, if pinned down to give it a name, calls it
hitu ("here"), and he calls his co-regionists *tago hitu* ("people of here"). The
Kalinga uses the borrowed Iloko word *ili* ("town") to designate it, and that, too,
is inadequate. The Kalinga gives each territorial unit a particular designation by
naming it from its principal barrio, and so, to a considerable extent, does the
Ifugao.

what isolated village, and its relations are more cordial with Mongaiyan, to which it is near and with which it has intermarried much more than with Kiangan Valley. Likewise the villages of the upper end of Kudug Valley are on more cordial terms with those over the ridge in another geographical unit, Piwong, than with those at the lower end of their own valley, down by the river. Thus propinquity and intermarriage are what matter most in determining any individual's home region, not geographic bounds. But in Kalinga the last are determinant. The bounds are vague and shifting in Ifugao, definite and stable in Kalinga.

There is another difference. Ifugao home regions are, in general, though subject to modifications by numerous circumstances, the center of a series of concentric rings, which I have called, from home region outward: (1) the neutral zone, a ring of regions with which the home region is at peace and greatly intermarries; (2) the feudist zone, beyond the neutral zone, with which there is less intermarriage and with which there are numerous interkinship-group feuds; and (3), beyond this, a war zone, almost any of whose people will be killed if a good opportunity presents. There is not this zoning in Kalinga.

In the Ifugao home region there is only the delicate, amorphous, almost invisible embryo of political organization. The Kalinga region has a political organization that is rather feeble so far as domestic affairs go but has a hard crustacean shell with respect to foreign affairs.

Lubwagan Region is an oval valley having diameters of about seven and five kilometers. It faces northeast, being backed in the south, west, and north by mountains. Its open end and steep eastern side lie along the Chico River, a large tributary of the Cagayan. Just beyond the mouth of the valley lies the region of Tanglag. Elevation ranges from about 1,600 to 3,000 feet; most of the villages are located on or near the 2,300-foot line.

The valley's surface is considerably greater than it would be if it were flat instead of being convoluted. The population lives in fifteen hamlets or, as we shall call them, barrios, all but four of which are concentrated within a circle about a kilometer in diameter at the southwestern end of the region. Excluding lowlanders, the population is about 2,400.

Over the mountain to the west, about four kilometers distant, is Uma (population 852), which constitutes an extrusion of Lubwagan outside the valley both as a political and as an endogamous unit. We have already explained how this came about (p. 35).

Thus, except for this satellite, Lubwagan is marked off from surrounding regions by strong geographical features except in one case, Tanglag. The bounding regions, beginning in the north and proceeding clockwise are: Ableg, Kagalwan, Tanglag, Mabungtut, Sumadel, and Ginaang.

Kalinga institutions appear all to be genetically related to institutions that are to be found among the Ifugaos, yet the custom laws and procedure of the two cultures differ remarkably.[2] The principal reason is that two of the institutions common to both societies have become highly specialized in Kalinga and much more effective than in Ifugao. At the same time, and probably because of the effectiveness of these two, other common institutions are decadent in Kalinga. Before examining Kalinga institutions in detail, we shall make a general comparison of a few of these common institutions. We shall begin with a consideration of an indemnity whose significance to a great

2. [There are also important similarities between Kalinga and Tinguian institutions, the nature of which requires further comparative study. Mountain Tinguian villages represent in part an overflow from Kalinga.—F. E.]

extent escaped me until recently, namely, the *tokom* in Ifugao, the *pasoksok* in Kalinga.

Inasmuch as Ifugao society is based almost exclusively on blood kinship, neither the individual Ifugao nor a kinship group will ordinarily intervene in a matter that concerns a nonrelative or in a dispute between other kinship groups. That is to say, the unrelated individual and kinship group will usually remain neutral. An Ifugao will ordinarily intervene to prevent an offense against a co-regionist only in case the latter's life is directly and immediately threatened by an alien—and not always then. In some other cases he might obstruct a wrong against an absent neighbor (in the sense of a man whose house stood alongside his own), but he would not be nearly so likely to interfere in the interest of a nonrelated person who lived at the other end of a village of, say, twenty-five houses and probably would not interfere at all in behalf of one from another village only 200 meters away. The most he would do would be to ask *tokom*, a kind of indemnity, from the offender, if the offense happened to be committed in his presence or under certain special circumstances. Thus, if he saw somebody seizing his co-regionist's child to sell as a slave or stealing his neighbor's pig, he would always, if a kadangyan or of kadangyan blood, demand *tokom*, and he frequently would if of lower class. So far as he is consciously concerned, his demand probably amounts to an assertion of dignity by showing the malfeasors that he is a man to be reckoned with when somebody is profiting by an irregularity. The *tokom* demanded might be a bolo if the man were stealing a pig, or might be the promise of a pig and two or three chickens if a child were being kidnapped. If his demand should not be complied with, he would obstruct the carrying-out of the offense, or, if the other party were too strong for this, he would later, backed by his kinship group, enforce his demand for *tokom*. For some reason, I cannot help associating the demand for a *tokom* from a tortfeasor with the "coming-out" of villagers to demand a cut of meat from a hunter (p. 85).

Now regardless of the individual's motives in the case— for the sociologist in his study of the beginnings of institutions, like the Freudian in his analysis of the sources of virtues, learns at first to hold his nose and later to be able to get along without even that—the practice of demanding *tokom* signalizes an advance beyond the tribal principle of social organization in that it establishes the right of an outsider to intervene in what, in a strictly tribal society, would be none of his business. And out of the right there is plainly growing a *duty* to intervene that is incumbent on the most powerful stratum of the population. And that duty is the beginning of police power, and police power is the beginning of the domestic aspect of the state.

My previous interpretations did not entirely miss the mark—they merely mistook the ideological, reinforcing rationalizations for the essence. For the indemnity does rationalize itself on the ground that it compensates for a magical injury or a disagreeable circumstantial linking of the *tokom*-demander with the offense committed. Lists I have compiled show *tokom* to have been demanded: by the owner of a field in which a woman was kidnapped; by a man who loaned a basket to a boy who was kidnapped while wearing the basket; by a person who was kidnapped by mistake for another person; by a trader whose companion was seized to be sold as a slave; by witnesses of various offenses against unrelated persons; and so on. Any circumstantial connection whatever gives an Ifugao the right to demand *tokom* as an evidence of noncomplicity (so the rationalization has it) and as the price of nonintervention, and some circumstances make collection of the *tokom* obligatory in order that what is received may be shown the kindred of the offended as an evidence of noncomplicity.[3]

The *tokom* must be demanded by a member of the aristocratic (kadangyan) class if an offense be committed in his presence, else he loses face (prestige). A poor man will, unless the circumstances be such that he would otherwise be blamed as a participant in the offense, use his discretion about intervening, but a kadangyan in his own home region loses prestige unless he demands *tokom* or even, it appears, if his near-relative who may himself be poor does not demand it.

Thus, the *tokom*, sometimes a mere bribe and always a sharing of the spoils, is a faint malodorous beginning of the police power of the state; it is vested in the upper, the wealthy, class more than in anybody else. It reflects an incipient territorial principle in society. The police power of the modern state, be it noted, sometimes smells strongly of just such an origin as we have shown in Ifugao.

Now let us notice this payment in Kalinga. I learned about the Kalinga's more advanced political organization before I learned of his *pasoksok* (which is what he calls his form of *tokom*), and I was surprised that a group having so much apparent local unity in some respects should have so little neighborliness as to countenance a wrong against a neighbor if given a bribe. The following questions and answers show the status of the payment among the Kalingas:

Q. If a Kalinga sees a man stealing from a nonrelated man's house in his barrio, what does he do?

A. He goes to the thief and says, "Ah! I have caught you! Give me something." "Yes," the thief will say. "Come to my house and I will give you something." Then he will go, and if it is a pig that was stolen

3. See R. F. Barton, *Ifugao Law*, pp. 83 and 89; *Philippine Pagans*, pp. 158, 159, 163–65.

the thief will give him a nice piece of meat or a chicken if he'd rather have it, or a bolo. This is called *pasoksok*.

Q. And if he gets this, will he tell who the thief was?

A. He will not.

Q. Suppose the thief refuses to give *pasoksok?*

A. Then he will go to the owner whose pig was stolen and say, "Give me something, and I will tell you who stole your pig."

Q. Will a kadangyan ask *pasoksok?*

A. If he is a good man, he will not. Probably he will not, even if he is a bad man, if somebody is looking.

Q. Well, suppose that two or three persons come upon a thief in the act; what will they do?

A. They will all demand large *pasoksok* because they are less afraid than one man would be.

Q. Do all Kalingas ask *pasoksok?*

A. Probably the pangats do not, and if a commoner is a good man, maybe he doesn't.

It is only justice to add that the Kalinga's attitude is more cynical than the Ifugao's, which is merely naïve; the Kalinga's attitude is a degeneration, made possible I think by the fact that Kalinga society has a degree of political organization that is regulatory in domestic affairs. The Ifugao *tokom*, it seems to me, in the absence of any kind of political government, reflects a positive trend, while the Kalinga *pasoksok*, in the presence of a fairly efficient mechanism of regulation, is decadent.

Two duties are delegated to the Ifugao go-between by the public opinion of his region: (1) he must kill or wound a man from one kinship group that attacks a member of another while he is mediating a controversy between the two and (2) in some regions of Ifugao, if he finds the case not "go-betweenable" and decides to withdraw from it, he must impose a truce during which he will punish the side that commits an aggressive act against the other.

Breaking the peace while a case is being mediated by a go-between is the sole crime or *public* wrong, strictly speaking, in the Ifugao code. All other offenses are against kinship groups and are torts; this one is against what little police power the region has and is, therefore, a crime.

It is a crime, too, in Kalinga, but, among the records of over a hundred cases of controversy and "troubles" I have recorded, there is not one of infraction of the peace while a case was being mediated. I have repeatedly made inquiries and have sent my best informant to make inquiries regarding such an infraction. No one ever heard of such a case— not even the old blind man of Mabileng, who would know, they say, if it had ever occurred. And they all say that the Kalinga go-between would not pay weregilds in such a case.

Among the Ifugao two men of distant regions sometimes enter into a highly formalized and ritualized pact which makes them *biyao*, trading partners, with definite obligations to each other. Each will trade with the region of the other through the other only. Each will avenge the killing of the other or his people accompanying him or sent by him if that killing occurs within certain limits agreed on. Their "trade" is carried on more, probably, for the sake of the prestige and ceremonial visits and interchanges of gifts and the accessory ritualizing it entails than for profit. Such pacts are usually short-lived; the principals and even more their kinship groups get tired of the effort and exactions they impose. The pact then loses force, and the regions are left without one until other individuals are minded to enter into the relationship. While it lasts, and if the trading partners be strong characters, backed by sufficient prestige, the *biyao* pact has almost the effect of a peace pact between the two regions. But usually it is whimsically undertaken by the two men on their own initiative and never has back of it the entire sentiment of the regions concerned.

The Kalingas have developed the peace pact into one of the most admirable and efficient primitive institutions I have ever seen or read about. We shall devote several pages to it later on. At present, I wish to point out that it appears to have developed by fission from a *biyao* or trading-partner relation similar to that of the Ifugaos. The function of the latter as a mechanism of trade is embodied in the *abuyog* relationship (see p. 134)—*abuyog* is almost certainly the Kalinga cognate of *biyao*—while its function as a peace-maintaining institution has become the *budong*, or peace pact, which is guaranteed by the pact-holder, the *mangdon si budong*.

The Ifugaos have an upper or aristocratic class called kadangyan. The kadangyan is a person, almost always the first- or second-born in his family, whose principal and almost sole social functions are the leadership of his own kinship group and, when invited, mediation between other kinship groups. Though the kadangyan's influence is often great with nonkindred, he rarely rises to a position of leadership of a *locality*.

Class stratification is the same in the two societies except that, in Kalinga, exceptional individuals have risen above the kadangyan class and taken on a function that responds not only to the blood tie but to the territorial one—that is, a political function. The classes are:

KALINGA

1. Kapus, the poor
2. Baknang, the well-to-do; the affluent[4]
3. Kadangyan, wealthy aristocrats, leaders of kinship groups
4. Pangat, selected men who exercise functions that are political

4. *Baknáng*, "rich man" by original meaning, is almost certainly a borrowed word, now used in more or less confusion with kadangyan to denote persons of middle status. As a matter of fact, both Ifugaos and Kalingas appear formerly to have recognized only two classes: the kadangyan, an upper class by reason of having inherited great wealth (or of being descendants of a conquering race?), and the *nawatwat* (lit. "passed by in the distribution") or *kapús*, whose derivative meaning I do not know. The Ifugaos are coming into a consciousness that there is a middle class, but they hardly know what to call it. By derivation, *natumok* one of the terms used, means "attached"—to the kadangyan, by reason of being younger brothers?

IFUGAO

1. Nawatwat, "the disinherited"
2. Natumok, the middle class; *mabitil*, "those who will become hungry"
3. Kadangyan, wealthy aristocrats, leaders of kinship groups

Thus the difference between the two cultures in this respect is that the Kalingas have this specialized subgroup, drawn mainly from the highest class. It is true that, when an Ifugao kadangyan acts as a go-between, he does, in some aspects of that office, fulfil a political function. It is also true that the Kalinga pangat is still largely bound by ties of kinship. Quantitatively the difference between the two is not great, but it is enough to bring about an important qualitative difference: (1) the pangat performs his function as moderator in his region all the time, and (2) he not infrequently coerces erring kinsmen in order to bring them back into some sort of correct relation to folk who are not his kin. His stature is sufficient to raise his eyes above the rim of the kinship tub—he has *out*look. The Ifugao kadangyan acts is the first function only fortuitously, and in the second rarely or never.

Kalinga society reflects in the pangat, in the peace pact with pact-holder to enforce it, in its defined boundaries, in its definite citizenship, with provisions for formal change of citizenship, and in its detailed and humane treaties with other regions a higher political development than any other Philippine people, so far as has been reported. The virility of these institutions and the hold that they have on the Kalingas are manifested by the fact that they function almost or quite as efficiently and extensively now and underground, after thirty-odd years of foreign rule, as they did before that rule, so that, as has already been said, the Kalingas are really subject to two governments, one native, one foreign. One reason for this persistence is the

Kalinga attitude toward paying indemnities and were-gilds. If an indemnity be plainly required by custom law and expected by public opinion in the case, a Kalinga and his family would be ashamed not to "do the right thing." And after the painful part of paying is finished (or perhaps even before that) they boast about the largeness of the indemnity.

Governor Walter A. Hale ("Sapao" to Kalingas, Ifugaos, and old-timer Americans) perceived the genius of several Kalinga institutions, fortified them, and gave them a field wherever they could be useful. So, too, did his Filipino assistant and successor, Governor Thomas Blanco. But succeeding native governors have looked on them as resistance to Filipinization.

THE PANGATS

Pangats are powerful individuals who have been selected by a long informal process whereby they grow in popular influence and recognition and are elevated to the rank in which the domestic aspect of the Kalinga state is lodged.

In the eyes of the people, the pangats' main function is to make peace when trouble arises—they are sometimes collectively called "The Peacemakers" or "Right-determiners" (*manlilintog*). But people go to them for advice and assistance in all kinds of matters. Every pangat holds at least one or two peace pacts and helps to determine the regional policy when emergencies arise. Formerly at least, the pangat, knowing that people were afriad of him and wanted to stand well with him, was not backward about requesting labor services or about "borrowing," or simply intimating that he needed this or that.

Selection of a pangat.—No form of election or voting has ever been reported from any native culture in the Philippines.[5] No native culture has gone further in political development than community government. Elevation to rank and power in the community is a gradual process of emergence in which the power is attained before the rank is acknowledged by the people. So it is in Kalinga.

Wealth, lineage, family connections with other pangats, personality, co-operativeness, fairness (meaning suprakinship vision), oratorical ability, a record of having settled cases of controversy between kinship groups, and above all a reputation as a dangerous man were formerly the principal factors entering into selection. Nowadays the last factor is, perforce, of diminished importance and its place has been taken by our own American darling, "go-getting." According to Mr. Dakauwag, "If a man has nothing, people just won't listen to him when he speaks in any gathering. Even if he is wealthy but has only lived on his wealth without winning more, then no matter how good his reasons are, they can be refuted by jeering, 'What have you acquired?—nothing! Therefore your reasons are no good.' And what can the fellow say? He has to shut up."

Until the Americans came, the contradiction was sharp in Kalinga society that the road to stoppage of homicide began with—homicide! The route to pangathood lay as follows: (1) the youth would kill somebody in order to get his tattoo and a right to voice his opinions among men; (2) then, seeking dominance, he would kill more people and

5. Voting in the Philippine Assembly and Senate differs radically from voting in American legislative bodies. A majority does not press through a vote as soon as debate is concluded. There still has to be a lot of "arranging." Influential opponents have to be appeased somehow or other—by swaps or favors such as creation of jobs for relatives—else they will cherish grudges and sooner or later make trouble. Consequently a vote is postponed until everybody who matters is "convinced." This might be construed as a safeguarding of minority rights if the appeasement were organically connected with some principle or with the measure itself, but good observers declare that this is not often the case. It is apparent that the processes that underlie modern Philippine legislation are continuative from native, Malayan society.

thus inspire fear among the folk; (3) he would intervene to settle disputes between kinship groups, incited to this course, no doubt, by the demand of public opinion that the powerful do this, and he would be successful because feared by the people; (4) if in these settlements he were fair and acted "for the good of all the people," and if during his life he should not have offended too grossly against the community ethics, then a few of the people would begin to call him pangat. And right there was the critical point in selection: if the rest followed, he was selected and would be accepted by the pangats as one of their own number. If they did not follow, then even those that had begun it would quit.

Nowadays the pangats play a greater role than formerly in selection: they may invite a prominent man to join them in consultation once or twice, after which the people are likely to accept their appraisal of him.

The eldest pangats are called *kamalanan* and enjoy a little more respect and influence, presumably, than the others. Lubwagan has three such, Galamoy and Maddalum, both well over sixty, and Kanao, a little younger.

The sort of co-operation the pangats of a region were capable of rendering the colonial government if given a chance is shown by the following case from Magnao. I should explain that in the northwestern part of the subprovince, Kalingas pay a bride-price to the fiancée's relatives that is enormous—quite comparable to the Ifugao *hakba*.

47. Refusal to discontinue studies and marry; bansak *required to be returned* (ca. *1928*).—L. of Magnao was engaged to be married to a girl when both were quite small, and his kindred had delivered the *bansak* to her kindred. When the Americans came with schools, L. developed a thirst for learning and, when the time came for him to marry, refused lest it interfere with his securing a higher education. His kinship group demanded the return of the *bansak* gifts. The bride's people refused.

Thereupon L.'s father went to the *presidente* of the municipality, at Tabuk, and complained. The *presidente* submitted the case to the pangats of a neutral neighboring region for decision. The pangats decided that the *bansak* ought to be returned. Then the local pangats in Magnao concurred and confirmed the decision, so the bride's people had to obey.

TABLE 1

LUBWAGAN PANGATS IN APPROXIMATELY THEIR ORDER
OF POWER AND INFLUENCE

| NAME | ORDER OF BIRTH | NO. OF BROTHERS AND SISTERS | AGE* | RANK OF FOREBEARS | | | NO. SLAIN BY HIM | KINSHIP CONNECTIONS: PANGAT (a) BY BLOOD (b) BY MARRIAGE |
				Father	Paternal Grandfather	Maternal Grandfather		
Kanao......	1	(4)	42	Pangat	Pangat	Kadangyan	None†	(a) 7 (b) 4
Dugyang...	4	(4)	35	Pangat	Poor	Baknang	None	(a) 6 (b) 2
Galamoy...	Only	child	60	Pangat	Kadangyan	Baknang	7 or 8	(a) 4 (b) 7
Damag.....		‡	50	Pangat	Pangat	Poor	1, for which imprisoned	(a) 4 (b) 8
Aklinon....	Only	child	45	Pangat	Pangat	Baknang	1	No data
ManaLtag..	1	(4)	40	Kadangyan	Poor	Pangat	None	(a) 5 (b) 6
Maddalum..	Only	child	70	Kadangyan	Baknang	Pangat	5 and wounded 1	(a) 5 (b) 7
Agpaowan..	5	(5)§	55	Poor	Poor	Pangat	1	No data
Wakas.....	1	(5)	43	Kadangyan	Poor	Pangat	1 and wounded 1	No data
Gasatan....	2	(6)	38	Pangat	Pangat	Pangat	None	(a) 8 (b) 4
Iwag.......	3	(5)	40	Pangat	Pangat	Pangat	None	No data
Liaban.....	2	(2)‡	42	Kadangyan	Baknang	Poor	None	(a) 1 (b) 7

* Age estimated or calculated by the author.

† Considering the fact that the Americans came and interfered with killing some thirty years ago, the poor record in this respect of men under fifty years of age should be excused; it is to be assumed that they would have done better had they had an opportunity.

‡ Children of dagdagas.

§ Son by second marriage of Kanao's paternal grandmother, who was of pangat rank, to a poor man.

The twelve pangats of Lubwagan region are listed in Table 1, together with certain data concerning them which will enable us better to understand how they have attained the rank.

It is apparent from the summary in Table 2 that inherited wealth and prestige are important but not decisive factors. Family circumstances such as order of birth, number of children, and so on have an important bearing, since they affect inheritance. Three of the pangats were only children, and so inherited estates of both father and mother, and five were either the first- or second-born and so had preferential rights in inheritance. Dugyang, although the youngest of four children, also had such rights, for his brother died, and so it was the same for him as if he had been the oldest male—he inherited his father's property. Actually only three of the lot worked their way up from relative poverty, namely, Iwag, Damag, and Liaban, the last

TABLE 2

RANK OF FATHERS AND GRANDFATHERS
OF LUBWAGAN PANGATS

	Pangat	Kadangyan	Baknang	Poor
Rank of father...............	7	4	....	1
Rank of paternal grandfather...	5	1	2	4
Rank of maternal grandfather...	6	1	3	2

two being children of mistresses. Iwag was third in his family and inherited little, though son and grandson of a pangat on both sides. His rise to wealth is said to have been largely due to the fact that he is an expert gambler, but he is also "shrewd in property deals, never quarrels with people, and is nearly always correct."

Pangat Dugyang, or one of his friends, when reading my manuscript, took umbrage at the passage relating to him above and crossed it out violently, inserting the following, instead: "Duguiang is the youngest son of Pallayoc. It was impossible for him to inherit the properties of his brother unless he does not kill animals. It is a fact that Duguiang was shared one field and one gusi, but they are untouchable till now—never sold and used as capital. Duguiang increased his inherited property because of being a business-man, farmer and servant of the government."

Mr. Dugyang's touchiness reflects the bourgeoisization of the aristocracy. Early in the American regime, one of the worst insults that could be thrown at an Ifugao kadangyan (Ifugaos have been fined for it) was the accusation that his wealth was mainly acquired property, not inherited. I suspect that there used to be the same touchiness in Kalinga. But now the emphasis is on acquiring and not on inheriting. And now a *sine qua non* of elevation to pangat rank is that a man must have added a good deal to his inherited properties. I have several times been told, when inquiring why a certain kadangyan had not made the grade to pangathood, "He never added to his inherited property —he just lived [vegetated] on it." I feel certain that this attitude is due to acculturation during the American regime. It may be added that Dugyang is cunning, quick-witted, and has added so much to his inherited wealth that he is second in riches among the pangats.

Kanao,[6] to whose sister, Lufina, Dugyang is married, has a reputation for magnanimity and generosity, is a good speaker, level-headed, and has a mature, somewhat cynical sense of humor that makes him an agreeable companion. He is the wealthiest of the pangats. Galamoy is a peace-maker, a diplomat, good speaker, and, in these latter, mature years, has good judgment. Also he has killed seven or eight persons (for one such instance see Case 58).

A number of the pangats are distantly related in Gi-naang. It came about thus: a wealthy Lubwagan man married a woman of the same town, and a daughter, Ukang, was born to them. But the wife was such a heller that, rather than continue living with her, the man preferred to

6. [For more recent news of Kanao see the Epilogue.—F. E.]

surrender all his property to his child and divorced the mother. He married again, became wealthy again, and had eight children. When this wife died, he married a third time and had five. The Lubwagan people were afraid to engage their children to the daughter by the first marriage on account of the mother's temper and tongue. Even after Ukang had become a beautiful young woman, the young men of the place feared the mother.

However, a Ginaang man who came to attend a pact-drinking, saw the girl and was fascinated by her beauty. He decided that her many half-brothers and half-sisters would give him a large "party" in Lubwagan and that he might safely renounce his citizenship in Ginaang and take that of Lubwagan. This man was the ancestor of several of the pangats, among them Maddalum. Maddalum has quite a head-hunting record, although he is really a timid man. He was dismissed from the office of mayor a few years ago on a charge of some sort of malfeasance and is now living with a youngish dagdagas in the most distant of Lubwagan's barrios.

I met Maddalum one morning soon after arriving in Lubwagan for my second stay. He greeted me as an old acquaintance and borrowed forty cents on the ground that his child was hungry and he had no bread for it. A week or so later, he brought me a prized heirloom head ax which, he said, he must part with owing to pressure of biting necessity. In order to make it attractive to me, he recited its head-hunting record. There is no doubt that it is old, for it is derived from cast iron and is of the stern, practical, Bontok shape rather than the elegant Kalinga one.

Maddalum's father inherited the ax from his father-in-law, Walis, the man who married the daughter of Ukang and the Ginaang man. In those days a man had to inspire fear in order to have "influence" with the people; he would set his goal at ten killings—or woundings, which count as killings.

Walis began his career by killing two women in Uma. He did not take their heads because Lubwagan intermarries with that settlement. He killed them "just to show that he was brave"—"also to get his tattoo." Balugan of Talgao came to Lubwagan to earn rice or pigs, "but because Walis wanted to kill many people, he slew him." Because of this act, the Lubwagan pact-holder for Talgao killed a relative of Walis so as to preserve the pact. Next Walis killed Mali of Lubo on a head-hunting expedition carried out by ten men from Lubwagan. Next he killed Bokad and Dulauwan of Dakalan. They had come to trade in Lubwagan; Walis saw them going around and "just killed them."

His next victims were Balungay and Daluwai, of Sumadel, killed in war (*baluknit*). The warriors of Sumadel met those of Lubwagan in a place called Lopnak. Maddalum claims ten were killed on each side and that on the Lubwagan side Walis killed two. Next he went with a head-hunting party to Mabungtut and killed Ulnagon and Naganag as they were working in their fields. Next he killed Malgik, a co-citizen of Lubwagan, who lived in Dangoy barrio only half a kilometer from Tiwod where Walis lived. He had already killed his ten, but he killed yet another "to get renown."

Now it is to be noted that he went head-hunting (which is dangerous) only twice and that Maddalum claims for him in each instance all the men who were killed by the entire party. He went to war (which is possibly still more dangerous) only once, apparently, when he claimed to have killed two out of the ten victims. He slew three fellow-citizens. He slew a man from a town with which there was a peace pact who had come to Lubwagan in order to work

for wages. He slew two from a town with which the pact
was ruptured who had come to Lubwagan to trade but who
had drunk water in Walis' house. Truly he was a dangerous
man, but he does not seem to have been a very brave one.
His wealth gave him the advantage of being able to pay
weregilds, save his own skin, and go on killing.

Killing within the town, though less dangerous to effect
than killing abroad, contributed more to a man's influence
than killing outside it, which indicates, I think, that the
upper class was striving for control over the people. It was
called *patoi si biloBo-oy*, "killing within the town." For all
his killing within the town, however, Walis did not achieve
the rank of pangat. The reason was this: in those days
when a trader came to a town he would go up into the
house of one of the "influential men," make straight for the
water jar, and take a drink of water. That made him the
influential man's guest. The two men from Dakalan had
done this in Walis' house, yet he had killed them. The
people did not trust him or consider him fit to be a pangat
after that.

Maddalum's father, who was later to marry the daughter
of Walis and inherit the head ax, began his career by killing
a man and his little daughter in Gaang, a barrio of his home
region. His motive was "to get his tattoo and attract
girls." He had been engaged when a child, but his tendency
toward dagdagas (a family trait of the Maddalums) had
led to rupture of the engagement. Next he went on a head-
hunting expedition (*kilib*) and killed Bugod and Mamanao
of Kagalwan, the pact with that town having been broken.
Finally, he killed Takloy of Lubwagan, who had wounded
a relative of his.

Maddalum inherited the ax. He got his tattoo by killing
Sanggui of Lubwagan. Sanggui was sitting in his house one
morning, and Maddalum threw a spear through the open

door. The reason he did so was that Sanggui had relatives too in Ginaang, and one of these had killed one of Maddalum's Ginaang relatives. Being wealthy, Maddalum's family was able to give the victim's kindred all that was demanded as weregilds, and Maddalum remained in hiding until these were paid, which, he says, was within a very short time. Next he claims to have killed three "Kristiagang"—Filipino soldiers who fled before the Americans from Abra in 1901 and led a precarious life of semistarvation and terror in the Lubwagan region until killed off by the Kalingas or captured by the Americans ("rescued" was the word one of them used in telling me about it). The story of how Maddalum killed them is as follows: A childless widow was induced to tempt some of them to her house by an offer of food. When they laid down their arms to eat, Maddalum and companions grabbed the guns, threw them into the brush, and then dispatched the "Kristiagang" with spears and head axes.

Q. Why had she to be a widow and childless?
A. If she had had a husband, he would have been obliged to take vengeance on those who killed his guests. If she had had children, these would have been obliged to do it on growing up.

Maddalum next accompanied a large punitive expedition led by the lieutenant-governor to a certain region, which at his request shall be left nameless, because relatives of a man he wounded are in a mission school here in Lubwagan at present and might avenge if reminded, but the inhabitants, being forewarned, fled before the party so that only one man was wounded—and that one, of course, by Maddalum!

Maddalum's next victim was a prisoner who broke jail after wounding two other prisoners. "Sapao," he says, told him (he was *presidente* at the time) to kill the man, so he cleft the fellow's skull with this head ax.

THE REGIONAL UNIT 157

Reciting the list of its glories has, I see, made the old man reluctant to part with his ax, and, since I do not want it anyhow, I charge him with not really wanting to sell it. He admits the fact but says that there is nothing in the house for his child to eat and "would the Apo . . . ?" Well, poor old man with a youngish dagdagas. . . .

Before leaving Lubwagan, I tried for a while to collect, but he would always put me off with an awfully-sorry-haven't-got-it and a what-after-all-is-a-little-matter-like-that-between-old-friends-like-us?

On returning to Lubwagan, I learned that the old fellow is still quite rich. I had supposed he had stripped himself for his children. "Then why doesn't he pay his small debt to me?" I asked.

"Oh," I was laughingly informed, "that is an old-time custom of the pangats. If they wanted or needed something, they would go and ask for it as a loan—and what could the people do?"

Even so, hardly such a sinecure for aristocrats as the Polynesian taboo system.

The culture was well implemented to encourage killing: the tattoo, favor of women, privilege of participating in stylized, chanted boasting recitals, and, most powerful of all, perhaps, attainment of status among men all depended on it.

Only a killer's opinions had weight in Kalinga conversation, and, even today, it is an impudence for a nonkiller, unless he command a lot of respect as a man who is rapidly getting rich, to advance his opinions in the presence of men who have killed. A young man, though he be a high-school or even a university graduate, feels this suppression keenly. If occasion arises, he will go along with the rest on an expedition lest his age-mates get ahead of him in distinction. Being present on an expedition that kills or wounds credits him with a killing.

The present assemblyman from this district, the Honorable Saturnino Moldero, a Spanish-Igorot mestizo who has lived for many years among the Kalingas, told me of attending a boast festival, way back in 1918, at Tinglaiyan. The man who had killed the most people began his boasting recital (*palpaliwat*) first, saying, in substance:

"I am the most influential man in Tinglaiyan, for I have killed more people than anybody else." He then, for half an hour, recited the list of his killings. He was followed by another man who began his recital in this tenor: "I cannot equal your killings in number, but I do not believe you could have killed some of the men that I have killed." He chanted his *palpaliwat* for about half an hour, attempting to make out a qualitative superiority, since a quantitative one was impossible. And so it continued for hours, with the warriors speaking in the order of their reputation. When the last warrior had spoken, somebody turned to a lazy fellow who had never killed anybody, but who was tolerated because he was thought to be queer in the head.

"Hey, Dunug, speak up and boast of *thy* killings!"

"As you know," said Dunug, "I am a lazy man, too lazy to fight, too lazy to work. Yet I think that in valor I am not second to any of you, as the following exploit of mine will prove. At least it is something I am sure none of you have ever done.

"Last year, at a time when all you brave and industrious people were leading your carabaos around and around in your fields to prepare them for planting, I was sitting in my house near the road, because I am lazy. There came through the town an American, the supervising teacher. He was hiking to Lubwagan accompanied by a cargadore from Bontok, whom he had agreed to discharge at Tinglaiyan. He required a cargadore to replace this man and, seeing me, ordered me to come. I refused, but he grabbed me and gave me a kick, placed his suitcase on my head, and told me to get along. When we came to a place where the road is very steep, my anger mounted as the sweat began to drip, and I contrived to get him ahead of me. I then threw his suitcase down, whacked him with my staff where he had kicked me, and disappeared into the jungle. [Yells and laughter.]"

The killing of people, among the Kalingas, adds renown almost without respect to the means; it has considerably less connection with valor or bravery than money-getting among ourselves usually has with productive, constructive, or initiative activities.

A few years ago a lowlander of Tuao, Cagayan Province, had trouble with his wife and left her. Having acquaint-ances in a barrio of Pinukpuk, Kalinga, he went to live among them, where he was known as "Ankwan" (Juan). He had lived with them over a year on amicable terms, with no disagreements and without making any enemies. One day the Kalingas there tied him to a tree and, all par-ticipating, slowly jabbed and sliced him to pieces. This deed was unknown to the authorities for about two years and came to light through the Kalingas' inability to refrain from their *palpaliwat* boasting. At the trial the Kalingas denied all malice or unpleasantness and said that they had killed only because it was their custom and because the victim was so conveniently at hand.

The pangats never meet as a village council; they meet at all officially only in great public meetings, with their fellow-citizens, to consider troubles that have arisen with regions with which there is a pact or to consider conclusion or rupture of pacts. Anybody has a right to appear and make speeches, and the pangats harangue the citizens.

No votes are taken, and there is no action until the whole people are persuaded. A meeting of the pangats is called *among da papangat* or *mimiting da papangat*—into what language has the English word "meeting" not made its way!

In dealing with domestic matters, the procedure is quite different: the pangats do not meet together in a way even faintly resembling a session. They are not a council; they are a "counsel" if I may use the word so. They are moderators—using the word literally in the sense of "those who moderate." Only in serious cases or in a small town will all of them ever participate in settling a dispute—this would very rarely happen in Lubwagan, where there are twelve of them. Let us illustrate the procedure of settling a minor case.

Let us suppose that A thinks a chicken of his has been stolen. A will go to a pangat who is living in his barrio, or who is his relative, or, failing such a one, to the pangat with whom he is on the best personal terms. He will relate the circumstances, and the pangat will say, "Wait—I'll see if I can arrange the matter." If detective work needs to be done, he will tell his most dependable relatives and henchmen to keep eyes and ears open. Finally, suspicion fixes itself on Z. Then the pangat will go to Z and talk to him in the way he thinks best under the circumstances. He will suggest to him that the matter be arranged "simply" and quietly by the return of twice the equivalent of the chicken—that is, of two chickens. "Otherwise," he will say, "they are likely to demand a carabao." If Z denies the deed, he will inform a pangat who is related to Z of the evidence, and this other pangat will talk roughly to Z. If Z still denies the deed, they will talk about calling Kaiyabo from Balatok to do the ordeal and will mention the expense and publicity that such a course will involve. If with this warning he doesn't pay up, other pangats will probably enter the case, and they will entertain A's formal demands, which will have grown possibly to a fat hog, and they will give A to understand and Z's relatives to understand that they consider A's demands justified and that he may seize a gusi or valuable heirloom or a rice field unless the demands be met. They will suggest an ordeal. If Z refuses this, one of his relatives will pay to avoid trouble, and Z cannot resist repaying his relative. I doubt that an innocent man is ever punished unless erroneously indicated by an ordeal.

In cases where serious trouble is brewing, as, for example, adultery, advances to a married woman, homicide, wounds, or in less serious ones which lead to assemblages of the two kinship groups in a fighting mood, several pangats will be notified by mutual relatives of the two principals who rush to them terrified and breathless (see p. 71), and the pangats will intervene in greater numbers than in minor troubles. Those related to either side will go to their relatives and counsel moderation and calmness.

The two parties may or may not be assembled within sight of each other. On each side will be the related pangats, counseling according to the circumstances and their feelings in the case, but *always* striving to prevent hasty, ill-advised action. Other pangats will be passing to and fro between the parties, consulting with their fellow-pangats and with the influential men in either party, carrying news of the other party's attitude, always counseling moderation, then returning to the other party and repeating the process. They practically always maintain the peace.

Perquisites of pangats.—The pangats do not ask a fee for their service: I doubt that their qualm is similar to that which long prevailed in the medical profession about submitting a bill; they claim to "act for the good of the community, to prevent trouble"; and I will not say that there may not be something of *noblesse oblige* in the case. Still, "if a man expects ever to need their help again" (and what man knows how soon that will be?), "he would better give them something." Thus, in our hypothetical case, above, of the chicken-stealing, if the one pangat arranges the case "quietly" on the basis of the return of two chickens, it is not absolutely necessary for a man to give the pangat the extra chicken (though that would be the handsome thing to do)—he may keep the chicken and provide basi enough to get the pangat drunk. If the case should go further, so that other pangats are needed to arrange the case, and if a large pig be received as indemnity, then a man of propriety will either kill the pig for a feast for the pangats or will keep it and kill a small pig, thus retaining a little something for himself from his trouble. For preventing bloodshed, no fee is required, but, if weregilds be collected, then there will be a big feast for pangats and people, with plenty of basi. In general, if a case of theft is settled on the basis of *sukat* (usually the stolen thing or its equivalent plus twice its value as an indemnity), then one of the three units ought to be given to the pangats. The pangats of a village receive choice cuts of meat whenever an animal is slaughtered. In the distribution of ceremonial gifts a pangat is awarded as if he were a first cousin even though he be a third or fourth (see pp. 204–5).

Death of the pangat.—A killer his whole life long, a pangat would formerly, when on his deathbed, intrust a near-relative with the task of killing somebody as a post-funeral victim, called *alang*. Furthermore, the period following the death of a pangat was believed to be the most auspicious possible time for anybody to go head-hunting. Such head-hunting was called *dinson*. As I write, in Pongol region, the body of Alumbaiya, a woman of pangat rank, who died about a month ago, rests on a high scaffold, wrapped in blankets. The body will not be buried until somebody kills her *alang* victim. The scaffold is also called *alang*.

Reasons for failure to reach the rank of pangat.—Despite the oftentime ridiculous shortcomings of late in the government of these mountain tribes, one important gain remains to them from foreign rule: walking around killing people in order to gain "influence" over them is no longer a road to pangathood. To a considerable extent, attainment of leadership has been shunted to the path of oratorical ability and even more to "acquiring." This is apparent in a partial list which I made of kadangyans who had failed to reach the coveted goal and the reasons for their failure. Their names were given to me, but out of a fellow-feeling for them, I designate them by letters. Such individuals are about three times more numerous than the pangats.

A, son of a commoner, married the daughter of a pangat who inherited several peace pacts; is wealthy, doesn't gamble, but he "never did any good for the people." Lacks the boldness to speak at meetings.

B, son of a pangat and wealthy, but unenterprising; depends for his living entirely on his inherited property, to which he has not added. Doesn't gamble; indolent.

C, was wealthy but "gambled his property."

D, son of a kadangyan, wealthy, but does not talk fluently or convincingly; "never arranged any troubles."

E and F, wealthy, but do not speak at meetings called by the mayor to consider the public good; do not try to settle troubles between kinship groups; have not added much to their inherited properties.

G, very wealthy, but is a liar and very tricky [see Case 28].

H, very haughty, an oppressor of the poor [see Case 74].

I, very wealthy, but what he says gets nowhere. When he talks, he argues for one side and then for the other. He says a thing and then shows that it is not true. As the Ilokanos say, "He spits and then licks it up." "No cases can be settled from this man's reasons." [A liberal!]

THE GO-BETWEEN ("MANGI-UGUD")

By derivation, the Kalinga word *mangi-ugud*, which I translate as "go-between," means "advocate," "conferrer." The derivation thus implies far less power and greater limitations than the Latin *arbiter*, less, too, than the English word "arbitrator." This implication is correct so far as power in settling disputes is concerned, for in that respect the go-between's function is only "trying to arrange a settlement" between kinship groups involved in controversy, but in another respect his power and duty are vastly greater. For all that, the Kalinga go-between is not nearly so important a functionary as the Ifugao, for the reason, probably that much of his function is performed by the pangats.

In all-important or serious cases there is a go-between, and often there are two of them, on each side. Go-betweens are functionaries of the territorial social unit, as well as of kinship groups. If selected by the pangats, they are formally so, of course. But they are essentially so in any case. For, however selected, they are, as has been said, in honor bound to punish infractions of the peace by either side *while mediation is in process* with death or wounding; also they are in honor bound *not to pay weregilds* in such cases. That is to say, they carry out an execution sanctioned by the whole region.

The following are the necessary general qualifications of a go-between: he must be a mature man of much experience in dealing with men; a man of influence, having a strong family backing and, formerly, renown as a killer. If there be only one go-between, he should preferably be related to both sides in the dispute or else to neither. In homicide cases, if there be only one go-between, he may not be a relative of the offending party, else the offended might reject and kill him when he came to them. He may be a distant relative of the offended if acceptable to the offenders.

In cases of homicide or wounding, the go-betweens are likely to be selected by the pangat. In adultery cases there will probably be only one—sent by the offender. The husband will be all rage and venom, ostentatiously seeking to kill, and declaring it beneath his honor to accept a price in satisfaction of his wife's betrayal. For even if he should have an eye open for the indemnity (the whole of which he will keep for himself), it is good tactics for him to fume and go looking for somebody to kill. In cases involving minor injuries, it is most likely to be the injured party who sends the go-between.

The Kalinga conception of the tort approaches our own more nearly than does the Ifugao conception. The Ifugao regards nonpayment of a debt as being a tort—he considers that it injures him magically and that it is an offense to his pride, whereas the Kalinga looks upon it simply as a broken contract. And, yet, the Ifugao does not put unpaid debts in precisely the same category as other torts—for example, he will more often call the go-between he sends in bad-debt cases a *mombaga*, or "dunner," than he will call him a *monkalun*, or "admonisher."[7] Still, nonpayment of a debt constitutes an offense to him. In Kalinga the creditor does his own dunning in cases of debt and minor torts such as injuries to property due to negligence. Thus the Kalinga uses a go-between in fewer cases than does the Ifugao, namely, in cases where what we would call a "criminal element" is apparent.

The Kalinga go-between's typical handling of a case of wounding or killing was thus described:

7. Another distinction and a more important one is that he can still eat, drink, and chew betels with the debtor, whereas he cannot do these things with a tortfeasor.

He first goes to the offender's group and says, "Let us make the weregilds."

"All right," they will say—for they are in fear of being killed.

Then he goes to the other side and says, "Let us make the weregilds—otherwise they may kill you very soon."

"All right," they will say—for they want to live.

Then he tries to get from the offender and his brothers what the offended and his brothers demand. If they do not have it, he tries to get it from a wealthy cousin. "They are aroused and dangerous," he will tell that cousin. "I am afraid they will be satisfied with no less a man than yourself if I should be unable to arrange the case." The cousin will be afraid and will pay. Then he tries to get the first cousins of the offender to buy off the first cousins of the offended. Then he goes to the second cousins and the third cousins, and with these it is not so difficult because the second cousins of the offended side will be satisfied with a blanket or two each, and the third cousins with a dog or a knife. Yes, of course, the *mangi-ugud* will try to get the demands reduced if the offenders really cannot pay.

If the go-betweens cannot "arrange" the case, they will be disgusted at all the hard work they have put in on it to no avail, and maybe they'll say, "Now go ahead and kill each other." They inform a pangat of their withdrawal, which is called *na-unat*. Then the pangats become active again and give warning and probably they will send other go-betweens. But nearly always the first ones are ultimately successful, although it may take them months or even sometimes years to arrange the case.

If the peace be broken during the negotiations, the go-betweens take back all weregilds that have been paid and return them to the payers. No weregilds will be paid in such a case—the attempt or attack balances the original offense.

To a great extent, go-betweens and pangats are judges of what is a correct indemnity. They try to keep indemnities "regular." The go-between takes to each relative what he thinks is right, and, if the relative is not satisfied, he argues with him. He may have to go back to the offenders for something more, but he will try to keep the extra amount down to a peso, a chicken, a dog, or a small pig.

Compensation of go-between.—The go-between receives gifts (*gunsud*) from all those that receive substantial payments. Thus, in a case involving weregilds, the offended person himself, if living, and the brothers, sisters, parents, uncles, aunts, and first cousins, would receive fields, gusi, gold earrings, carabaos, and large pigs. The receiver of a large field ought to give him a carabao; the receiver of a field or gusi worth five carabaos ought to give him a large pig; the receiver of a carabao ought to give him 2 pesos. The gifts will run at about 5–10 per cent of the value of the thing received. Sometimes he receives something from the other side, also. The go-between's pickings are very good in a large case.

THE PACT-HOLDER ("MANGDON SI BUDONG")

The peace pact, *budong*, enforced by a pact-holder, appears to be a specifically Kalinga development. Pangat Dugyang and Mr. Dakauwag have the feeling that it is comparatively recent but can give no reasons for the belief. The following consideration argues in favor of the view that it is a comparatively late institution, although it undoubtedly reaches back before the coming of the Americans: the nature of the institution is obviously such that it would propagate itself rapidly, and, indeed, it has expanded its area during even American times. That it has not covered a greater area may be regarded as indicative, perhaps, of its comparative youth.

Its development in Kalinga is much more definite, complete, and complex than at the margins of its distribution. In Abra, only the towns bordering on Kalinga have it.[8]

8. [It actually is found over most of Abra. For a preliminary reference see Fred Eggan, "Some Aspects of Social and Cultural Change in Northern Luzon," *American Anthropologist*, XLIII (new ser., 1941), 11–18.—F. E.]

I am informed by Deputy-Governor Klaver, a Benguet Igorot married in Bontok, that in Bontok Subprovince it reaches as far south as Kayan, but I suspect that it is a purely ritual institution in regions south of the town of Bontok. In all Bontok towns as far down the Chico River as Sadanga, its only feature is a guarantee of peace, with provision of a pact-holder for punishing infraction; these pacts lack the provisions of the Kalinga treaty with respect to care of the sick or wounded, trade, collection of debts, and so on.[9] The map (Fig. 6) shows the pact's general distribution.

One ground for looking upon the peace pact with enforcement by a pact-holder as a development from the trading-partner institution rather than on the latter as a degeneration of the former is that the trading-partner institution has a rather wide distribution in the Philippines, Borneo, and perhaps other parts of Indonesia, while there is no report in the literature, I think, of an institution similar to that of the Kalingas.

There is no specific rite of blood brotherhood for making the pact-holders "brothers," but they are considered to be such, and on that account their children may not marry—in fact, all the marriage prohibitions are binding on their kinship groups. There are also obligations of assistance on ritual occasions such as funerals, marriage of a son or daughter, etc.

Lubwagan has over forty pacts with other towns. Some of them are recent, and yet one of them—with distant

9. In Bontok the pacts are held by various wards (*ato*) for the whole town. That is to say, a ward will name its man to hold the pact with the other town and will back him, thus exercising the function which in Kalinga is exercised by the kinship group of the pact-holder.

Citizenship is a matter of residence in Bontok; there is no formal change. If a man marries in another town and goes to live there, he becomes a citizen of that town. Thus, perhaps, there appears to be no distinction between citizenship and residence.

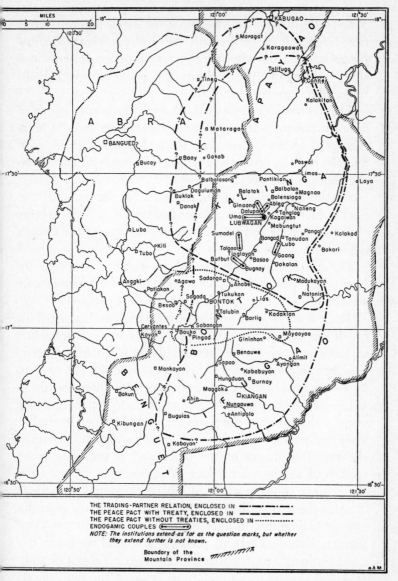

Fig. 6.—Distribution of trading-partner relationships and peace pacts in the moun-
in province.

Kalitkitan, in Apayao—has been inherited and antedates the coming of the Americans. Several pacts with distant places arose from the *abuyog*, trading-partner, relationship. Lubwagan's pact-holders and pacts on which I obtained data are listed in Table 3.

The pact-holder has a dual office: (1) he is spokesman of his own region in its relations with another and (2) he is the agent of that other town in its dealings with his own and the righter, often the avenger, of wrongs against it. In the pages of this work, "pact-holder in (*or:* of) . . ." designates the first office and is followed by the name of the pact-holder's own region; "pact-holder for . . ." designates the second office and is followed by the name of the foreign region.

The thirty-nine pacts listed in Table 3 are held by twenty-six pact-holders. Of these, fifteen are pangats or are the mother, sister, widow, or son of a pangat.

The office of pact-holder is inherited and allotted in much the same way that property is. There is a tendency to favor sons somewhat, yet daughters frequently inherit, too. Agwak allotted two of his pacts (he still holds two) to his two married children, one of these a daughter. Six pact-holders are women (one of whom holds four pacts), and I suspect that some of the pacts attributed to men in the list were really inherited by their wives: the husband performs the principal duties of the office and is therefore often spoken of as the pact-holder. Widows hold the pact for their minor children who will inherit them and sometimes cling to them after their children have grown up, as in the case of Gaiyampo, mother of Lubwagan's most powerful pangat, Kanao. There is, perhaps, a special reason in her case: Ginaang's pact-holder for Lubwagan is also a woman. It is said that years ago relations between the two regions were such that no man in either place wanted to hold the

TABLE 3

Lubwagan Pact-holders and Manner of Obtaining Pacts

Lubwagan Pact-holder	Manner of Obtaining Pact	For Region of
1. Gaiyampo	Chosen	Ginaang
2. Pukao	Inheritance from her father, who was chosen because his brother had been slain by Balatok people	Balatok
3. Lisking	Inherited from Agwak, his father	Tanglag
4. Sindung	Inherited from Agwak, her father	Mabungtut
5. Agwak	Inherited from his father	Lubo
6. Galamoy	Chosen	Bangad, Magaogao
7. Kagaid	Inherited from father	Sumadel, Mallango
8. Wakas	Chosen	Bilang
9. Pataotao	Inherited from father	Dananao
10. Pataklang	Inherited from father	Talgao
11. Pukao	Inherited from her father	Butbut
12. Pukao	Inherited from her father	Paswai
13. Iway	Inherited from father	Balensiagao
14. Gaiyaon	Inherited from her father	Puapo
15. Palangya	Inherited from father	Pantikion
16. Lumangyang	Inherited from her father	Magsilay
17. Vacant	Pact ruptured by Lubwagan on account of inactivity of the Kagalwan pact-holder in punishing cattle thieves and cattle wounders	Kagalwan*
18. Vacant	Pact ruptured by Lubwagan on account of the wounding of one of its citizens (see Case 62)	Dalupa-Ableg*
19. Palangya	Inherited from father	Salegseg
20. Dugyang	Inherited from father	Linos
21. Likadang	Inherited from mother	Naneng
22. (a) Pagatpat (of Uma)	Inherited from her father	Balbalasang†
(b) Palangya	Inherited from father	Balbalasang
23. Pulitud	Inherited from father	Mangali
24. Addum	Inherited from father	Taloktok
25. Banutan	Kinsman of slain by Tinglaiyan (see Case 63)	Tinglaiyan
26. Banutan	Inherited from wife	Pangol

* There is *alasiu*, or truce, between Lubwagan and these regions. Kagalwan's spear is being held by Kanao; he has held it for about five years. Dalupa's spear is being held by Mabwaki, brother of the boy whose wounding led to rupture of the pact; he has held it about four years. It is said that soon the pact will be drunk between the two regions.

† This is the only instance in which Uma holds a pact separately from Lubwagan.

TABLE 3—*Continued*

Lubwagan Pact-holder	Manner of Obtaining Pact	For Region of
27. Agwak..............	Chosen	Dakalan
28. Bakuli..............	Chosen	Osiga
29. Pulitud.............	Inherited from father	Magnao
30. Paliyo..............	Inherited from her father	Buaya
31. Maddalum..........	Chosen	Mabaka
32. Ngaiyaan............	By gift from half-brother, Maddalum	Dauwangan
33. Pukao..............	Inherited from her father	Manibu
34. Maddalum..........	Chosen	Patok
35. Wakas..............	Chosen	Bontok
36. Buung..............	Chosen	Tukukan
37. Galamoy............	Chosen	Magaogao
38. Pikut...............	Chosen	Kabugao (Apayao)
39. Iwag...............	Inherited from his father	Kalitkitan (Apayao)

pact. Then Gaiyampo, wife of Pangat Alundai, said that if a certain woman of Ginaang would hold the pact there, she would hold it in Lubwagan. It was done so, and there has since been peace between the regions. Pass her house most any time, and you will see it full of Ginaang people, mostly women, who have come to Lubwagan to sell and buy and who have dropped in to chat and rest.

Lubwagan's peace pacts have spread far to many regions with which there was no pact until after the Americans had come and made it the capital and center of a system of trails and highways, consequently both a political and a trading center. Thereby arose the necessity for distant regions to conclude pacts with it.

Pikut, who holds the pact with Kabugao in the Sub-province of Apayao, six days' hike distant, was formerly a very rich and enterprising man. At present he is well-nigh impoverished through paying the gambling debts of his son and is suffering from tuberculosis besides. In 1917 or there-abouts, having heard that precious beads were quite cheap in Apayao, he assembled a few kinsmen and, carrying 400 pesos, started for Kabugao, with which, at that time, Lubwagan had no pact. At Salegseg, which had a pact with Kabugao, he hired two men to accompany him in order that they might confer a degree of safety on the party. Then he continued to Mabaka, which also had a pact with Kabugao, and picked up two more. Arrived at Kabugao, he stopped at the house of Sigon, a wealthy man. Sigon purchased beads for him advantageously; the two agreed to become trading partners. After that, five trips were made by one or another to the town of the other, the Apayao always bringing gusi and ancient beads and carrying back money, the Kalinga always taking money and buying gusi and beads through his trading partner.

As happens frequently, the trading partners initiated a pact, with themselves as the pact-holders.

The Kalinga greatly enjoys the honors, limelight, and ceremonies of the office of pact-holder, but it is a risky one, for nothing can so blast a man forever as failure to enforce it. Now that it has become a less dangerous office, many men crave it who lacked the courage to undertake it formerly.

The word "chosen" that heads one column of our list does not mean that the pact-holder was chosen only by Lubwagan. The region that makes overtures for a pact where there has been none before, by the very ceremony by which this is done, nominates a man in the other region, as we shall soon see. If the nominee be willing to serve, the pangats of the place will ordinarily confirm the nomination, for it is well for the permanence of the pact to have a man who is *persona grata* to the other side.

But when a pact has been ruptured and the suit is for renewal, both regions, especially the offending one, will want as pact-holder the most influential man who can be drawn from the nearest kin of the victim of the deed that led to the rupture. If such a one accepts the office, he cannot afterward undertake revenge, and he, more than any other person, can hold the rest of the offended kindred in check. If he should fail in this, then he would be obliged to retaliate on his own group or somebody more or less connected with it. In like manner, the preferred pact-holder on the offending side is the very culprit whose act caused the rupture of the pact! There is invincible logic in these preferences. Making the persons who have the greatest grudge against each other pact-holders and, by the fiction of the institution, "brothers," is the surest way to attain a secure peace (see Case 63).

It needs to be emphasized that the pact is held by an individual *and* his or her kinship group *and* the kinship group of his or her spouse. The situation is well set forth in the speech on page 182. The reason that a woman, who cannot engage in major trade, take the lead in ceremonials or debates, "arrange" troubles, detect offenses, punish or execute violators of the pact or perform any of the more important functions of the pact-holder, can nevertheless hold a pact is explained by the fact that her menfolk do these things for her and that in reality the kinship group is the pact-holder.

As one informant stated the case, "The pact-holder's relatives and following are his soldiers and spies. If a man hasn't a strong 'party,' he has no business being a pact-holder. If it is hard for him to discover who has committed an offense or aggression against the other region, his relatives and followers listen everywhere—and finally they hear something."

THE PEACE PACT

Overtures.—There are two cases to consider: first, a situation in which there has never been a pact between two regions and, second, one in which there has been a pact and it has been broken.

In the first case an influential man in one of the towns has personal reasons for wanting a pact: possibly he aims at the honor of holding it, or he wants to trade or collect a debt. He talks the matter over with the pangats and if he receives encouragement from them, he sends his spear as a bid for peace (*sipat*) to a man of the other region, thus nominating him as opposite pact-holder, as just explained above. As messenger (*mansipat*) he will have to choose a townmate who is related in the other town or else secure the good offices of a citizen of a region that has a pact with both his own and the other region, since it would be unsafe for anybody else to go—there are no tokens by which a messenger carrying peace overtures may be distinguished.

On receiving the spear, the influential man in the other town will go to the pangats and say, "Do you want me to keep the spear? If you do, I am willing to accept, provided you promise to help me." The people, having heard the news, will assemble and talk the matter over. Special notice will be carried to the kinship group of the person last slain or wounded by the suing region. If the pangats want somebody else than the receiver of the spear to hold the pact, they will say so, but this rarely happens. Finally, the receiver of the spear will stand before the meeting (probably holding up the spear) and say to the people: "Shall I accept it? If any man object, let him speak."

Conditioning since childhood by a vengeful kinship-group ideology, intrenched and implemented, makes it hard for a Kalinga to renounce vengeance. But vengeance is dangerous to accomplish, weregilds easy to take. Besides, silence at this time spells no final renunciation of vengeance: it merely initiates a period in which one will be coaxed to accept weregild—he can enjoy the solicitation of go-betweens, be an object of attention for a while, and still refuse them if he wants to. Unless some citizen, because of recent injury, be hell-bent and raging for vengeance, there will probably be no objection raised at this time. If there should be, the spear is sent back to the sender. If there be none, the receiver sends his *own* spear, or sometimes a Chinese bowl back to the initiator. The token returned is called *alasiu*, and its bearer, *mamalasiu*.

Acceptance of a spear initiates a truce, called *alasiu*, during which weregilds can be arranged between kinship groups having unavenged accounts. The *alasiu* is rather more than a truce—it is almost equivalent to a peace pact *pro tempore;* intercourse is opened between the regions, though visitors and traders, a little doubtful still of their safety, usually come in large groups. *Alasiu* sometimes lasts for years. The pact with Kagalwan was broken seven years ago because the Kagalwan people were said to have wounded cattle belonging to Lubwagan and because the pact-holder there did not fulfil his duty of detecting and punishing the culprits. The Kagalwan people after two or three years sent their spear, and it was accepted by Pangat Kanao, but negotiations have not gone to completion. Thus, *alasiu* has lasted four or five years. Pangat Kanao states that the reason for the hitch in the conclusion of the pact is the nondetection of the culprits and the lack of persons willing to act as pact-holders.

When a pact is to be renewed, there is the same procedure of sending a spear as if there had never been a pact, and the overture will almost invariably come from the offending side. In only one instance on our list of peace pacts, that with Dakalan, a few years ago, did the offended make the overtures—that was because they could afford no longer to be cut off from Lubwagan, the center. They were willing to forego weregilds for the victims of Lubwagan's aggression, but the kinship groups of the Lubwagan aggressors considered that they would be unsafe if Dakalan people were allowed to come freely to their region with the account unsettled, and so offered small weregilds which were accepted.

Formerly, too, when a peace pact was broken, there would always be a battle or series of battles if the regions in question were sufficiently near that they could get at each other, and sometimes there is even now. If one region was consistently worsted, it would sue for peace, and the stronger region before accepting the overture would rub its victory in by demanding a victim called *kompaLa* to be nonfatally wounded on the boundary between the regions. Usually the victim sent was an old woman. This practice embraced the Magnao-Naneng area as well as that of Lubwagan and the towns to the south. Lubwagan, on various occasions, has exacted *kompaLa* from the neighboring regions of Mabungtut, Tanglag, Ableg, Kagalway, and Dalupa. It has always lorded it over these weaker regions and still does.

The period of "alasiu."—Two men are appointed on each side to act as go-betweens, *mangi-ugud*, in arranging weregilds to even up the various debts of life. If this be the first pact between the two regions, there will be old, dormant feuds, and these will be easier to arrange than those freshened by a recent act. The latter may prove impossible of settlement—there may be one or two relatives who cannot be bought off from taking vengeance. The co-regionists will, of course, exert strong pressure on them to accept weregilds. But if they remain obdurate: (1) the pact may be given up and the weregilds paid to date returned, after which the *alasiu* is terminated, or (2) the two communities may go ahead with the pact, merely leaving the objectors and those whom these wish to kill outside its operation. The latter is the usual course.

In settling accounts in order to initiate a pact, if one kinship group has killed or wounded four and the other only one, three sets of weregilds have to be paid in order to bring about *amano* or "balance." If each side has taken the same number of lives, then the case is *babbalus*, evenly avenged, and *amano* exists without payment of weregilds.

The renewal of a pact that has been ruptured is much easier to accomplish: if one region has slain seven *in battle* and the other side only one (or even merely wounded one), there will be no weregilds—the death or wounding of one is regarded as avenging all seven slain by the other side. This change from the old blood-feud reckoning of the debt of life by summation and subtraction to the new regional or community way of reckoning must have been essential to the success of the peace-pact institution, to its diffusion, and to the development of the foreign aspect of the community state.

The change was certainly not a legislated or negotiated one. It came about, I think, inevitably, logically, and without recognition of its significance, as an outgrowth of the fundamental attitude and concepts of kinship society. We have already noted that the Kalinga claims as his own any victim taken in a head-hunting or war party. To us, of Western, individualistic attitudes, this seems like braggadocio. To the Kalinga it is not, for, as we have also noted, the Kalinga so completely identifies himself with his kinship group that even in ordinary conversation he is always getting his *I*'s and *we*'s mixed up. This identification carries over into war between communities. The kinship groups retain their integrity to a great extent in the community's army, and each kinship group regards a victim slain in war as balancing its *own* loss. Accordingly, one victim balances the loss of any number of kinship groups: at least so long as a group loses only one life. It would seem that it ought not to be so if it loses more than one, but I neglected to ascertain how such a case stands. A little thought convinces one that such a case would happen exceedingly rarely. I suspect that the group that lost two of its number would insist on the war continuing until two had been killed on the other side.

Not all those apparently grave contradictions which we from time to time have seen the tribal principle of social organization so tenaciously withstanding proved so fatal to that principle as this, its own attitude in the personalities of its carriers. It is as if the territorial principle had sneaked into the kinship fortress by an open back door.

Drinking the pact.—When nearly all the weregilds have been paid or reliably and definitely promised, the pact-holder of the region that received the overtures sends a messenger to invite the pact-holder of the other region to come with his people, both men and women, for a feast called *inum di budong* ("drinking of the pact"), where unsettled debts of life or other outstanding questions may be discussed, as well as the terms of the treaty to be made between the two communities. If the invited pact-holder accepts, the messenger rolls bark on his thigh and makes two strings, then ties a knot in each for each day intervening till the appointed date, keeps one and gives the other to the pact-holder. Each day a knot will be cut off. In these days, the messengers often carry letters of invitation written in flowery terms in English or the native language—probably typewritten![10]

On the appointed day, the folk of the invited region will observe their omens early in the morning with great care.

10. I made repeated inquiries for such invitations, but was unable to obtain any. They would make capital museum specimens!

If these are bad, they will send word that the omens are bad and that they cannot come till tomorrow. If they are good, men and women who desire will proceed to the other town. Many of them will be carrying *patanggok*—segments of bamboo of lengths varying from 30 to about 50 centimeters, with a node at the proximal end and with the rind on one side cut diagonally away in the distal half. Near the node is a small hole. This device, when beaten against another piece of bamboo or the head ax, gives a musical note

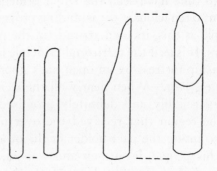

FIG. 7.—Side and front views of *patanggok*

that can be varied by stopping and unstopping the hole; numbers of them of different sizes and lengths, of course, give a great variety of tones (see Fig. 7).[11]

Of course, the visitors may be turned back by bad omens before they arrive, in which case they will try again next day. One informant told me that if the early-morning omens are good, they try not to see or hear bad ones on the road, and that the purpose of the *patanggok* described above is to prevent bad omens from being heard.

11. The Ifugaos have a device which is probably either the prototype of this or a degeneration—a stick of hard wood which they carry in their processions at the funeral of a person slain by the enemy, called the *bangibang*. The Kalinga *patanggok* faintly suggests certain bamboo instruments (*anklung*) of the Javanese orchestra.

When the guests have arrived at the house of the pact-holder, two pigs are slain in order that the omens of their bile sacs may be read. The old men interpret these: (1) if the bile sac be on the same level as the liver and be transparent, they say, "The peace will be long, clean, and inherited by the children"; (2) if it be black and deflected to the right side, they say, "The peace will be short and will be broken by the wounding or killing of somebody of the region of the host," so the visitors are informed that they will have to come at a later date; (3) if, on the other hand, the bile be black and deflected to the left, it is indicated that the peace will be short and will be ended by the killing or wounding of somebody from the visiting town. Since it is the old men of the host's region who read the omens, they report them to the host. If the omens be bad, the fact may be suppressed, and they may be reported to the people as satisfactory. The Kalinga does not greatly fear remote omens, such as these. He hopes they will not prove true or that something can be done in the meantime to ward off evil. The host will have gone to great expense in preparations for the feast and will not want to repeat it. Furthermore, if the news should be given out that the pact would be short, the people on both sides would say, "Oh, he is no man to be pact-holder! He will be unable to control his people. Our pact will be weak." Finally, the loss of life that is foretold is for the *other* side!

But the Kalinga still fears and heeds proximate omens. If anybody sneezes while the food is cooking, that prognosticates brawling, wounding, or loss of life during the feast itself, so the guests are sent home and told to come another day. At a "pact-warming" I attended I was especially cautioned not to sneeze at this time.

Prolonged flowery greetings couched largely in terms of self-belittlement are exchanged and pass gradually into a discussion of the differences between the regions. The speeches are made in a more or less metric form and constitute a style of oratory known as *dangdango*. Kalingas are very polite and dignified at this time, do not interrupt each other's speeches, and listen attentively to what is said. It is improbable that agreement on all weregilds will have been reached at the time of the first pact-drinking. Dancing will begin after a while, and matters will be left in abeyance until the second feast of the sort. Class distinctions are not observed in dancing unless the pangats manage it so. This used to be done much more frequently than at present. The pact-holders also harangue their respective kinship groups in the following strain:

Now that I am a pact-holder, it is an honor to you as well. But though you, my relatives, and you, the relatives of my wife, share the honor with me, you also share the responsibility of restraining anyone from unfriendly acts. Had it not been for the confidence and trust they have in you, the pangats would never have let me become the pact-holder. Being a pact-holder is a serious business, and I intend to enforce the pact fearlessly and preserve my honor, which is also your honor. You must consider it your duty to me and to our kinship groups to prevent the necessity of my having to resort to extreme measures, for be assured that I shall resort to them even against my own blood if necessary.

Cakes of *dikEt* (glutinous rice) are passed around. Many carabaos and pigs, contributed by the receiving pact-holder and his own and his wife's kindred, are slaughtered. Rice wine and basi flow freely. The guests stay two days—days of dancing, singing, gorging, drinking, and possibly of flirtation, but days of nagging worry for both the pact-holders and for their relatives, who must be constantly vigilant lest incidents occur to mar the occasion, incidents which, if serious, would have to be retaliated by the killing or wounding of a co-regionist.

On the second or third day, the receiving pact-holder will present the visiting one and his kindred with gifts that he and his relatives have gotten together for the purpose. Then the visitors go home.

As has been said, it is unlikely that all outstanding questions will have been settled at this first feast; that may require weeks or months or years. When that time comes, the other pact-holder will invite the former hosts to a second drinking of the pact, which is in all respects similar to the first one except that the terms of the treaty will be announced. Announcement of these terms is supposed to be a solemn moment, and everybody is expected to listen attentively.

After the treaty goes into force, there will be another exchange of visits, ratifications at which more animals will be slaughtered than at the past drinkings; this is called *lonok*. Then, every two or three years, one of the pact-holders will invite the other and his region to a *dolnat*, or "pact warming." This is especially required if any trouble shall have occurred between the regions. At one pact warming I attended, the cause of the occasion was an unjust accusation of carabao stealing. The pact-holder of the accusing region invited the other. At this *dolnat*, I saw something I have not seen subsequently: a man from one region would dance with a woman from the other; of this pair, the one from the host region, whether man or woman, would present the partner with a piece of money, a blanket, gee-string, skirt, or other textile. Gifts were numerous, and all were recorded in a notebook by a clerk sitting at a table, to whom they were turned in. The guests would distribute them among themselves when they returned home. When the guests invite their present hosts, gifts will go back to the other side. The clerk's record will enable them not to give less than they received.

Another pact warming I attended had no special reason for existence, so a matter was invented—a claim was advanced for refund of weregilds already paid that everybody knew was specious; it was argued in flowery language for at least twelve hours. I recorded the gist of the first speeches as they were translated to me; some airplanes were roaring overhead just as the complimentary speeches began to be exchanged:

Balbalan pact-holder (the guest): What a happy day when we can visit you! And how auspicious that airplanes roar overhead and a man from America is present to write about the customs of our fathers and to make speeches to us!

Balensiagao pact-holder: Although we may not be able to feed you the food that you like best, yet we are here to give you greeting and to pay you honor and respect.

Balbalan man: We thank our grandfathers for having arranged the pact, because if they had not done so, who can say what would have happened?

Aged Balensiagao man: Yes, we arranged the pact because we pitied the young generation. No man has two heads, so that if he loses one, it is a great pity for him. And if he destroys the pact, he loses one.

Balbalan man: Though a man be a high-school graduate, if he does not review he forgets—therefore we are gathered here to review the peace pact between Balbalan and Balensiagao. [He then recites the history of the pact.]

Balensiagao man: If we should offend against the pact, our fathers who are in the heavens [*Ngato*] would look on us and weep.

Balbalan man: Indeed they would. Therefore if we have offended in even the slightest thing, heedlessly and unknowingly, it is well that we be charged with it so that small things may not grow into big and cause tears to the fathers.

Balensiagao man: We do not think of anything at present and if we did we should not charge our guests with it until they have had the chance to charge us. [Turning to a group of twelve men from Sumadel sitting apart, who have come to the region seeking to work at building fields or irrigation canals in return for a carabao:] You men of Sumadel, you had better come and join us, for you are neutral and if our friends have complaint against us, you will be able to act as moderators. [The Sumadel men did not accept the invitation; they kept on sitting where they were.]

Balbalan man: So far as the present years are concerned, there is no complaint. Our regions adjoin, but there is no complaint. But in its incipiency there was an injustice, an injustice though unintentioned. For most of us men of Balbalan lived formerly in Gubang, in Abra.

A treaty was made between Gubang and Balensiagao and we paid weregilds. Then we moved to Balbalan and had to join in paying weregilds again when a treaty was made between that place and Balensiagao.

Balensiagao man: The people of Balbalan had killed some of us, therefore they paid weregilds.

Balbalan man: They who slew the men of Balensiagao did so before we came to Balbalan, yet we contributed to their weregilds. We ask a refund.

Balensiagao man: The only thing to do now is to forget the matter because our forefathers settled it.

Balbalan man: Our fathers in *Ngato* will be weeping because our account is not paid.

Balensiagao man: Oh, no! They will not weep, because we settled all accounts long ago and made peace.

These remarks initiated long-winded speeches that continued on and on the rest of the afternoon, all night, except for about three hours, and half the forenoon. Everybody knew the claim had little or no merit, including those who advanced it; everybody knew it would lead to naught. But they needed something to keep up the tradition of arguing wrongs, something to exercise their oratorical and poetical ability on, and this was the best they had.

The treaty.—As has been said, in the Bontok culture area, pacts are limited to a single function—that of bearing witness that all accounts of blood vengeance are settled between the two regions and that there is mutual agreement to maintain the peace henceforth. Kalinga pacts seem to me deserving of being called treaties, for they contain a number of general and particular provisions, and sanctions for enforcing them are taken for granted according to the custom.

Lubwagan's treaties all contain eight uniform general articles aside from those that cover particular cases. The general articles are:

1. Statement of the boundaries of each region. (These have to be defined whether the region be adjacent to or distant from each other,

because they define the people for whom each pact-holder will be responsible.)

2. Each pact-holder will be responsible for the acts of citizens of his region, and for all acts within his region, that affect citizens of the other region.

3. Neither region will pollute the soil of the other with foreign blood (each region will respect the neutrality of the other). Neither region will permit a third region to stain its soil with the blood of the other.

4. Each pact-holder guarantees visitors from the other region shelter and food.

5. In the event of illness or of accident to citizens of one region within the bounds of the other, the pact-holder where this occurs will return the persons to their home region, or to an adjacent intermediate region, providing carriers or attendants as the case may require. In case of serious illness or death, the person will be returned wrapped in blankets.[12]

6. Each pact-holder will assist traders from the other region. If requested, the pact-holder will appoint reliable agents to execute commissions for the visiting trader or will undertake them himself.

7. Money stolen from or lost by a citizen of the one region within the other region will be restored him by a collection from the citizens of the place where this occurred.[13]

8. Pact-holders will facilitate the collection of debts owed citizens of the other region by citizens of his own and seizures (*taliwan*) to cover such debts.

I am informed that the treaties of northern Kalinga regions regularly include a ninth article which provides that each pact-holder try to restrain his co-citizens from

12. The swanky thing, in the case of dead aliens, is for the pact-holder to give them a funeral feast before sending the body home; if he does not do this (and it depends on his financial ability whether he does—no such feast is stipulated in the treaties), he will at least send a contribution for the funeral along with the corpse. The same is true if the alien died in another region and is delivered thence to the pact-holder to relay further.

13. *Q*. But may a man not say he lost money when he did not or that he lost more than was actually taken?

A. [Pangat Kanao]: A man wouldn't do that. If he did, it would be found out and he would be punished severely. But he wouldn't do it.

Comment: A Kalinga has no privacy; his life is an open book. The pact-holder of his home region would be notified if he put forward such a claim, and he could not withstand the circumstantial investigation that would follow if his claim were not well founded. But, aside from this consideration, I think that Kanao is right in saying that a Kalinga would hardly do that sort of thing.

taking a dagdagas in the region of the other and to compel them to do the right thing by the girl if they do.

48. Attempt to contract dagdagas relationship; intervention of pact-holder; marriage (1925).—Abauwag, a policeman of Salegseg, was attracted to a schoolgirl of Magnao. He sent her the *banat* gift [see p. 60], and she retained it. When this came to my knowledge [C. Lammawin, pact-holder in Magnao for Salegseg region, speaking], I communicated the fact to my Salegseg colleague, and he placed the matter before some of the Salegseg pangats. Councilor Balikao, the most influential of the pangats, summoned Abauuwag and advised him to marry the girl. Abauwag did so.

Besides the general articles of the treaty, there may be particular ones covering such points as the following: inclusion in the pact of citizens living outside the region, determination of cases of dual citizenship, also of the status of policemen, constabulary soldiers, and governmental officers, whose acts in most cases are declared outside the scope of the pact-holders' responsibility if correctly performed as a part of their official duties. That is to say, if a policeman, the citizen of one region, kills or wounds a citizen of another in making a proper arrest, then his pact-holder is not obliged to avenge the deed or to collect weregilds. Where children of two or three or more regions attend the same school, pact-holders are often, likewise, relieved of responsibility in the case of children's playground rows in which blood is drawn.

Sometimes there are demands on the part of individuals to be excluded from the pact. If, for example, the Z's of the one region have slain or wounded a relative of A, of the other, and if A and some of his kindred have not received or have refused to accept weregilds, A will come forward at a drinking of the pact and demand that he and certain of his relatives be excluded from the pact and that the Z's or certain of them be excluded on the other side. That is to say, he reserves for himself and his kinsmen the right to take vengeance on the Z's and serves notice that this vengeance must not be construed as an infraction of the pact, since he and his kinsmen will remain out of it. Exclusion, if granted (and it has to be granted unless he be somehow "convinced"), protects him and his relatives from punishment by the pact-holder of his region if he should carry out his revenge.

Every attempt is made to settle such cases so that the two towns may enter into the pact without exclusions. Pressure is brought to bear on both sides, and weregilds offered. Needless to say, discussions of such cases are likely to become heated and to end in bloodshed. Sometimes pacts are concluded with definite exclusions of kinship groups. A powerful family can usually veto the pact.

Some treaties contain an article to the effect that if either region be engaged in a battle with a third, it will respect *bakdoi* (see p. 192) laid or planted by a citizen of the other region.

The article on "shedding foreign blood" is to be taken literally. Taking a prisoner (*biyag* or *biLag*) on neutral soil does not violate neutrality unless the man be wounded.

49. Capture on foreign soil is no violation of neutrality; ransom (pre-Spanish).—The Balensiagao people went head-hunting to a barrio of Poswoi, where they pursued a group of people, all of whom escaped except one, who was taken in the adjacent region of Asiga. The head-hunters dared not kill him, so they brought him alive to Balensiagao and danced around him there as around a head taken in war. They kept him for three months, after which time, his home region, Poswoi, sent five carabaos as *siwat*, ransom. Since the capture was effected without bloodshed, the Asiga pact-holder did not send "strong words" to his Balensiagao colleague.

In the Magnao-Naneng district the taking of captives was frequent, not only when they could not be killed because overtaken on neutral territory, but also in their own regions. The captives were enslaved or held for ransom,

baiyuga. The great-grandfather thrice removed of my
Magnao informant captured two or three Negrito families
in this way and brought them to Magnao. They grew into
quite a community through their own multiplication, became somewhat civilized, and were utilized by the Magnao
people to do "most of the hard work." Indeed, it is my observation that wherever the Negritos live with other
peoples, they do far more work individually than the
people they live among.[14] Finally my informant's grandfather died and his son succeeded to the pangatship. Some
Naneng people killed some of the Negritos, and the latter
were seized by fear that the young pangat did not intend
to protect them; consequently, they fled in the night to the
mountains and were never seen again. The place where
they had their settlement is still called Agta, the Kalinga
word for "Negrito."

50. Neutrality maintained (1904).—Naneng people went on a revenge
expedition [*kilib*] through Lubwagan territory to Sumadel, where they
killed some people. They then hastened back to Lubwagan with the
Sumadel people hot in pursuit. The Naneng people went to the pact-
holder for their town, Salikanto, the father-in-law of Alundai, who fed
them. The Sumadel people went to the house of the pact-holder for
Sumadel, Alilom, who likewise fed them; thus the two parties were eating at the same time within a few hundred meters of each other. Alilom
talked very seriously to the Sumadel people, warned them against
spilling blood on Lubwagan territory, and detained them a little to
minimize the danger of a clash but not sufficiently to frustrate their
chances of overtaking their enemy. He also mustered his kindred and
the whole town so as to punish them while they were within the region
should they violate its neutrality.

The Sumadel warriors followed the Naneng people across Lubwagan
territory and across the territory of Kagalwan, respecting its neutrality,

14. Two months' observation of the Negritos of the east coast of Luzon
brought me to the conclusion that a large factor operating to keep the Negritos
distinct, forest people is the scorn and ridicule they encounter whenever they
venture among the Filipinos. I have several times seen them standing patient and
silent in a jeering ring of these and have seen them quiver and wince at some of
the things they have been compelled to hear.

too, and attacked only after reaching Neneng itself. Several men from Naneng were killed.

Comment: Maintenance of neutrality does not imply prohibiting the passage of war parties from other regions to make an attack on a region with which the home region is at peace.

Q. You told me once that a host is obligated to avenge the death of a guest wounded or killed on his way home. Was Salikanto obligated to avenge the slain Naneng men who had been his guests?

A. No. The obligation of a host extends only to the limits of his region or to acts committed by his fellow-citizens within or beyond those limits.

51. Violation of neutrality indemnified; distribution of indemnity (1939).—A Talgao man lay in ambush on the Lubo-Lubwagan trail within the territory of Lubwagan and speared a man from Lubo. Through their pact-holder, Pataklang, the people of Lubwagan sent "harsh words" and a demand for an indemnity of seven carabaos. This was compromised and a *dalus* of 100 pesos was paid in money "for their having polluted our soil with foreign blood." The indemnity was collected by the Talgao pact-holder from the kinship group of the offender. The distribution of the 100 pesos was as follows

To Pataklang as a gratuity..................................	₱25.00
Used to purchase galvanized iron roofing for communal use, especially as shelter or sunshade, according to the weather, for the guests who attend funeral feasts. [The sheets are laid above on a temporary scaffolding outside the bereft house]..............	25.00
To the various barrios according to their population, sums ranging from ₱5 to Linas and Mabileng, the most populous, down to ₱1.50 for Dognak, Gungungung, and Gaggatong, a total of..........	22.50

The remainder was presented to the eleven pangats, and they divided it among themselves. It was given them on the ground that they had often contributed to benefit "the whole people."

The various barrios deposited their quotas with Pangat Dugyang to be held until such time as they should grow to such amount as might purchase more galvanized iron.

Meanwhile everybody uses the seven or eight sheets bought—they save a great amount of grass-pulling and are a highly prized convenience.

Comment: Kalingas frequently, when speaking of a violation of a pact or a violation of their neutrality, use some such phrase as "spilling foreign blood on our soil" or "infecting our soil." Possibly their regional endogamy may make alien blood a vile thing to them, but I am convinced that this manner of speech is a case of *post facto* rationalization in order to explain and bolster pacts and neutrality. Foreign blood appears not to be considered vile if they spill it themselves, and there are no rites of purification whatever.

52. War on account of insult to pact-holder (ca. *1900*).—About twenty Naneng people went to Sumadel to trade during a period while the pact between Naneng and Bangad was broken. Their presence in Sumadel must have been shouted to Bangad, for on their way back they were attacked and pursued by Bangad people. They reached Lubwagan territory without wounds or loss of life. Lubwagan prohibited the Bangad men from violating its neutrality by fighting on its soil and turned them back.

"Criticism and insulting words" were sent to Lubwagan by the Bangad pact-holder. Lubwagan was indignant, and the pact-holder there for Bangad sent back the *banat*, a Chinese bowl, by a passer-by as a token that the pact was broken. Then he assembled his townsmen and went to a place about a kilometer from Bangad called Kallitong, and they shouted a challenge to the Bangad folk. A battle ensued in which Lubwagan lost one and Bangad two, with several wounded on each side.

Two days later, Lubwagan went again to the same place and renewed the challenge. In that fight, each region lost one man dead. "The man killed on Lubwagan's side was my mother's brother, Pasungao. When I was a little boy my mother told me this story many times. The tears would come, and she would sob and tremble all over as she told it, and she would tell me about my duty to avenge. But, of course, I never shall, for I am an educated man [Mr. Auwiyao speaking]."

On the following day, MaLangan and Bokad went into Bangad territory and killed a woman working in her hill farm. However, avengers rushed out, overtook them, and sliced them into small pieces.

On the following day, Lubwagan went to Kallitong and challenged. In the battle that day, Lubwagan lost one man, who was drowned in the river, Bangad lost three men, and several were wounded on each side.

Two days later, the Sumadel pact-holder for Lubwagan brought here the trunks, legs, arms, and many small pieces of the two men who had been killed invading Bangad territory and delivered them to their relatives. The relatives gave him two small pigs for his good services and feasted him and his party.

After the burial, Lubwagan went again to Kallitong and challenged. None were killed, but several were wounded, more on Bangad's side than ours.

Bumusao of Bangad shouted, "You men of Lubwagan, stop coming to Bangad to fight. Let us make peace!" On the next day, he sent a Sumadel man with his spear. It was accepted, and because he was related to every man who had been killed, Galamoy, a mere stripling at the time, was chosen for pact-holder. Bumusao held the pact in Bangad. The peace has lasted ever since [see Case 58].

Bakdoi.—There is an interesting right to stop a battle that is possessed by any neutral who cares to intervene, a right called *bakdoi.* The neutral shouts his name and citizenship and goes between the warring parties. They will not spear him because he is a neutral and probably also because they welcome what he is going to do. He lays a stick or pole down between the two parties and declares *bakdoi.* It is believed that any warrior of either side who advances beyond the extended line of that pole will be instantly killed by the other side. Experience has shown that this always happens, and it is easy to see why it should. For, because of the custom and belief, all men's eyes are riveted on the *bakdoi,* and he who dares step across it will step into a shower of spears. Often, the *bakdoi*-layer will make a speech in which he tells the two parties that they have both fought valiantly but that he sees that they are exhausted and that it is time for them to go home.

If a battle is fought near a boundary line and transfers itself to a neutral region's territory, the violation of neutrality is condoned as *awat*—"accidental." But the pact-holder of the neutral region for one of the two parties will almost certainly lay *bakdoi*—partly, it is said, in his own interest, because if many of the region with which he holds the pact should be slain or wounded, his own expenditure in blankets in which to transport them home would be heavy (see Article 5 of peace treaty). In such a case, if, ignoring the *bakdoi,* the two sides should continue the battle, the pact-holder would muster his co-regionists and severely punish them, but such a contingency is purely hypothetical because such a continuance would never occur. They always stop fighting when *bakdoi* is laid.

53. Bakdoi; *neutral pact-holder stops battle (pre-American).*—Taloktok and Tinglaiyan were fighting near the boundary of the region of Mabungtut. The former town pressed the latter into Mabungtut territory;

Tinglaiyan was getting the worst of it. Bulaiyao, Mabungtut pact-holder for Tinglaiyan, went between the warring parties and laid a stick declaring *bakdoi*. He shouted to the warring parties and told them they were both tired and that whoever of either party crossed the line of that stick would be killed.

That did not mean that he would kill them himself—it meant that the other side would. It has always resulted, whenever men have tried to continue the battle, that when the warrior has advanced toward the other side past *bakdoi*, he has always been killed and then the rest are afraid to infringe the *bakdoi*.

In the present instance, Dangangao of the Taloktok side went past the *bakdoi*, and he received a fatal spear wound. In fighting a long time ago between Talgao and Lubo [not the recent battle reported in Case 90], a man from each side crossed the *bakdoi* and both were killed.[15]

54. Pangat lays bakdoi (ca. *1900*).—Mangali attacked Kagalwan and lost five men and three wounded while they succeeded in wounding only one man of Kagalwan. They fled into the territory of Tanglag, the Kagalwan warriors in hot pursuit. Uduk, a Tanglag pangat, saved them from further losses by laying *bakdoi*. He shouted, *Adi-yo lasoyan di bakdoi-ko* ["Do not trespass my *bakdoi!*"].

55. Naturalized citizen of warring town sticks bakdoi (ca. *1883*).—A broken pact between Magnao and Ambukaiyan was the occasion of annual battles for several years. The two regions always met for this battle in a chasm called Binokan. After two or three of these annual battles, the women on each side began to accompany the men in order to cook for them, for the battles came to last several days each year. Sometimes a champion would advance from each side, and, after the battle of the champions, it might be that there would be no more fighting that day.

There was a man from Magnao who had married in Ambukaiyan and became naturalized there. He always remained neutral, taking no part in the fighting. After having consulted the pangats on each side, he went one day between the two warring sides, stuck up a stick, and proclaimed *bakdoi*. Fighting ceased and a pact was thereafter arranged which has been respected to this day and inherited at least twice.

"*DuwaL*."—In order to prevent a battle or an attack on a town, *duwaL* is sometimes given. The following is an instance:

15. The violation of the *bakdoi* at the Talgao-Lubo battle is said to have been accidental. The line of battle was so long that the men who advanced across the line of the *bakdoi* had not heard the shouts of the *bakdoi*-layer.

56. Murder and robbery of a tradesman; duwaL (*a victim*) *given to buy off from an attack* (ca. *1903*).—In the time when a baldheaded American [Volkmar] was governor in Bontok but before the Americans had established a governor in Kalinga, Lakpao, of Daowangan region, went to Tollang, in the present municipality of Pinukpuk, to sell some valuable beads. There was a pact between these two regions.

Doyak, a man of Tollang, murdered Lakpao and ran away with the beads. Bulaiyao, the pact-holder of Daowangan for Tollang, demanded retaliation and the return of the beads. Ambong, pact-holder of Tollang for Daowangan, killed Lataowan, a younger brother of Doyak, but probably really could not return the beads because Doyak had absconded with them.

Then Bulaiyao led an expedition of Daowangan men against Tollang in such force as to be able to well-nigh exterminate the Tollang people. To save themselves, the Tollang people caught the mother of Doyak, Bagoyan, and gave her as *duwaL*. By order of Bulaiyao, the oldest male relative of the slain Lakpao was given the privilege of the first blow. He was followed by other relatives in order of rank, age, and nearness of relationship. The woman was hacked to pieces with head axes right in Tollang in the presence of her own people, and her head, arms, and legs were carried back to Daowangan.

Duties of the pact-holder.—The pact-holder supervises the relations of his home region with the folk of the region with which he holds the pact. These, on visiting his region, will usually proceed at once to his house and will eat and sleep there unless they have trading partners or friends in the town with whom they prefer to stay.[16] I have noticed that Pangat Kanao's house is nearly always full of Ginaang people—his mother holds the pact with Ginaang; not many of them sleep there, but it is their assembling place. If a man brings something to sell, the pact-holder may undertake the commission himself, or he will recommend somebody to undertake it. If a man comes to seize property to

16. Often the visitors bring gifts of food or dainties to the pact-holder. One rainy afternoon I saw folk from Magaogao arrive at the house of Galamoy, Lubwagan pact-holder for their town. Soon women from houses round about began to visit Galamoy's house, each carrying a bit of banana leaf. On making inquiry, I was told that these were relatives of Galamoy or of his wife who had come to get a share of the *dikEt* cakes that the visitors had brought.

cover a debt, he may consult with the pact-holder on the question of whose property it would be best to seize. That is the usual practice at present, but it was not always followed formerly and is not obligatory today.

If an offense be committed by one of his co-regionists against a person of the other region, the pact-holder is obliged to detect the offender and punish him. Failure to do this will cause people to complain against him to their own pact-holder, who may be moved to break the pact. The pact-holder of the offending region and his relatives thus lose face and honor in their own town.

If a man of his region slays or wounds one from the other region, the pact-holder is obligated to slay or wound the offender or one of his relatives.

Let us suppose that a Lubwagan man slays a man of Sumadel. The Sumadel pact-holder will come himself or will send a messenger with "harsh words." He will not break the pact right away—he will give his colleague plenty of time in which to do what ought to be done. The latter will investigate and unless he finds that the act of his citizen was fully justified—and in the investigation he will actually lean toward the side of Sumadel, because rupture of the pact would spell loss of his own prestige—he will pursue either the first or the second of the following courses:

1. Immediately kill or wound the offender or a relative of the offender. This course will save the pact. Some pact-holders consider that their honor demands that they shall not pay weregilds to the kindred of the slain in such a case; others are "cowards" and pay.

2. (*a*) Collect weregilds for the relatives of the slain Sumadel man; sometimes he will send an advance on the weregild from his own property so as to show his Sumadel colleague that he means to do the right thing.

b) Collect also a small weregild for himself, for, since there is the fiction that he is a brother of his colleague and so a relative of the Sumadel people, a weregild is due him.

c) He will carefully select the relative of the offender who may most cheaply be killed or wounded and will do one of these to him.

d) He will pay weregilds to the kindred of the victim.

I think that the first course is the older of the two alternatives and is still the more honored. An aged pact-holder told me, "If a man breaks my pact, I will kill him; I will have none of this weregild business. It is a device of cowards. If an offender against the pact came to me and offered weregilds, this is the answer I would make him: 'So-o? You thought you could break the pact and go free because you are rich?' "

Even when weregilds are paid, as seen under No. 2 above, there must, in theory, be a victim, but the job of killing or wounding may be postponed or passed on to the pact-holder's sons. If the latter does not do it, somebody will taunt him: "Fine pact-holders ye are, the whole tribe of you! So-and-so broke the pact with such-and-such region, and your father did not avenge and ye have not avenged. What kind of family is that to hold a peace pact?"

Informants say that the pact-holder will not kill those of the offender's relatives who pay weregilds. Nevertheless, they say, the pact-holder will always kill a relative of the offender.

Q. But you said that if they pay weregilds they will be safe.

A. Yes, that is correct. But always there will be some who do not pay—even if only third cousins.

Q. He will not kill a relative of the offender beyond the third degree of relationship?

A. No, he has no right to—those are outside the offender's kinship group.

It is evident that there is here a conflict of customs. I think the situation came about thus:

The ancient pact was an extension of the kinship principle. It established in each region a fictitious kinsman of the other, the pact-holder, and gave him a spear from that other with which to avenge wrongs against it. In that epoch, the pact-holder, as a fictitious relative of the other side, killed the offender, and that was all there was to it.

But later came the weregild system of buying off from vengeance, and the growth of this custom within the region made inroads on the more primitive retaliation so that it became acceptable to the offended region in lieu of killing. However, the old tenet that a pact-holder must maintain his pact by killing continued on, and killing was still necessary to the preservation of his honor. But payment of weregilds served to save the pact and make it possible for the pact-holder to go about the dangerous business of killing in a discreet way or take an easier course and pass it on to the next generation, which may, if not too often reminded, forget about it altogether, so that the weregild system grew in favor. Before the Americans came, a pact-holder probably always killed even when weregilds had been paid, for killing was the fashion of the day and added to a man's prestige and control over his people. But the coming of that peculiar folk greatly increased the wealth of the Kalingas, so that payment of weregilds was easier than before and possible in a greater number of cases.

The coming of the Americans, with their puzzling prejudice against the killing or wounding of people who were no kin of theirs and their equally puzzling assumption of the sole right also to avenge wrongs for groups that were no kin of theirs, made it dangerous for a pact-holder to retaliate and so gave added impetus to the practice of collecting weregilds and postponing retaliation. Or there was another device that might be resorted to, and it exists among the Kalingas, although they hardly recognize it yet—that of token woundings (see Cases 63 and 96).

Thus there are three courses open to the pact-holder today: (1) the old custom, forthright killing or wounding; (2) the new, weregilds plus a deferred killing or wounding that may never come off; or (3) a present token wounding.

One reason that may account for the continuance of retaliatory slaying even though weregilds have been collected is the superstition that unless such retaliation be taken, the pact-holder's belly and testicles will swell. The Kalingas are relatively an unsuperstitious people, so that I doubt that a pact-holder ever acts from the motive of shunting such a calamity from himself. But the superstition is a superb vehicle of ridicule and scorn and probably drives him to retaliatory action in order to obviate questions from his fellow-citizens about the condition of his private parts.

The question arises: Are the slayings of a go-between privileged above those of the pact-holder? For the go-between, it will be remembered, does not pay weregilds if he slays in retaliation for an aggression committed while he is mediating a controversy. Even one of my informants knew that "he is punishing a wrong against all the people." But the pact-holder, as we have seen, frequently does pay weregilds, although he more vividly holds a commission from all the people than the go-between, for in public meeting he holds up the spear that has been sent him and asks, "Shall I accept it? Does any man object?"

In the theory of the custom—if custom can be presumed to have a theory—I think that both functionaries are equally privileged but that circumstances have led to a variance in practice. Certainly, too, it is a feather in the cap of the pact-holder if he does not pay weregilds for his victim. I am not so sure, either, that some go-betweens would not pay weregilds; I have only the people's opinion for it that none would; there appear to be no cases. Mediation is surely an older institution than the peace pact. No doubt in the old days, go-betweens did not pay weregilds—probably there were no weregilds. Long habituation to mediation, its importance for the domestic peace, and the tradition that offenses against mediation will surely be punished have disciplined the people to it, and they do not offend. An offense of the sort would arouse tremendous indignation solely as an unheard-of, outlandish thing. On the other hand, the very frequency of offenses against pacts tends to minimize public sentiment against them, so that the pact-holder has less backing for his executions than a go-between would probably have, and so has the greater need in the interest of his own and his group's safety to pay weregilds.

The student of primitive law will, I think, agree that the slayings by both fall into the category of legal executions, since both are agents of the regional unit, of the police power of a budding state.

57. Pact-holder punishes offense against pact (pre-American times).—Sumaíl of Lubwagan had a dagdagas at Tanglag with whom he passed much of the time. He also had an old fuselock. He carried it with him to Tanglag one time, and, while proudly practicing at a target before the Tanglag people, he accidentally wounded a Tanglag woman.

Sumaíl fled, and he and his relatives went into hiding in Lubwagan immediately, but, "luckily," Agwak, the pact-holder, was able to find one of them, a woman, under circumstances that allowed her to be killed. Agwak received *lotok* from Tanglag.

58. Pact-holder slays accidental offender against pact (pre-American times).—A Lubwagan man traveling with his head ax stuck between his body and his gee-string accidentally wounded a Bangad man while squeezing past him on a narrow trail which overhung a precipice. The Bangad man was not honest and reported the event unfairly to his pact-holder. The latter sent a strong protest to Galamoy, the Lubwagan pact-holder.

Galamoy summoned the Lubwagan man, who came to him with a perfectly clear conscience expecting no danger. Galamoy beheaded the man with one stroke. The wound received by the Bangad man was very slight and is said to have been purely accidental.

Galamoy paid *pakan* but no weregilds; Bangad gave him a *lotok*.

Whenever a pact-holder kills or wounds an aggressor against the pact, the aggrieved region pays him *lotok*, just as a kinship group pays *lotok* to an avenger of one of its members.

59. Advances to married woman; pact-holder protects alien (1925).—Aiyangyang, of Lubwagan, went to Sumadel to the house of his *abuyog* [trading partner] with a carabao which he gave to sell on the *tokdai* [see p. 133] basis. The trading partner went to sell the animal, leaving Aiyangyang alone with the wife. It grew late, and the trading partner had not returned, so the mistress of the house lay down to sleep and advised Aiyangyang to do the same. The woman was very pretty, and Aiyangyang could not sleep for "thinking of her beauty." Believing the woman was already asleep, it occurred to Aiyangyang that he might possibly be able to "steal" from her without awakening her. He tried it, but "unfortunately" the woman did awaken, and she began screaming. Aiyangyang fled to the house of a neighbor, who summoned the pact-holder. The pact-holder protected Aiyangyang from the irate husband and took him to his own house.

Next morning, the pact-holder summoned the pangats and these arranged the matter "amicably" and informally by assessing an indemnity of only three Kalinga blankets plus 10 pesos. The pact-holder got nothing out of the case because he wanted to settle it quickly lest the Sumadel people harm Aiyangyang and so cause the breaking of the pact.

Comment: Compare this trifling indemnity with the domestic settlement of similar cases, for example, Case 94, or with the way the pact-holder mulcted his fellow-citizen in the following case.

60. Theft of rice by alien; pact-holders' share of indemnity (1928).—A poverty-stricken Sumadel man came to Lubwagan hoping to work for wages. Being disappointed in the hope of finding work, he started to go back home early one morning. On the way he opened the granary of Magayam and stole five *lakom* of unthreshed rice [worth one-half a peso]. Magayam discovered the theft from the faulty way in which the door had been closed, trailed the man, overtook him, questioned him, and ascertained that it was, indeed, his palay. He returned home and complained to Tambulong, the Lubwagan pact-holder for Sumadel. Next morning, Tambulong went to Sumadel and informed Alnag, their pact-holder for Lubwagan, about the case. Alnag settled it thus: Magayam received 50 pesos as indemnity for the theft; Tambulong received a carabao; Alnag a carabao. The relatives of the culprit paid for him, practically enslaving him until he should work out his debt. "In such cases, the offender has to fear his own relatives almost as much as his nonkindred," remarked by informant.

Q. What kind of cases do you mean?

A. When a man is poor.

Compensation of the pact-holder.—The principal compensation of the pact-holder is in his own enjoyment of the authority and prestige of the office. This office is a road to the rank of pangat if one be not already a pangat, and it raises the pangat's prestige if he has already attained that rank. The expenses of the position are considerable, and it is questionable whether the pickings from the job suffice to repay them, although the pickings are not to be sneered at. They are more numerous than can be enumerated or classified and depend a good deal on the pact-holder's own enterprise, avidity, and cunning.

The more regular sources of compensation are: (1) He and his relatives are in a preferred position for carrying on trade with the region for which he holds the pact. (2) He usually shares in the so-ol of fields seized and of heirlooms sold between the regions. (3) If he avenges aggression against the pact by slaying, he receives weregilds from the slayer's kinship group and also *lotok* from the offended region. (4) He always shares in indemnities collected from his own people for offenses against the other region and often shares in those collected from the other region for his own people (Cases 58 and 60).

Rupture of the pact.—A violation of the pact is called *buguy* and a rupture of the pact is called *gopas*. A pact-holder notifies his colleague of a rupture of the pact by sending the latter's spear or a Chinese bowl back to him. The messenger will sometimes, after delivering the spear, go to a safe distance on his return road and then shout a challenge (*gaiyagai*) to battle (*baluknit*), naming the date and place.

The reasons for declaring the pact broken are various. The more frequent are: homicide, wounds, robbery, failure of the colleague pact-holder to detect and prosecute injuries, and offenses against citizens of the region, stoning or beating of citizens or failure of the pact-holder to protect them, dispute about the boundary line, insult to pact-holder, and the breaking of any of the terms of the treaty.

61. Dispute over boundary; war (1939).—The land near the boundary between Bangad and Tinglaiyan is good land that might be converted into rice fields. Consequently, each region wants it for its own. In the "month" called *mankikipkip* ["fish-trapping month"] the Bangad people placed some fish traps in the Chico River near the boundary. As a way of precipitating a boundary dispute, the Tinglaiyan people ordered them to take away their traps. The Bangad people did not do this, although they were sent word to do it several times. The demands appear to have been a pretext, rather a thin one at that, for they were not in the least justified by the custom with respect to fishing.

Tinglaiyan sent a messenger who handed back the spear and informed Bangad that the pact was broken. When he had got to a safe distance on his way back, he turned and shouted, *Whao! Whao! Dakayu'n iBangad, intako mamaluknit si bigat id BisiLa* ["Whao! Ye people of Bangad, let us have a battle tomorrow at BisiLa"].

Next morning Tinglaiyan warriors to the number of about a hundred proceeded to the place named for the fight, where they found no Bangad warriors, but only the people of that place dismantling and carrying away their houses as rapidly as they could, to be transferred later to the main town, Bangad. These ran away, but the Tinglaiyan people were able to overtake an old man, whom they slew. They hacked the body into many pieces—the young men, especially—thereby earning the right to be tattooed.

The news of this deed was shouted by relay to Bangad, and the people there knew almost right away what had happened. The whole of Bangad, including the other barrios of the region, took their spears and head axes and went to do battle.

Three Bangad men were killed and three wounded. Tinglaiyan lost four killed and several wounded. At present, one sees numbers of young men in Tinglaiyan and Bangad with fresh tattoos on their arms. "The officers of the law ought to imprison those fellows and send them to Bilibid along with those already there, because it is a confession that they killed, wounded, or carried away a part of the corpse."[17]

Informant also says that the management of this affair by the provincial authorities was more than ridiculous. Neither the pact-holder nor the mayor was prosecuted. He believes that both of them fought

17. A young boy may tattoo the back of his hand and usually does, to be as much like a man as possible and to see if it hurts. The tattoo on arms, breast, and back can be had only by the procedure shown on p. 238, n. 8. The Lubwagan people do not now observe formal requirements for obtaining the tattoo nearly so strictly as those of the western parts of the subprovince.

along with the rest. It ought to have been their duty to inform the constabulary as soon as the pact was broken so that measures could be taken to settle the dispute and prevent fighting. The court also, he says, was to blame for allowing a few young men to be made the goat and for letting the "influential men" go unpunished. Furthermore, the officials have not even arranged a peace pact or settled the boundary line. "They are lush plants that draw and draw up water, but produce no fruit."

Q. I went to Bangad not long ago and noticed that the houses are frightfully close together. Is that because the outlying barrios have moved into it?

A. Yes, that is the reason. I went there as a census-taker and noticed that the town is in very unsanitary condition owing to crowding [see Pl. IV].

It requires years to renew a broken pact. Lubwagan utilizes its superiority of strength and its advantage of location as a trading center and subprovincial capital and necessary transportation point to oppress weak towns:

62. Peace pact broken (1938).—A funeral feast in Dalupa was attended by some Lubwagan people related to the deceased through the same ancestor as Maddalum's [see p. 153]. Sakleo, a boy of about fourteen, attempted while drunk to climb the ladder into a house while carrying a bolo. He accidentally inflicted a slight wound on the hand of a boy of twelve who lived in the house. Frightened, he ran away without explaining that it was an accident. His victim had not cried out, but some other boys told the injured boy's father and relatives. These without investigating or questioning the wounded boy [I am giving the Lubwagan version] overtook Sakleo and deliberately wounded him in the same way as he had wounded the other boy, namely, in the back of the hand. The cut was made by Lisales, uncle of the wounded boy.

The Lubwagan people all started home. On reaching the divide, one of them shouted a report of the incident which was relayed by shouts and which reached Lubwagan in the following form: "The people of Dalupa have killed one of us." Thereupon the inhabitants of Linas, who were nearly all relatives of Sakleo, as well as many people from near-by barrios, grabbed their spears and rushed to avenge. "Unluckily," they did not kill anybody but turned back fearing the stock of "paltiks" [illegally made guns from the Ilokos provinces] that the Dalupa people were reputed to have. Next day, the constabulary brought the Dalupa people in for investigation. As they passed Linas, Sabado, a second cousin of Sakleo, wounded a Dalupa man, relative of Lisales, right under the noses of the constabulary.

Talon, the pact-holder of Lubwagan, sent a Chinese bowl by these men who had been called in for investigation to Kobao, the Dalupa pact-holder, as a token that the pact had been broken. The pact-holder there cried the news through his town, *Nagpas di budong id Lubwagan* ["The pact is finished with Lubwagan"].

After the lapse of some months, a bowl was sent to Mabwaki, brother of Sakleo, with a plea for renewal of the pact. The Dalupa folk argued that two men had been wounded on their side and only one on Lubwagan's. The bowl was rejected and a demand made for weregilds. Dalupa countered with a demand for weregilds on account of Sabado's act, but Lubwagan rejected this demand on the ground that Dalupa had begun it all. Dalupa had to yield before Lubwagan's superior strength and advantageous location. The pangats of each region named two go-betweens, not closely related to either of the principals, and these began working for a settlement.

That was nearly four years ago. Dalupa people come to Lubwagan in groups, not individuals, since they do not trust Sakleo's party, which is large, and have clearly shown that they have no respect for the constabulary.

A letter written in English by Mr. Bumugas, vice-mayor, who lived in Dalupa, was sent to Mr. Wailan, the mayor, entreating his good offices in renewing the pact. Mr. Wailan read it to the Lubwagan people, but they said, "Wait till the weregilds are paid, please."

The weregilds have now been partially arranged, to wit:

Sakleo receives a field and a gold earring worth six and two carabaos, respectively

Mabwaki, Sakleo's second brother, one gong worth six carabaos

Gopai, Sakleo's oldest brother, a field worth six carabaos

Gopai's children, three in number, receive only *pakan* ["for eating together"] of one carabao each because their mother is a relative of Lisales, who committed the assault on Sakleo

Gopai's wife receives nothing because it was her uncle who committed the offense

Sakleo's mother receives a field worth five carabaos

Sakleo's father receives a field worth five carabaos

Binto, brother of the father, receives a gong worth five carabaos

Idao, brother of Sakleo's mother—a gold earring worth three carabaos

Pangat Dugyang, first cousin of the mother, was given a field worth two carabaos

Pangat Maddalum, cousin of Sakleo's mother—a field worth two carabaos

Aiyangdu, cousin of the father—a Chinese bowl worth 10 pesos and one carabao

Pangat Galamoy, second cousin of the father, reckoned as a first cousin because he is a pangat and because the father has few cousins—two carabaos

Tumolnok, first cousin of the mother—one carabao

Palangyan, first cousin—one carabao

Bakilas, first cousin—one carabao

Three children of deceased first cousin, Pinading—one carabao

Two children of deceased first cousin, Bananao—one carabao

Jackson, a second cousin ["he is becoming a pangat, and they fear him"] reckoned as first cousin—one carabao

Umaiyao, son of Maddalum, second cousin, also becoming a pangat and treated as a first cousin—one carabao

Four children of Bantiag, deceased second cousin—one carabao

Gilfillen, first cousin—one carabao

Likadang, first cousin—two carabaos

Pangat Iwag and brothers and sisters, second cousins—a gold earring worth three carabaos

Pangat ManaLtag, second cousin—20 pesos

Pangat Gasatan, second cousin—30 pesos

TOTAL PAID AND PROMISED TO DATE: 60 pesos plus a value equal to sixty-two carabaos

Some of the carabaos were immature, but all will be matured by the time the weregilds are paid. We will reckon them as worth on an average 25 pesos. Then the total of weregilds paid or promised to date is 1,610 pesos. There remains about 500 pesos to pay. The go-betweens say that the kinship group of Lisalis is really stripped bare and must be given time to "acquire." Compare with the amount of these weregilds the total accumulation of the divorcing spouses for fifteen years that is listed on page 56.

We may make certain inferences from the list of payments above. It is apparent that the size of weregild a kinsman receives depends on: (1) nearness of relationship; (2) rank; (3) the amount of fear he inspires. It is not necessarily so much that they fear that he himself will avenge as that, being influential, he will stir up the rest. We see, too, that minor children whose related parent is dead receive collectively what that parent would have received had he been living.

For an explanation of the *pakan* payment mentioned above see page 242. Only Gopai and his children received *pakan* because only they will continue going to Dalupa (where they are related); it is not necessary in the case of the others.

63. Peace pact broken (1920).—Pumusan, a Bontok man, while serving in Lubwagan as a soldier in the constabulary, became a friend of Puttiyao, a wealthy young Kalinga. After Pumusan's discharge, the two became *abuyog* [trading partners]. There was talk between them that Pumusan should sell a certain jar in Bontok. Pumusan, having found a buyer in that town, came to Lubwagan to get the jar and, finding Puttiyao not at home, took it in his absence with the consent of the latter's wife. Puttiyao, however, had changed his mind about selling the jar and, on learning that Pumusan had taken it, set out after him and overtook him at Tinglaiyan about nightfall. As it was raining, the two decided not to return to their respective towns that night but to sleep on the roofed bridge near Tinglaiyan. A number of other wayfarers also slept there that night.

Pumusan, the Bontok man, had hereditary enemies in Tinglaiyan, and a premonition of danger made him arise and go during the night to sleep on the other side of the bridge. His premonition was correct, for a Tinglaiyan man from among the enemy kindred came to the bridge and slew Puttiyao, mistaking him, from his position on the bridge, for Pumusan.

Next morning, the news was shouted to Lubwagan, where everybody suspected Pumusan of having committed the murder. Puttiyao's kindred, together with some unrelated men rushed to Tinglaiyan, found that Pumusan was in the *presidencia* [town house] under arrest, began to destroy the place and would have taken him except that the constabulary arrived, took Pumusan to Bontok, and kept him under arrest. They also arrested the Lubwagan warriors.

Pumusan, however, told a straight story and steadfastly denied his guilt. The Lubwagan people began to threaten to march on Tinglaiyan to avenge; the Tinglaiyan people were afraid to come to Lubwagan. Finally, a meeting of the Lubwagan people was held in Linas, and Mandit, the pact-holder, told the people he was minded to declare the pact broken since he was afraid that the kindred of Puttiyao would commit an aggression on Tinglaiyan—which would oblige him to kill one of them. This meeting did not reassure him with any promises, so he sent back the spear and ruptured relations.

The Court of First Instance found Pumusan guilty and sentenced him to five years' imprisonment. He appealed and died in prison about a year afterward, before the Supreme Court had acted on the appeal.

Tinglaiyan had a strong and capable man, Pa-ao, as pact-holder. The peace between Tinglaiyan and Lubwagan, both strong regions, had never before been broken. The Tinglaiyan pact-holder felt the disgrace deeply. He had done all he could do, now, except one thing to clear his honor; now he did that—he found the real culprit. His relatives "listened and listened," and by and by "they heard something." Gunut was the murderer. He confessed when confronted by the pact-holder with the evidence against him. He was arrested and sentenced to six years' imprisonment.

The Lubwagan party who had gone against Tinglaiyan had meanwhile been sentenced to short periods in the calaboose for the damage they had done to the *presidencia* there.

The Tinglaiyan pact-holder collected 300 pesos for Puttiyao's kindred from the relatives of Gunut. Before distributing the money, the relatives paid the lawyer's fees of those nonrelatives who had acted with them.

The Bontok people also put in a claim for the court expenses of the innocently arrested Pumusan. The pact-holder collected these from Gunut's relatives. He then collected a small weregild for himself—he took all there was left. Next he "accidentally" wounded one of Gunut's kindred in a very clever way. He placed his head ax between belt and body with the blade turned at just the right angle, and backed hurriedly into one of them. The beauty of it was that everybody knew perfectly well why and how he had done it and that if he should be arrested the case would easily be made one of accident.

The pact was not renewed for six years. The Tinglaiyan people were afraid to come to Lubwagan during that time. When Gunut came back from prison, they made him the new pact-holder.

Q. Made Gunut the pact-holder! Why?

A. For his safety's sake and for the permanence of the pact.

Q. How could that be?

A. Perfectly simple. You remember the pact-holders are "brothers"? Well, one pact-holder will not kill another pact-holder on that account. It is thought that if he did he would get big belly and die very shortly. That makes Gunut and his relatives safe from the Lubwagan side, and there are no other cases outstanding—you remember the peace between Lubwagan and Tinglaiyan lasted from almost time immemorial until Gunut killed Puttiyao by mistake.

Q. How did Pa-ao, the Tinglaiyan pact-holder, discover that it was Gunut who did the killing?

A. Probably several little things. All that I heard of was that Gunut went to Bangad to a feast of some sort, got drunk, and could not refrain from boasting. He thought he was boasting very cautiously; he said, "I once saw an eagle flying downstreamward." One of the Bangad men who was a friend of Pa-ao thought, "What can he mean? He must mean the soul of Puttiyao flying homeward." So he told Pa-ao.

Now, in this case, if I [Mr. Dakauwag speaking] should avenge my cousin, Puttiyao, who is related to me on my father's side, then the pact-holder, who is also related to me on my father's side, would kill a relative of mine on my mother's side. He would not kill one of his own relatives. He would choose a distant relative on my mother's side so as the less to enrage me and my mother's kin, and he would choose one who had a weak kinship group, so as to lessen the danger to himself and lessen the amount of the weregild.

ALLIANCES

If there be a contemporaneous rupture of the pacts of a region with two others, those two are likely to unite forces in expeditions against it. Such an alliance has occurred several times. The alliance is always temporary and solely for the duration of the hostilities.

CITIZENSHIP

In Kalinga, as also in the civilized world, two factors determine citizenship: residence and blood (descent). Owing to the Kalinga's strong regional endogamy, the two factors rarely come into conflict. But in different districts of the subprovince, there is a difference in the relative weights given them and, consequently, a difference in attitude toward citizenship and a difference in the procedure of changing it.

The language has no word for citizenship. The prefix *i-*, meaning the same as the English suffix *ite* (as, for example, *iLubwagan*, Lubwaganite; *iBangad*, Bangadite) indicates residence and nearly always citizenship as well. But if one wants to be explicit, one must use the phrase, *manitkom si budong ud Lubwagan . . . ud Bangad* ("included in the peace pact of Lubwagan" or "of Bangad").

There are also evident in Kalinga the same two attitudes toward citizenship as exist in the civilized world, namely, the "citizen" attitude and the "subject" attitude. I have heard it said that the citizens of a place are "owned" by the pact-holders and, again, "we belong [meaning in respect to relations with foreign regions] to our pact-holders." However, the strong principle of equality handed down from kinship group society, the relative separation of the apparatus for controlling foreign relations from that for controlling domestic matters, and the division of the "foreign office" of the regional unit into numerous mutually independent sections (pact-holders), all favor the "citizen" attitude.

Changes of citizenship.—In the Lubwagan district changes of citizenship are under the control of the pact-holders and may be made at any time the two of these that are concerned permit. In the Magnao-Naneng district changes of citizenship must be added as amendments to the treaty between the regions concerned and may have to wait two or three years until the two regions meet together in a *lonok* celebration (a re-ratification when the pact passes by inheritance) or a *dolnat*, a "warming of the pact." The Magnao people explain their procedure by saying that, in their district, people are so inclined to abide by their ties of kinship rather than yield obedience to regional policy that changes of citizenship ought to be talked over between the two regions assembled together before being allowed. They say, for example, that if A goes from Magnao to Naneng and if he be allowed lightly to take Naneng citizenship, and if he there be killed or wounded by a Naneng citizen, his kindred in Magnao are very likely to take vengeance and so break the pact between Magnao and Naneng. There is here apparent a greater weight attached to descent as compared to residence than in Lubwagan and a greater ownership by the region of its citizens—a "subject" attitude rather than a "citizen" one.

Change of citizenship is publicly announced in both the region of nativity and the region of naturalization. If a Lubwagan man were to decide to marry in Tanglag, reside there, and change his citizenship, the following forms would be observed. He would take a gift befitting his station—if he were a wealthy man, a blanket—to the Lubwagan pact-holder for Tanglag. The pact-holder would display the blanket in one or two barrios, announcing: *Dakayu'n tagu! Si* [name] *initdon-na 'naiya 'n kaboy tai pi-on-na maniTanglag. Adi pon manitkon si budong id Lubwagan* ("Ye people! So-and-so has given me this *kaboy* blanket because he wishes to be a Tanglag-ite. He will no longer be included in the pact as of Lubwagan"). *Mutatis mutandis,* the same announcement would be made in Tanglag.

Women as well as men have citizenship:

64. Change of citizenship of woman who marries alien must be applied for (1925).—Manganip, a wealthy man of Mabungtut, came to Lubwagan and married a poor but very pretty girl,[18] the daughter of a dagdagas. He married by a simple *palanos* [feast] with no other formalities. He took her to Mabungtut with him.

After a short time the woman was found to be pregnant; it was accordingly presumed that the marriage would be a permanent one and that she would stay in Mabungtut. Thereupon Manganip went to the Mabungtut pact-holder for Lubwagan and gave him 2 pesos—1 peso to be kept and 1 peso to be sent the Lubwagan pact-holder for Mabungtut. The Lubwagan pact-holder kept the money when it was sent him, and that meant that the woman might renounce her citizenship in the region of her birth.

The question arises whether the gifts made to the pact-holders are an indication of a theoretical ownership by these of their people and anywise indicative of contacts with the tribute serfdom of the Malays. It is impossible to say, but I think that the gift-giving may more safely be attributed to a universal oriental attitude: officials in the orient, including the Philippines, are generally reluctant to act unless given a present. The fact that both pact-holders are given a present adds to the probability that this attitude explains the gifts.

18. In no other of these tribes does wealth play so little role in the choosing of a bride and beauty so great a one. I asked informant, "Why did Manganip marry in another town, contrary to custom?" and he answered, "It was his fate, because he saw how pretty the girl was and was attracted."

When a man changes his residence, the considerations that confront him with respect to changing citizenship as well are very serious ones. They lie, I think, at the basis of the Kalinga's regional endogamy. A surprising feature of this endogamy is its relative lack of snobbishness; the Kalingas seem to me to be much less snobbish than the Ifugaos, who, despite that attitude, are free to marry and do marry anywhere. Kalinga endogamy is certainly not based on a feeling of superiority to other peoples.

Let us assume that a Lubwagan man is going to marry a Tanglag woman and live in Tanglag. *If he changes citizenship:*

1. He protects his Lubwagan relatives if he should become involved in trouble or a feud in Tanglag, whereas if he should live in Tanglag as a Lubwagan man and should kill somebody there, even though he acted in self-defense, the Lubwagan pact-holder for Tanglag would be obliged, in order to save the pact, to kill one of his relatives in Lubwagan.
2. He can freely fulfil his duty to his wife's relatives, acting with and supporting them and killing for them. If he did this without changing citizenship, he would be a Lubwagan man killing Tanglag citizens, which would break the pact between the two towns, whereupon, the Lubwagan pact-holder would have to kill one of his relatives. In this connection it is to be remembered that it is the prime duty of a husband to avenge his wife's death.
3. He can keep up relations with his Lubwagan kindred, can come and go safely at all times and despite all happenings, because, even though his own brother may have killed a man there, the kindred of the slain will not dare kill him or even throw a stone at him—he is a citizen of Tanglag, and they dare not.
4. But he imperils his life if there be some Tanglag people having hatred toward a branch of his own kinship group. The latter could kill him as a Tanglag man without danger from the Tanglag pact-holder. Of course, since there is a pact between the towns, ancient grudges are supposed to have ceased. But who can tell what an adolescent boy, anxious to get his tattoo, will do?
5. If he gains wealth and honor, he may become a pangat and hold a peace pact for the Tanglag people.

On the other hand, *if he retains his Lubwagan citizenship:*

1. He will be able to render active help to his relatives in that region, and he can do this with greater safety than if he resided there. He can avenge them either in Lubwagan or in other towns and escape to Tanglag. If he were to change citizenship, he would henceforth be able to help them only in a material way.
2. He enjoys the immunity of a privileged foreigner in his relations with the Tanglag people. The pact-holder is obliged to protect him, no matter what he does.
3. His own safety, as has been explained, is considerably greater in case his kinship group has ever had a feud with any Tanglag groups.
4. By retaining his citizenship, he will be able to accompany a party of Tanglag people to a region with which Lubwagan has no pact or whose pact with Lubwagan has been ruptured—to a region he would not dare penetrate as a Lubwagan man—and there kill with impunity, provided he can escape to Tanglag or Lubwagan.

65. Abuse of immigrants' immunity (ca. *1900*).—Diyug, the son of Koitig, "my grandfather," a powerful pangat of Lubwagan, married in Tanglag without changing his citizenship. After having lived there about a year, he accompanied a party of Tanglag traders to Salegseg, a region whose pact with Lubwagan was broken. He there killed a man on the trail, and the party turned back. Diyug, however, turned off the road, leaving his party, and came back to Lubwagan. He did not want to go back to his wife in Tanglag, for he had had no children by her—he had married her probably for the purpose of carrying out this exploit. The Tanglag pact-holder for Salegseg punished the Tanglag companions of Diyug for not having restrained him. Diyug, being a citizen of Lubwagan, might safely have gone back to Tanglag, however, had he wanted to continue with his wife. [Informant: DAKAUWAG.]

Q. Why did Diyug kill the Salegseg man?
A. He did it in order to add to his reputation for killing people.

In considering a man's application to change citizenship, the pact-holders ponder over the same items as the man himself but from a different angle, namely, that of probable effect on the pact. If the applicant be a braggart and a bumptious individual, likely to get into trouble, or if his kinship group has had a feud with any Tanglag folk, both pact-holders will be anxious for him to change his citizenship—they will not want to be responsible for him. But if the Tanglag pact-holder suspects that the applicant intends to use his new citizenship in order to gain access to his enemies and is thus likely to cause the rupture of his region's pact with a third region, he will reject the application.

Malefactors and refugees who come fleeing from feuds or threatened feuds in other regions may safely enter any region with which their own has a treaty. Neither asylum nor exclusion nor selection nor expulsion enters into regulation of immigration: these have not been invented. Usually the immigrant enters the household of a rich man who will subsist and sponsor him. But the pact-holder will not often, until after the lapse of some time, entertain the immigrant's application for citizenship.

Let us suppose, for example, that a Lubwagan man flees to Sumadel. If he should be allowed to change citizenship, and if the relatives of him he slew in Lubwagan should kill him, that would spell a rupture of the pact. If, however, he should be killed as a citizen of Lubwagan on Sumadel territory, that would involve no rupture, being Lubwagan's own deed and domestic concern.

If the immigrant marries and has a child, he will usually be accepted by the local pact-holder as a citizen. Suppose, however, that he does not apply to change citizenship. He still acquires, through his child, a sort of quasi-naturalization. Inside Sumadel both pact-holder and his in-laws must protect him. He may safely go on trading trips to any place that has a pact with Lubwagan, the region of his nativity. There is, of course, the danger that a trading party from a town having a pact with Sumadel but none with Lubwagan may kill him right in Sumadel. Suppose that an in-law, in such case, on the spur of the moment, kills one of them or, trying to defend his brother-in-law, is killed himself. Great trouble for the pact-holder! Suppose, though, that only the immigrant is killed. The in-laws will want the pact-holder to break the pact. He will not do this, but he will worry a lot lest the in-laws carry out their kinship-group obligation to avenge.

Or suppose that the immigrant should return to the region of his citizenship, Lubwagan, and be killed by feudist enemies. His child and wife's people would appeal to their pact-holder for Lubwagan to declare the pact broken, and the latter would have a hard time expounding the new, *political* law to folk in whom the ancient ideology of blood-tie society is ingenerate. The possibility of their retaliation would be a threat to the pact.

And yet another threat. Suppose his feudist enemies in Lubwagan regard his child as a Lubwaganite on account of the father's citizenship and so fair prey for their vengeance? But both by residence and by the mother's blood, the child is a citizen of Sumadel. Truly law is complicated from its very beginning.

These threats of great troubles—of loss of many lives if war ensue, of irruption of feuds, of retaliations by pact-holders, of cessation of trade, of women having to work their hill farms in danger of being speared from the brush all around, of mulctings by weregilds—will have been due to the fact of intermarriage between the two regions and a consequent clash between kinship-group custom-law and political law. The practice of regional endogamy avoids them. It avoids not only such threats to the pact but also another kind of trouble such as is illustrated by the killing of Sanggui by Maddalum (see p. 155). These two men were descendants of intermarriages between Lubwagan and Ginaang. When, some generations later, fighting occurred between their kindreds back in Ginaang, Maddalum spread it into Lubwagan by killing Sanggui (see also Case 62).

In nearly all cases, though, weregilds will be paid in the trouble that led to an immigrant's flight, or else the score of vengeance will be evened. The immigrant will apply for citizenship, and his application, if persisted in, will be granted by the pact-holders.

66. Refugee immediately accepted as citizen (Spanish times).—One night Basingat and Bataowang, in Lubwagan, went to the granary of GaLisi to steal rice. GaLisi, however, was watching and speared Bataowang, killing him. Then he ran and went into hiding. Palaiyok and Basingat, relatives of the slain, tried to find GaLisi and, failing in this, wounded GaLisi's father.

Their thirst for vengeance was not satisfied by this retaliation— probably it was the more avid because of their having been discovered as thieves. Therefore, GaLisi took his sister and her two daughters and fled to Balbalasang.

The pact-holder in Balbalasang, taking all circumstances under consideration, concluded that there was very little likelihood of further feud, since the score was even and since Lubwagan was very far away. Accordingly, he accepted one of GaLisi's bowls and sent the other to the Lubwagan pact-holder, who also accepted.

Q. Was GaLisi justified in killing a man who had come to steal his rice?

A. What else could he have done? If he had cried out, the two of them would have killed him to prevent their being publicly disgraced.

67. Refugees retain citizenship (1927) (continuation of Case 4).— Bangibang killed a kadangyan, Basingat [not the Basingat of the preceding case], and fled with several of his relatives—for the family was poor and small—to Balbalasang. They chose this region because they were related to GaLisi, of the preceding case, already in refuge there. Bangibang was arrested, convicted, and died in prison. His relatives did not change citizenship. Two relatives of Bangibang who remained in Lubwagan were slain by Basingat's kindred.

One of the refugees has recently returned to Lubwagan because she has a field here.

Sometimes a man's relatives in his native region oppose the change of citizenship and bring pressure on the pact-holder of their region to refuse his application:

68. Change of citizenship opposed (ca. 1903).—My uncle was not a wealthy man, and he had killed a son of one of the pangats. His cousin, Topag, being fearful for his life, fled to Ginaang, where he took service as a *puyong* under one of the wealthiest pangats there. His master, at Topag's request, took two Chinese bowls worth about half a peso each to the pact-holder and asked him to send one to the Lubwagan pact-holder for Ginaang "as a change" for Topag's citizenship. This was done, and the bowl was accepted.

The years passed and three children were born. About eleven years after he went there, the weregilds of my uncle were paid up, and Topag's relatives went to Ginaang and persuaded him to come back with his family to Lubwagan. After being in Lubwagan about a month, Topag gave a bowl to the pact-holder to be sent to the Ginaang pact-holder with the request for Topag's change of citizenship back to Lubwagan. The Ginaang pact-holder raised objections: "His wife is from here—better wait—perhaps they will want to come back." The bowl was sent twice more before the Ginaang pact-holder accepted it.

All informants are agreed that permission to renounce citizenship cannot be indefinitely withheld, except in the instance of a refugee whose feud in his native region is unsettled.

Multiple citizenship.—The citizenship of the mother is as important as that of the father, and, when the sole element of descent operates to determine the citizenship of the child, there results a dual citizenship. Thus, if a Lubwagan man marries a Bangad woman in a neutral region, say Baguio, the child born to them there has a dual citizenship, and, if he should be wounded in that or any other region than the two concerned, the pact-holders of both parents will send "strong words" and a demand on his behalf for the customary retaliations. If the parents should come to live in Lubwagan and if the mother retained her citizenship in Bangad, a wounding of the child in Lubwagan would result in such a demand by the Bangad pact-holder on his Lubwagan's colleague.

Q. Suppose the Lubwagan man to have been a widower having his child with him in Baguio when he married the Bangad woman. He goes to Bangad with his family and changes his citizenship. Does his change of citizenship also change that of his child?

A. It is impossible to say. There have never been such cases.

Q. Well, whether or not that child's citizenship were affected, suppose the child were wounded or killed in Bangad. Would the Lubwagan pact-holder demand the customary punishment in such cases and, failing satisfaction, rupture the pact?

A. There have been no cases. It is exceedingly probable, though, that the relatives of the child [in Lubwagan] would bring very strong pressure to bear on the Lubwagan pact-holder to follow such a course. So I think it would be as you suggest, although, in general, we like to see people citizens of the region in which they live. The fact that all the child's relatives except the father lived in Lubwagan would probably lead Lubwagan to consider the child as a Lubwaganite.

Instances of dual, and one probably of triple, citizenship arose in the Magnao-Naneng district in this way: the boundaries of the regions of Magnao, Limos, and Naneng as defined in their treaties did not include a roughly triangular uninhabited region which lay between them. A few young married couples moved into this "free" region, one being made up of a Limos man married to a Naneng woman, another of a Limos woman married to a Magnao man. The individuals of the settlement were especially enumerated in all peace pacts as citizens of their respective regions, and their children were included as having citizenship in the regions of both their parents. Informant thought that one of the children of the Limos man and the Naneng woman married in Magnao, and that the children of this marriage had a triple citizenship. This, he said, would have been quite in line with the attitude prevailing in the district with respect to citizenship. The region has been again uninhabited for several years.

The same informant also stated: "The pact-holder of Naneng for Limos is a relative of mine. Now if I, a citizen of Magnao, should be killed or wounded, the pact-holder would send a strong protest and demand for payment of weregilds or for vengeance."

Q. If there were no compliance, would he break the pact?
A. I don't know. He might—especially since I am a pact-holder, myself.

Chapter V

RESPONSIBILITY; PROCEDURE; PUNISHMENT, TORTS AND CRIMES

RESPONSIBILITY

A WHOLE kinship group is responsible for an act, whether contractual or tortfeasal, of one of its members. There is a tendency to center what we would call "civil" responsibility on the offender or his nearest relatives. Thus, seizures of fields are made from the offender himself if he has a field—otherwise from one of his brothers or sisters; failing these, possibly from a first cousin. Blood retaliation, however, may be inflicted on any member of the offender's group, male or female, although it is considered a bit thick to kill a third cousin. Inasmuch as the retaliating group will expect to pay weregilds, they will for the sake of economy—if they act deliberately—choose that member of the group who has fewest near-relatives (see pp. 80 and 233–34).

Within the town, minor children are excluded from the penal responsibility of their group. Children of enemies play together. If, for example, A has killed B, then B's children are obligated when adult to kill A or his relative, and, if they eat A's rice, they break the strongest of all taboos, that against eating the food of their father's slayer, and will get *butut*, "big belly," and die soon. Therefore, if, someday, A's children and B's are playing together and if A's children run into the house and get some tidbit, such as *dikEt* cakes, A will protect B's children against breaking the taboo; he will tell his wife or his own children, "Oh, don't give them any; they have no right to eat here," or "They will get a big stomach." This is not entirely because of pity for the children: if he should let them eat, then their father's kindred, believing them doomed because of the broken taboo, might assemble and attack A or even one of his children. One informant states that A's children are quite safe from B's kindred so long as they stay within the region but that, if they should be found outside the region, they might be killed. Another informant denies the latter part of the statement and asserts that the feeling against holding minor children responsible is founded on what we might call "public policy." "Everybody has children," the people, he says, reason, "so if we begin to kill off each other's children, the vengeance will never end, and there will be no people left."

There is a range both of opinion and of practice in the matter of the age at which a child begins to participate in the collective responsibility of his group. If we place the median at the wood-getting (*mangaikaiyu*) stage of growth (eleven to thirteen years), we shall not greatly err. The group's responsibility for the child begins much earlier, but demands in serious cases are mitigated according to the age, circumstances, and personalities of the parties, while light offenses may not be punished at all.

69. Offense by minor of maba-on *age (1939).*—Informant's daughter [eight to ten years old] had a row with a playmate at school and stabbed her with a pencil. Informant went to the child's father and said: "It depends on you whether you want something, but for my part I consider it an 'accident.' "

The Kalinga use of the English word "accident" is a translation of their own word *awat*, which means more nearly an excusable or unprosecutable offense. The father of the hurt child agreed that the aggressor child was too young to know what she was doing.

Q. Suppose the child had died?

A. I should have helped with the *utong* [funeral feast] as one does in case of mad-dog bite.

Q. Would you not have been afraid they would avenge?

A. [*Hesitating.*] Not after I had contributed to their *utong*.

70. Offense by minor of wood-getting age (1931).—About 1922 the father of Paligan, of Sumadel, murdered the father of Sapao,[1] both Paligan and Sapao being at the time babes in arms. Sapao was reared on the story of how Paligan's father had murdered his own when he was a baby and was often told of his duty to avenge. One day, when he was about eleven years old, he went with his head ax to the house of Paligan and saw him sitting by the door. He slashed him in the side with his ax causing immediate death, "since the intestines rolled out." Sapao and his relatives were brought by the constabulary to Lubwagan, and the relatives of the slain were taken to Tinglaiyan. Both parties were put to work in different road camps for a while to prevent further trouble, and Sapao was sent to a reform school.

After about two years, Sapao came back from the reform school and before the end of another year he was killed by the relatives of Paligan. Then the relatives of Sapao accepted weregilds, and an intermarriage between the two families was arranged.

71. Feud between children (pre-American).—The people of Kalaiyan [Naneng Region], a village that has now been abandoned, encouraged the son of a pangat of the place, a boy of thirteen or fourteen years, to attack an old woman from a neighboring region as she was fishing in a creek not very far from Kalaiyan. The boy succeeded in wounding the old woman, and the Kalaiyan people paid weregilds. Nevertheless, Lammau, a nephew of the woman, a boy of about ten, avenged by killing an eleven- or twelve-year-old boy of Kalaiyan.

Factors which modify responsibility.—Accident, if clearly proved, excuses from punishment so far as the theory of the custom is concerned. However, the old tooth-for-a-tooth principle is so persistent that punishment is very often inflicted (Cases 22 and 27; note also Cases 73 and 74 below). As a matter of practice, a case has to be very nearly as clear as the one set forth immediately below, else the committer must feel frightfully uneasy until it is settled.

---

1. This boy was named after the pacificator of Kalinga Subprovince, Lieutenant-Governor Walter A. ("Sapao") Hale, so nicknamed because of his having accompanied an expedition of Igorots in the early days against the Ifugao region of Sapao.

72. *Accidental homicide* (awat) *excused* (*1939*).—A man in Mangali had to go at night to his field house to watch his crop against wild pigs. The field was located at a considerable distance from town, and the man invited his second cousin to come along with him, saying that they might probably get a wild pig. They went and by and by heard a wild pig in the adjacent thicket.

"You stay here in the fieldhouse," he told his companion, "so that there will be no accident, and I'll see if I can spear that pig."

He took his torch and went looking for the pig. By and by he heard a rustling in the grass and threw his spear.

"You have speared me!" groaned his cousin.

"Why! I told you to stay at the fieldhouse."

"Yes," answered his cousin, "I know you did—I don't know how I came to be here. Carry me back to the fieldhouse."

When they arrived at the fieldhouse, the wounded man said, "Now go and call my brothers and sons, but be careful not to tell them that you speared me."

The man did as his cousin told him. He told his cousin's nearest kindred that an accident had happened—he didn't know how—and they must hurry; he was afraid his cousin was dying.

When the brothers and sons had come, the dying man told them how it happened and that this was truly a case of *awat* [excusable accident] and that he did not want them to avenge—neither on the slayer nor on the slayer's relatives. Then they carried him back to the town, and he soon died.

The slayer furnished four carabaos for the funeral and gave a rice field to the sons, although these things were not demanded of him.

Comment: Slayers by accident always furnish a handsome *utong* for the funeral and often add a bit of weregild for greater security.

An interesting sequel of this incident is the explanation of it that is current. The constabulary sent investigators. These, it is said, found no human tracks leading from the fieldhouse but only a pig's tracks. They followed the tracks and found that they ceased and that human tracks began just before the place where the man was speared. The obvious conclusion was that the man dozed off to sleep and changed into a pig, as some of the people of one of the barrios of Ginaang region are believed often to do, and that just before the spear was thrown he had changed back to a man.

73. Accidental burning on land under apa not excused (pre-American).
—Lonagao, as he claimed, was unable to prevent a fire from spreading to the hillside declared *apa* in Case 27. He pled accident, but was mulcted a large pig and a gusi.

74. Accidental wounding not condoned; demand for exclusion from peace pact.[2]—[Informant Auwiyao speaking:] I was teniente of the barrio of Mabileng at that time, and, when I saw the fighting, I ran to call the constabulary. I met Basingat, acting mayor, and told him about the trouble. He said he would take care of it—never mind the constabulary—so we went back together.

I should explain that this Basingat was an overbearing man and that he had previously wounded Bangibang's father and had refused to give weregilds, although the pangats had advised him to. Basingat thought that he and his relatives were so strong that they need not fear Bangibang, who was a poor man and had few kindred. When Bangibang and his brothers grew up, they demanded weregilds several times, but Basingat rejected their demands.

Now when Basingat came to where the two parties were assembled, instead of trying to arrange their case, he slapped Bangibang. The latter started to run away and Basingat slapped him again. Bangibang drew his bolo, and slashed Basingat on the head, then ran toward the constabulary barracks.

The constabulary, having heard the uproar, were running into the barrio, their bayonets fixed. Puyao, one of them, was in the lead; behind him was Dalunag, holding his gun at his waist. The way was steep and slippery, and Puyao slipped and slid back into the bayonet of Dalunag and was wounded in the leg.

The pact-holders of the native towns of the two soldiers conferred and decided that the wounding was accidental.

After being discharged about a year later, Dalunag returned to his region, Puapo. There was a feast of that region to conclude a pact with a town in Abra. Present was Nalug, the pact-holder of Puapo for Kagalwan, the home region of Puyao, the soldier who had been accidentally wounded. Dalunag, being in his cups, began to boast that he had wounded a man of Kagalwan and—where was his kinsman whom the pact-holder for Kagalwan had wounded in retaliation?

Nalug, the pact-holder referred to by innuendo, resented these remarks and made a speech declaring that Dalunag ought to be excluded from the pact, whereupon a heated quarrel arose, during the course of which Nalug brought his bolo down on Dalunag's head, inflicting a severe wound. Nalug was arrested.

The relatives of Puyao contributed to pay Nalug's lawyer. It appeared to them that if Dalunag were boasting of having wounded

2. Continuation of Case 4.

Puyao, then the case could not have been one of accident. As pact-holder, Nalug had avenged it—therefore, he was entitled to *lotok*, as a pact-holder always is in such cases; the contribution to pay his lawyer was regarded by both sides as his *lotok*.

Nalug was sentenced to six months in the Bontok penitentiary.

75. Accidental wounding when butchering carabao condoned.—Bokali was butchering a buffalo. Palaiyuk came without being noticed and reached for some meat, but Bokali was bringing his knife down and wounded him in the hand. No action was taken. Yes, they were relatives, but even if they hadn't been, no action would have been taken.

Comment: The Kalingas say that they formerly had the free-for-all scramble, *gaiyamos* [called by the Ifugaos *giginut*], in cutting up a buffalo carcass in which each man secures whatever meat he can get away with. Among the Ifugaos, serious wounds that eventually cause death are sometimes received on these occasions, but they are never punished. If we compare the immunity in the case above with the great to-do made over a no more serious wound in the case that led to the rupture of the Lubwagan-Dalupa peace pact [Case 62], we are likely to conclude that the immunity of a wounder when butchering is a survival from the days of the free-for-all.

76. Accident during play.—Palikas and Naganag were making ties from bamboo for rice bundles. Naganag playfully poked his knife at Palidas but "unfortunately" cut his arm. The relatives told him to bring a chicken to sacrifice so that the arm would not swell. He did, but the arm did swell, and there was temperature. Next morning, Naganag came, found the patient with fever and brought a small pig and sacrificed it. No priestess was called: Naganag simply sacrificed the pig himself and said something like this: "Do not be so painful, heal soon. I did not do it intentionally. Kabunyan make it get well soon."

77. Theft by second cousin; "good, kind" policeman; amicable settlement (1930).—Lusingan, recently bereft of his wife, had nothing to feed his children, since he had spent everything he had on his wife's funeral and could not leave his children and go to work for wages. He went one night to the granary of Adao, his second cousin, and carried away a load of unthreshed rice. Next morning, Adao's wife went to get rice and noticed the theft. She screamed, "They have stolen our rice," and the relatives assembled and looked for clues. About mid-forenoon they found the rice in Lusingan's granary.

Lusingan's relatives assembled, and the two parties were about to fight, but a "good, kind" policeman interfered and was conducting them to the mayor's office for investigation when I met them. I told them that they ought to settle the matter between themselves, since they were second cousins. Adao, my first cousin, "was convinced," and so I told Lusingan, my uncle, to return the rice to Adao's granary and to

butcher a pig and feed the people who had gone searching for the rice
and to get basi for them to drink. It was done so, and the case was
settled. [AUWIYAO.]

Forbearance toward kindred hardly reaches third cousins and is thin by the time it gets to second cousins, but
Kalingas will usually manifest it when reminded of their
kinship after their first anger has cooled a little. Note that
the policeman is called "good, kind" because he interfered
to prevent trouble between kinship groups. The informant
plainly did not conceive this as a policeman's duty.

78. Homicide; first cousins killed and wounded (1935).—At a marriage
celebration in Madukaiyeng, everybody was drunk. Shouting was
heard, somebody was seen pursuing another, and DundungEn, recog-
nizing the pursuer as his first cousin, ran and seized him to prevent
trouble. The cousin, however, tried to spear DungdungEn, so the latter
shoved him with his shield, forgetting that he was holding his head ax
in the same hand with the shield. Thus he accidentally wounded his
cousin slightly in the head. The cousin kept trying to spear DungdungEn, who ran away, but, on being pursued, turned and inflicted
another head wound. After that, those cousins of the wounded man who
were not related to DungdungEn killed two of DungdungEn's relatives.
DungdungEn's relatives retaliated by killing three relatives of the
cousin.

DungdungEn, who entered the affair in order to prevent trouble, got
plenty of it himself. The Court of the First Instance sentenced him to
eight years—"because he had wounded somebody before."

The case is not settled by Kalinga custom yet: it awaits Dungdung-
En's return from prison.

79. Advances to married woman; refusal to indemnify; homicide (1938).
—In the region of Mabungtut, Gaiyaman made advances to the wife of
Dalwigis, his father's second cousin. "But, because she knew somebody
was watching or else because she didn't like Gaiyaman, she did not consent." Gaiyaman's advances were observed, and also the woman told
about his conduct. Dalwigis and his brothers wanted to settle the matter
amicably on account of the relationship with Gaiyaman's father. They
asked an indemnity of only two fields.

Gaiyaman's relatives refused this. Thereupon, Dalwigis and his relatives attacked Gaiyaman's party. Dalwigis wounded Gaiyaman and
another, while his kinsman Manganip wounded Auwing, a relative of
Gaiyaman. Auwing was carried to Lubwagan Hospital, but, being convinced that he would die, he begged his brothers to take him back home.
They did, and his premonition promptly verified itself.

Dalwigis drew six months from the Court of First Instance, which would appear to blow hot and blow cold [see foregoing case], and Manganip, four months.

"This case is unsettled the Kalinga way, as the Mabungtut people cannot make peace and are always fighting. They are too poor to offer each other weregilds that people of any pride would be willing to accept for the death of a relative—and they have pride. Also when one pangat talks, the other pangat talks the other way—there are only two. So they go on fighting."

Except *possibly* in homicide, where the rule of retaliation tends to overwhelm all other considerations, absence of evil intent on the part of a *kinsman* tends to make his offense one of excusable "accident" (*awat*). Presence of intent on the part of a relative, however, is interpreted as malice and makes him liable to punishment, although not to so heavy punishment as would be levied on a nonrelative.

80. Father wounds child (ca. *1904*).—Z, an irritable old man of Lubwagan, ordered his child to get him a light for his pipe. The child did not obey. Z stood up with a going-to-do-something-about-it look, and the child, frightened, started to run away. Z swung at the child with his head ax and inflicted a slight wound. The child's relatives assembled in response to his howling, and they reported the affair to the pangat of the barrio.

The pangat strongly advised Z to kill a carabao as a feast for all the relatives in order to prevent more serious trouble. "Had the pangat not arranged the case, then the relatives of the wife would have killed one of Z's relatives."

Q. Might they not have killed Z, himself?

A. Killed the child's father? That would be very curious! That would make the child die.

Q. Why?

A. Because the child would certainly have to eat with his mother—that is to say, with the group that killed his father. But he who eats with the slayers of his father promptly dies.

My informant [Mr. Auwiyao] also pointed out two other contradictions that would be set in operation if the father should be made the victim, first, the obligation on the part of the relatives of the wife to avenge the death of her husband. If they should kill the husband, then they would have to take vengeance on themselves! Second, the child on growing up would have to avenge his father by killing somebody from the group of his mother.

In the case of an unrelated offender, absence of intent does not alleviate punishment of homicide. It may, however, alleviate the indemnity in minor offenses, although much depends on other circumstances:

81. Killing of domestic animal; settlement (ca. *1936*).—Kanao had some pigs living in the mountains, mostly on wild guavas. Once or twice a week he or his wife would go to the mountains with some *tiki-tiki* [rice inner husk with cracked grains of rice], would call the pigs, and would feed them. Only he or his wife could call the pigs; they were half-wild and would run from anybody else.

One night Okin went hunting and speared one of the pigs. Next time Kanao went with *tiki-tiki*, he noticed that one of the largest was missing. He somehow ascertained that Okin had speared it.

Kanao called Gasatan and Sumaal to act as go-betweens in demanding indemnity. They went to Wakas, pangat of Mabileng, Okin's kinsman. Wakas went to Okin, who claimed he had speared the pig by mistake and offered to settle. Kanao accepted Okin's story and was content with restitution. In this connection it should be taken into consideration that Kanao has political ambitions. Another man might have demanded *sukat* [three times the value] and a feast.

Q. Suppose Okin had denied the deed and had refused payment?
A. Since he was not hard-up, Kanao might have left it for his sons to collect.
Q. For his sons to collect?
A. Yes, we Kalingas frequently do that if we do not especially need the debt at the time.

Rank plays a minor role in degree of punishment. As informants have repeatedly stated, the go-betweens try to keep indemnities "regular." This is not to say that circumstances do not enter in; if an offender's group really cannot pay, the go-betweens will try to induce the offended to take everything they have and be satisfied, pointing out to them that this is more advantageous than imperiling their own security by retaliation.

Alienship of offender, in marked contrast to Ifugao custom, is a strong alleviating circumstance if the alien be protected by a peace pact; if he should not be, it would no doubt be an aggravating one.

82. Advances by alien to married woman; punishment (1923).—Sugao, of Uma, had a trading partner, Saiyud, of Bangad. One time, he took a string of beads to Bangad and gave them to Saiyud to sell on the *tokdai* basis, stopping, of course, at Saiyud's house until the latter accomplished a sale. Saiyud's wife talked "very politely," and Sugao concluded that he charmed her. So when Saiyud was late coming back that night, Sugao made an evil proposal and touched her nipples. The woman, however, screamed, and the news was shouted all over town. Pangat and pact-holder rushed to the house and prevented Saiyud from killing or wounding Sugao. Sugao told how he had "talked something about love, and it seemed to him that the girl had a feeling for him." But the girl explained that she had talked as she did only to show courtesy to one who was the guest and trading partner of her husband.

The pangat and pact-holder settled the case amicably by assessing an indemnity of a carabao, to be given to Saiyud, and a pig to be slaughtered for themselves and the pact-holder.

Sugao went back to his town and sent a carabao and money with which to buy the pig. He did not go back himself because he was ashamed to face Saiyud. Thus he lost a good business connection through not understanding women better.

While alienship of the offender alleviates punishment meted out in a foreign region, alienship of the offended, on the contrary, increases the offender's punishment in his own region (see Case 58). There is, of course, the same consideration back of both procedures, namely, the preservation of the peace pact.

Insanity certainly is no excuse against the rule of retaliation in cases of wounding or homicide, but I believe it would be in less serious offenses. In the settlement of the case stated below, family relationship was the mitigating factor.

83. Wounds inflicted by insane person; settlement (ca. 1932).—Bato, the husband of Simok, was blind. Husband and wife got along very well together. Bato, despite and perhaps because of his infirmity, probably helped his wife in her work more than any other Kalinga husband. The spouses had a son, engaged to the daughter of Palaiyok, a neighbor, and two daughters.

"Unluckily," Bato went crazy one night and arose and slashed at his wife with a bolo. His blows were not effective on account of his blindness. The neighbors, hearing his wife's cries, came to interfere, but the insane man slashed the wife of Palaiyok, prospective mother-in-law of his son, three times. Palaiyok, in retaliation, slashed Bato three times.

The pangats arranged the matter as follows:

The son of Bato gave only *pakán* to Palaiyok, since he was the latter's prospective son-in-law.

The relatives of Simok, the wife, demanded a large *pakán* from Bato, but the son of Bato begged them not to require it since to do so would take all of his properties. They insisted that they could never eat in his house unless they were given *pakán*, but they moderated their demands. Simok was required by her relatives to divorce Bato.

PROCEDURE

The procedures have to a great extent been illustrated in what has preceded. There remain only to mention a few special ones and to gather up the loose ends.

Fact-finding.—There is no formal taking of testimony. Pangats and interested persons listen and interrogate. Witnesses are not required to take an oath, nor do they confront each other unless the kinship groups of the disputing parties are gathered in one place.

The "palin."—The accused may fortify his denial with an oath, *palin*, in the following phrases:

My eyes will lose their sight if I am at fault; I shall die soon if I am at fault; I shall be drowned next time I cross a river . . . ; my two legs will be crushed by a stone . . . ; I shall fall off a precipice . . . ; I shall be seized by a pest . . . ; etc.—"almost any calamity one can think of."

The "sapatá."—When no evidence to guide has been revealed and when suspicion does not rest definitely on any man, all the men of the town may be summoned by a pangat to take a more vivid, what we might call an *illustrated*, oath:

84. Sapatá *of the* bulnay (*basi jar*) (*1938*).—The house of Pangat Damag of Linas was partly burned, and he suspected that the fire had had a malicious origin. Next day he summoned the pangats of the three barrios, Kimatan, Linas, and Mapitpitok, made a little feast for them, and talked things over. The pangats decided to have *sapatá*. They got a big basi jar, tied *gumamela* flowers around its belly and chicken feathers around its neck. They called all the men of the three barrios named.[3] Each man approached the jar, took a drink of basi, and repeated, *Bumulnai nan buang-ko no sakon di nanggob si be-oy Damag* ["May my stomach become large like this jar if I was the burner of Damag's house"]. Nobody's stomach got large in the weeks that passed; no culprit was ever discovered.

85. Sapatá, *"money toward the sun"* (*1919*).—Somebody stole 200 pesos from the trunk of Alundai, mayor and leading pangat. He called all his relatives and all the people of Linas to assemble at sunrise. Each man was called to the fore, and he would hold a silver peso toward the sun and pronounce the following oath: *PumiLak nan atak-ko no sakon di nangakao si piLak Alundai* ["May my eyes silver over if I was the stealer of Alundai's money"]. The money was never found, and nobody got cataracts. The thieves were believed to be his own nephews, who were gamblers.

The buyon is a rite of divination used in cases of theft or other crime to ascertain who was the culprit. A man takes the round shell of the *kimpulog*, moistens it with oil, and, placing it on the small end of an egg or on the pointed curved end of a head ax, commands it, "Stand there if so-and-so stole the money." The result has no status as evidence—it is purely a private guide to action.

The *buyon* is also used when a man intending to kill wants to ascertain which of several persons would be the most feasible victim. Hence the phrase, *Na-ibuyon-ka n matoi* ("Thou hast been omened for death").

The ordeal (*"du-u"*).—The ordeal spread into the Lubwagan region from Abra. The Lubwagan people say they know of only two men in the subprovince who know how to perform it, Kaiyabo and Daiyag of Balatok. These men have kindred in Abra who taught them the ritual and procedure. So far as I have been able to ascertain, Lubwagan represents the extreme eastward extension of the ordeal.

---

3. *Q.* Why didn't they call the people of Mabileng and Gotgotong on the other side of the town?

A. Those people never come to Linas at night.

Q. Why not?

A. There are enmities. Somebody might spear them in the darkness.

The northern and central Kalinga regions do not have it. Kaiyabo and Daiyag keep their knowledge a secret so that they have to be called and well paid if anybody wants to perform the ordeal.

86. Hot-water ordeal; leniency to kinsman (1909).—The money of Tawatao of Linas was stolen. He summoned Kaiyabo, who caused a *maLtaba* [large Chinese kettle-skillet] to be filled with water and brought to boiling. All the men of Lubwagan were called.

First, each of the pangats dipped a hand into the boiling water and took out an egg, then the rest of the people lined up to do the same. But a cousin of Tawatao slipped away to take measures to prevent his being injured by the water. He broke an egg and rubbed the yolk on his hand. Men were watching and saw this. After he had dipped his hand in, the witnesses brought the egg shell and told what they had seen. The man confessed. Since he was a cousin, he was let off with repayment of the money and payment of the costs. Kaiyabo received two blankets as his fee.

87. Rice-chewing ordeal (1905).—The carabao of a kadangyan of Ginaang was slashed by an unknown person. He sent a messenger to Balatok to summon Kaiyabo and Daiyag. When they came, the people of the town assembled, and the owner brought dry, uncooked rice. While Kaiyabo and Daiyag were repeating their prayers, it was observed that one of the men was trembling.

One by one the people came forward, chewed their mouthful of rice, and it was always wet. Then this man's turn came—he was still trembling, and after he had chewed, his rice was found to be dry. Kaiyabo and Daiyag charged him with the offense, and he confessed.

The offender was compelled to pay *sukat*, that is, three carabaos, and to give Kaiyabo and Daiyag two blankets each. The owner of the slashed animal did not distribute the indemnity among his kindred.

RETALIATIONS AND INDEMNITIES

Punishments, or perhaps we would better say "satisfaction for offenses," are of two kinds: retaliatory and indemnifying. There is not much difference in the Kalinga's attitude toward the two classes, for infliction of retaliation is regarded as an indemnification and collection of an indemnity as a retaliation.

The retaliatory punishments are: (1) homicide or

wounding, which are regarded as equivalent satisfactions,[4] and (2) tit for tat.

The indemnifying punishments are: (1) weregilds; (2) the *sukat;* (3) the *multa,* or *baiyad;* and (4) the *dalus;* the *pakan* and *sipat.*[5]

THE RETALIATORY PUNISHMENTS

Homicide and wounding.—Excluding cases when these acts are necessary for defense, are psychopathic, or are committed from a mercenary motive (which motive is exceedingly rare in Kalinga native culture), they are, in any society, always retaliations. Our society has the state which prescribes when the acts shall be excused as justifiable and which reserves to itself the sole right of inflicting punishment. The Kalinga has only a feeble, incipient state, so there is no differentiation between justifiable or punitive homicide and homicide as a crime. The result is that every homicide tends to be regarded as a capital offense by the group from which life is taken and as a justified retaliation by the inflicting side. Public sentiment and custom modify these attitudes, of course, but the groups concerned are restrained by a relatively ineffective police power and tend to take the attitude stated above.

It follows then that we must treat homicide and wounding—as *offenses* and as *retaliations* together—as private wrongs. To a certain extent, other offenses may have the

4. It has been noted that the same word is used for both—*patoi.* This works to the disadvantage of the Kalinga accused before the courts. If, for example, the court asks: "Did you intend to kill as a revenge?" when in fact the man intended only to wound in revenge, the question as translated and as understood is "Did you intend to wound as a revenge?" and is answered affirmatively. The result is a sentence for attempted murder, while the answer would justify only a *lesiones graves* or *minores* sentence.

5. The *pakan* and *sipat* are primarily ritualistic payments. In effect, however, they provide kinship society with an instrument for the punishment of kindred who offend (see p. 242).

same double character, for example, malicious wounding of an animal (see Case 100); but the kinship groups concerned do not become so wrought up about them, public sentiment is more operative as a restraint, and custom, with greater force, prescribes a reasonable mode of settlement. We shall, therefore, treat of these other acts that often have a retaliatory element along with other torts.

But we must consider as comprising a separate category the cases in which homicide or wounding is done by a go-between or pact-holder; both are officers of the regional state and are executing the will of the community. In the latter case they are sometimes privately compounded by weregilds.

Homicide and wounding are the most frequent . . . well, let us call them "troubles," as the Kalinga often does. Sex complicates Kalinga lives amazingly little—the folk take a normal, common-sense attitude toward it; they marry young, and the dagdagas is a sort of safety-valve institution. It appears that they are usually upright in their dealings with each other and that honor is no empty word with them. But they are proud and have been taught the sacred duty of vengeance from babyhood. Remembrance of old scores during a quarrel or when insulted is responsible for very many killings and woundings.

88. Wounds (1941).—In Kulung, a barrio of Uma, Ulibak went to Logao's house and dunned him for a one-peso debt. Logao, who was the husband of his mother's sister, answered rudely, whereupon Ulibak struck him with his fist. A fist fight ensued. A nephew of Logao's, remembering that years ago a brother of Ulibak had wounded his [the nephew's] father, exclaimed: "You wounded my father, and you have struck my uncle," and leaped for his spear. Ulibak, perceiving his intention, ran away. The spear overtook him, but because his velocity was in the same direction and nearly as great as the spear's, the wound was only about an inch deep.

The wounder, Sawatan, received a sentence of one month in Lubwagan jail.

I saw them carrying Ulibak to the hospital about a week after my arrival in Lubwagan. A few days ago, the sequel occurred. I heard tense cries in the village, walked to the window of my room, and saw an occasional brown body with shield and spear gliding up the mountainside. I grabbed my Leica and went to investigate. The news had been telephoned from the Uma gate that another kinsman on Ulibak's side had been speared—and it had been given out by the telephone office (government-operated)—to the Kalingas! The men going up the mountain were relatives of Ulibak on their way to do something about it. Two victims on one side were too many! But when they got there, they found that the news was incorrect, so they took no action. Ulibak had brought his head ax down on the skull of Logao, who was the husband of his aunt. First, nephew had speared nephew-in-law and now nephew-in-law had split uncle-in-law's head.

Drunkenness accounts for a good many homicides.

89. Homicide, wounding (1930).—A councilor in Uma celebrated his appointment by a feast which was attended by Pangat Wakas of Lubwagan. During a tug-of-war between the Uma people and Lubwagan, one of the Uma men was unnecessarily rough. Wakas resented this and struck the offender with his fist, whereupon everybody began to fight, and clubs began to be used. The Lubwagan people left the feast and started home, but Wakas had forgotten his hat and went back for it. One of the Uma men who had felt Wakas' club took a stick of firewood and brought it down on his head. His cousin and brother, seeing that he was likely to be seriously hurt, returned and helped him kill his attacker and seriously wound another man.

Wakas was given a four-year sentence, and his cousin was sentenced to one year of exile. On appeal to the Supreme Court, Wakas' case was remanded, and no further action was taken.

The councilor, as host, was bound to slay or wound the aggressor [a blow with the fist does not count as aggression] or one of his relatives. The councilor played safe with the law and his official position by "wounding" the corpse.

Mention has already been made of the considerations that govern choice of a victim, *when choice is deliberately made*, namely, that of minimizing as far as possible the likelihood of retaliation by the victim's kindred and that of lessening the size and number of weregilds to be paid. It should be added that, in harmony with these considerations, children of dagdagas are often chosen as victims of retaliation. On the mother's side, they are poor, and partly on that account "their family is small." Usually they have no full brothers and sisters. Their half-brothers on the father's side, while obligated to avenge them, look upon them with a tinge of condescending contempt and are, after all, only half-brothers and may be easily bought off.

Weregilds are always paid after infliction of a capital retaliation unless the other side retaliates immediately. Heads are never taken when a co-citizen is "executed."

To us whose society is so far removed from the tribal stage and so much more individualistic than the Kalinga's, it is almost inconceivable that the Kalinga should display no special preference for the offender himself when punishing an offense, but such is the fact. I am not sure that there is even a preference for a brother rather than a first cousin, and if there be a preference for a first cousin rather than a second, it is only a small one. As has been said, Kalingas hate to have to put up with a revenge on a third cousin but will do so if they cannot kill a nearer relative.

It is said that formerly the family unity was greater and that a relative was always right when he became involved in controversy. "Nowadays, a man had better consult his family and get permission to inflict a retaliation. A man's family will give this permission if he has been truly wronged. They may grumble when paying the weregilds, but, after all is settled, they will forget, and they will be glad they all stuck together, for they have increased the obligation of their kinsman and his nearest relatives to themselves should *they* ever get into trouble."

Extra-regional feuds.—The following history illustrates the origin and course of a typical feud:

90. Lubo-Talgao feud (1870[?]-1940 . . . ?).—Seventy years or more ago, some Lubo people went to Talgao to sell a carabao, not taking the animal with them. They found a purchaser, received the price and went home, telling the Talgao man to come for the carabao on the sixth day. The Talgao man went to Lubo and found there was no carabao yet. He went several times with the same result. This enraged the buyer, and he resorted to a ruse: he said that if they would get a carabao for him, he would pay them still more. They got an animal for him, and a day was appointed for the seller to come for the additional payment. He went on that day with a relative, but, while in Talgao, both of them were murdered. Relations were ruptured between the two regions for several years, but a pact was finally made anew. Then two Lubo men invited two Talgao men to come to Lubo to work in their fields. While the Talgao men were there working, some travelers from Mangali [only about 4 km. distant from Lubo] murdered these Talgao men. This violation of neutrality led to a declared war, and a battle [*baluknit*] followed between Lubo and Mangali, in which the latter region was the heaviest loser. Peace was resumed between these regions without collection of the *dalus* indemnity, for violation of neutrality because Mangali had lost more men in this battle than Lubo.

Some of the Lubo warriors went to Talgao to ask the *lotok* from the Talgao folk that was due them for having avenged the death of the two men murdered by people from Mangali. Instead of receiving *lotok* they were murdered.

One of these Lubo warriors left a baby son, Basitao. He grew up on the story of Talgao treachery and of his father's death. Also, he was childless. He married and divorced many times. His childlessness probably made him the more determined to take vengeance, for it is believed that spilling blood changes a man's luck in that respect.

Basitao went about the job systematically. His mother had spent all their properties in rearing him; he was poor. He got a job in the mines in order to lay up money with which to pay a lawyer. When he was about forty years old, he considered he was ready to realize his life's purpose.

He went to Salngaton, in territory not covered by any pact, and lay in wait on the trail used by the Talgao people when they come to Lubwagan. He went many times. Finally his patience was rewarded: three Talgao men came along. He rushed out and boloed the hindmost of them, Walai, in the breast. Walai shouted to his companions who had gone around a bend in the road. These returned and shouted the news to Malangao. Malangao, being an offshoot settlement covered by the same pact as Sumadel, shouted the news to the latter town. The pact-holder there for Talgao fulfilled his treaty obligations by ordering the Malangao folk to carry the man to the hospital at Lubwagan.

Basitao's lawyer must have been a disappointment to him, for the court sentenced him to four years.

"Unfortunately" Basitao had not killed his man: Walai recovered. After five months he went many times to Godai and hid in ambush to wait for some Lubo people. Godai is in Lubwagan territory on the trail used by the Lubo people when they come to Lubwagan. "Luckily" his patience was rewarded, and there came three Lubo people, headed by Gakaiyon, the mayor. Walai rose from ambush and speared the rearmost in the back, then ran away. The Lubwagan people fulfilled their treaty obligation with Lubo by bringing the man to the hospital. Lubwagan demanded and received 100 pesos as *dalus* for the violation of the neutrality [see Case 51].

Last year the Lubo people went to Talgao to wage war. They went at night and shouted a challenge. The Talgao people rushed out and killed two of them; the rest ran away. But when the Lubo warriors heard the cries that told them that the Talgao people were cutting their companions into bits, they turned on their pursuers, discharged their *paltik* [illegal, unlicensed Ilokano shotguns made of plumber's pipe], and renewed the battle. The upshot of the fight was that Lubo lost three dead and had seven wounded, while Talgao lost four dead and had six wounded.

We see from this instance how private vengeance (*kilib*) and war—or perhaps we should call it battle—are intermeshed. We also note a survival of the fertility cult that probably underlies head-hunting, the belief that bringing home a head brings general welfare, increases the fertility of fields, domestic animals, and women, and brings abundance of life generally. Here in Kalinga the element of the complex most emphasized is a faith that spilling human blood is a cure for childlessness.[6]

91. Murder as fertility rite? (*1941*).—The thirteenth of March this year, as I was passing by the constabulary cuartel, I saw a prisoner under guard, his head wrapped in bandages. Requesting permission to talk to the prisoner through Mr. Auwiyao, I heard the following story:

"My name is Bagay. I was watching my field yesterday night against

6. *June 22, 1941:* A woman from Pinukpuk has just been arrested for killing a nine-year-old boy of the same region. She had just lost her only child from sickness and had no other reason for killing the boy.

theft of water in my barrio, Manobel, a part of Tinglaiyan Region, along with many companions. We were all sleeping on a dry place when Onapol, a man whose children and first wife had all died, after which he had married again and had suffered the loss of his two children by the second marriage, arose and speared me in the temple. I ran away shouting for help. The other sleepers arose and ran, too. Bokakao, my second cousin, shouted to them, "Let us not run away—let us kill him." Onapol speared Bokakao in the thigh, then ran away to the forest.

"Early the following morning, my kindred and Onapol's kindred went searching the forest, trying to find Onapol—my kindred in order to slay him; his kindred in order to protect him from mine. My kindred had all the good fortune; they found him and sliced him into pieces.

"They carried Bokakao and me to the hospital. My wound was found not to be very serious, but Bokakao died when the doctor cut the spear out of his thigh."

[But Bagay's wound was serious, and he, too, died a few days later.]
Q. Why did Onapol kill?
A. We do not know; we think it was because all his children had died.

Private vengeance (*kilib*) was just the same in manner of execution among the Kalingas as among the rest of the mountain tribes: a band of usually about five or six men, mostly relatives, but including sometimes one or two unrelated young men who went along to secure glory and a tattoo, would lie in ambush in the enemy region until a member, male or female, of the enemy kinship group came along. Then they would take the head, hack off pieces of the body, and carry them home. The heads were set on a stake, and there followed a head feast at which the headtakers would drink the brains mixed with *basi*, re-enact in grotesque pantomime and dancing the taking of the head, and recite their exploits in still more grotesque chanting and posturing (*palpaliwat*).[7]

Kalingas do not keep the skulls entire but divide them into pieces which are kept in a sort of war chest in the attics of their houses.

7. Dean C. Worcester, "Headhunters of Northern Luzon," *National Geographic Magazine*, XXIII (1912), 833-930, gives an eyewitness account of a Kalinga head feast.

Rewards of the avenger.—As has been said, the society
bolsters its institutions: any son who avenges a near-relatives's death receives his parents' best field even if it has
been allotted to another child of the household. A more
distant relative or a nonrelative who avenges the death of a
member of the household must, if a citizen of the region, be
given a field. If the avenger is from a foreign region, he is
given *lotok* in the form of animals and heirlooms. After
Maddalum speared a man of his own town to avenge the
death of a relative of his in Ginaang, he received from the
Ginaang relatives of the avenged:

> *Lotok:* 2 valuable gusi; 1 carabao
> *Tungu:* 1 pig for a feast

The *lotok* a pact-holder receives from an offended region
for punishing an infraction of the peace is usually somewhat smaller than this. Indeed, Maddalum may have
exaggerated.

There were other rewards. There was the right to the
tattoo; formerly, a man got his tattoo progressively, part
of it for each man he killed up to five.[8] The avenger, too, if
at all wealthy, stepped into a position of leadership of his

8. If in killing or disposing of an enemy, a warrior fell into either of the following categories, he was entitled to one or any succeeding stage of the tattoo.
After having obtained the first five tattoos, he could have any or all the rest
without any further "killings": (1) wounder of the living enemy, *gimaiyang;*
(2) giver of the coup de grâce, *manela;* (3) taker of the lower jaw—it is taken
before the head is severed, *samí;* (4) taker of the head, *maNiwat;* (5) wounder of
the torso, *dumangin.*

The latter category lets the bars down to all members of the expedition who
do not fall into a former one. Some men (they are mighty few, I suspect) are said
to disdain taking advantage of it. Women have the right to be tattooed whenever
a male relative is.

The stages of the tattoo are: (1) back of the hand and wrist: men, *pinupungol;*
women, *iLuLunus;* (2) arms and forearms: men, *sinungdel;* women, *tinali;*
(3) shoulders and breast (men only), *biking;* (4) back (men only), *kinaLkaLpai-
yan;* (5) stomach (men only), *pinipingao;* (6) a "belt" across the juncture of
chest and belly (men only), *niLusok;* (7) a band across the throat, *manawat;*
(8) cheeks, *aiyang.*

family—perhaps he might become its chief leader. He was set on the road to pangathood—his influence began to extend beyond his family group. He was also, if unmarried, in an excellent position with respect to the women; he could aspire to marry a wealthy girl even though he were poor. The near-relatives of the avenged bore the expenses of the head feast, and at these he might recite and re-enact his exploit in the *palpaliwat* speech-pantomimes—no small reward in itself. In short, all roads to Kalinga success led through blood.

Tit for tat was the punishment for minor wounds when there was an absence of malice or intent:

92. *Tit for tat* (*1927*).—Tektek, a young man of Lubwagan, was passing a hill farm in that region. He plucked a runo reed, sharpened it, and, just for sport, threw it at what he thought was a stump. But either his eyesight was defective so that what he thought a stump was an old woman, or else his marksmanship was atrocious. At all events, it was an old woman he struck—right in the shriveled thigh—and the scream she let out summoned her kindred from Linas, a kilometer away. These caught Tektek and held him while the old woman took a sharpened stick and stabbed Tektek in the same place. Then his kinsmen grabbed the old woman and held her so that she could not stab again. [See also Case 62.]

THE INDEMNIFYING PUNISHMENTS

Weregilds.—These payments are, as the reader has seen, multiple; not a single, standard payment according to rank of the slain or wounded, as was the weregild in western Europe. The weregilds of each relative, or, perhaps we should say, of each degree of relationship, are agreed upon separately, with due regard to primogeniture, rank, and influence, for these qualities make some relatives more dangerous than others. Still, pangats and go-betweens succeed to a very great extent in keeping the payments "regular," so that the amount of weregilds paid depends more than anything else on the number of relatives to be bought off. Secondarily, it depends on the general status of the family of the offended. A rich family will demand weregilds of somewhat larger size than a poor one, and pangats always demand more than ordinary folk.

The reader will have found several evidences in what has preceded that the weregild is a more recent satisfaction than retaliation. The possibility of buying off gives wealthy families an opportunity to gain control over the people by killing and so may likely have led to an increase of killing, rather than a decrease, within the home region. It is a phenomenon of the rise of the wealthy to political control.

Weregilds are levied for homicide, wounding, adultery, and infractions of *apa* declared in connection with a death.

Payment of weregilds falls short of being a guarantee against retaliation; it makes the payer safer but by no means safe. It is merely a process which relieves the kindred of the slain of their *obligation* to avenge. But one of these may accept weregild and still take vengeance, and, it is said, a man who does so gains rather than loses in prestige. Hence it would seem that the weregild is only a payment which *makes it possible for a man to refrain from avenging* his kinsman without loss of prestige.

Longao, in Case 11, had received weregild, yet he wounded one of those who had paid weregild. Then he persuaded his younger brother to confess to the crime before the court. The motives of the false confession were several: it was hoped that Pulgao would get a chance at the culprits in prison; Longao was the bolder and more mature of the brothers and could better protect their father from retaliation; he was the better "acquirer" and could earn money to pay lawyer's fees and to send to his younger brother in prison.

Other indemnities.—*Sukat* is the payment due in cases of theft, property damages, malicious killing of animals, and the like. Normally it is a payment of three times the loss or damage. In case of informal settlements or of absence of intent (as in Case 81), the indemnity may be decreased to twice the loss or damage, or even to simple restitution. In event of malice and difficult settlement it may be increased by assessing a feast (*palanos*) for the pangats and the injured party.

Multa and *baiyad* are terms borrowed from other languages and are coming to be used to designate a great number of usually minor indemnities which have each a specific name. Sometimes *multa* is used to designate a mitigated *sukat*.

Dalus is a payment made by a region in order to "make the pact clean," as in cases of violated neutrality.

PEACEMAKING

If one from an offended group does not accept weregild, "look out for that man," say the Kalingas. Still, they continue also to distrust those who have accepted it, for, as we have said, acceptance is not a guarantee of future behavior—nearly always these refrain from retaliation—but *not* always. A man can feel safe only after he has eaten with his former enemy.

It is taboo to eat the food of an enemy. If you visit a Kalinga village, a pangat or influential man will shortly come to you and invite you to his house to eat, whatever the time of day may be. You must not refuse—that, today and for the white man, would probably be taken as ignorance or boorishness, but formerly it would have meant that you were an enemy.

The result of eating the food of an offender is believed among both Kalingas and Ifugaos to be bloating, short-windedness, and death. Ifugaos, when terminating even the most trivial controversy between groups, always perform a ritual to remove the taboo and the consequences of chew-

ing the betel, drinking the water, and eating the food of
him who has been an enemy. Until this ritual has been performed, it is even forbidden to eat at the same feast with a
former enemy.

The Kalinga does not interpret the taboo so strictly as
the Ifugao. The former enemies may eat at the same house,
provided they eat at different servings, or at the same feast
and serving provided they eat at a distance from each
other. The Kalingas have no inexpensive ritual like that of
the Ifugaos to remove the taboo but, instead, payments
that would be quite expensive if peace were made with *all*
the kindred of the offending group, payments that are
made in much the same way as weregilds. The larger units
are called *pakan* and the smaller ones *sipat*. When there is
an offense within the kinship group, it is necessary that this
be given, because otherwise the close relations that ought
to exist between kindred may not be resumed.

Unrelated persons do not ordinarily give *pakan*. On that
account they will not be able to eat at each other's houses
or simultaneously inside the house of a third person, but
they may attend the same feast if they eat, as has been
said, at a distance from each other. But among the relatives of unrelated principals there are nearly always mutually related kindred. These have to be protected—before
they may eat with the offender, they must be given *pakan*,
though it may be very small.

The *pakan* presents are greater, naturally, for the nearer
relatives, gradually petering out to almost nothing. For a
brother, in case of homicide, the minimum payment would
be a carabao and/or a large pig; for a first cousin, a smaller
pig; for a second cousin, a Chinese bowl; for a third cousin,
a cheap bead or two. The minor payments, to second and
third cousins, are called *sipat*. The children of the slain

might be given a carabao collectively.[9] If the case were one of wounding, the wounded man ought to receive at least a carabao.

The nearest relatives of a man who was slain may not accept *pakan* except when the slayer is a member of their kinship group, or when an intermarriage is arranged between the two groups, or when offender and one of the offended become pact-holders, as in the case of Banutan and Gunut (see Case 63).

When relatives of the offender attend a feast which is also attended by relatives of the offended party who have not received *pakan*, "they must respect them" by taking care to eat at a distance from them. Otherwise, they are likely to bring retaliation on themselves. Naturally, the relatives of the slain do not like the idea of a bloated belly and quick death from eating with a man whose group has slain a relative.

Intermarriage is everywhere the good old standby in settling feuds, and the Kalingas practice it frequently, but not so frequently as the Ifugaos. The reason may be that there is more fighting within the kinship group among the Kalingas, so that intermarriages are often hard to arrange outside the forbidden degrees.

93. Intermarriage to settle feud (1900).—Behind Sukao and Umnu, both of Lubwagan, there was a long feud, the last incident of which was the wounding of Umnu's father by a relative of Sukao. Umnu was a little boy at the time. When he grew up, he slashed Sukao's arm.

Weregilds were paid, after which the pangats arranged for the marriage of Umnu to Atagan, a first cousin of Sukao. Then *pakan* was paid, and the two married.

TORTS

Adultery (intokom).—Just as homicide and infliction of wounds are considered as equivalent in gravity, so also are

9. In Case 62 an uncle paid his nephews a carabao each.

adultery and improper advances to a married woman. In Lubwagan, improper advances to an unmarried woman are not punished, nor is fornication of a married man with an unmarried woman, since it is considered that only the wife's infidelity constitutes adultery. No other mountain tribe takes such a view of the case.

The indemnity due from a man who makes improper advances to a married woman or commits adultery with her is called *dosa*, which is the word for weregild. The payment is less than the total of the weregilds for homicide or wounding because only the husband's vengeance has to be bought off. But his weregild for adultery is much greater than the one he would receive if his wife had been killed.

The name of the crime appears to be derived from Arabic *hukum* (Ifugao, *tokom*), meaning judicial law as contrasted with the (Malay) *adat*, or custom law.

If a Kalinga is told that somebody has committed adultery with his wife, he immediately and without making any investigation sets out to kill the offender or one of his relatives. But—and here is what saves the situation—he will usually halt on the way to inform his relatives of his purpose, and these will usually restrain him until the charge has been refuted or sustained. And among these relatives, in any case, there will probably be some who do not want trouble ("cowards" the Kalinga informant called them), and these will let the accused know that he had better go into hiding or else demonstrate his innocence. The result is that an innocent man is almost never punished and that the guilty one usually is allowed to pay weregild after the husband's wrath has cooled. If a relative rather than the actual culprit be slain, it will always be a male relative—never a female. An offender caught *in flagrante* will always be killed unless he can outrun the husband.

Divorce is the only punishment inflicted on the wife; she

is never killed. If there are children, the husband will sometimes condone a first offense, but never a second. If there are no children, he will not condone even once.

94. Advances to married woman; weregild (ca. *1934*).—One day the wife of Tungdu, of Ableg region, went to the granary to take rice. Dalapas entered, thinking that nobody was looking. "Unfortunately" Tungdu was hiding near by and saw him enter. The woman, "thinking probably that her husband was watching," drove Dalapas out of the granary, and Tungdu pursued him. "But he could not catch him because Dalapas was a good runner." Dalapas went into hiding. Tungdu walked around the town looking for him. The relatives of each party assembled; those of Tungdu were urging him to kill Dalapas; those of Dalapas were urging him to indemnify. The pangats named two go-betweens, and these settled the matter thus:

> 2 fields worth 10 carabaos ⎫
> 5 carabaos ⎬ to the offended husband
> ⎭
> 1 carabao—slaughtered for a feast for pangats and people

The relatives helped Dalapas pay, *but he was compelled to repay* them, whereas in weregilds for homicide the offender pays only his share, that is, one weregild. There is no ritual connected with payment of weregilds; offender and offended do not even meet.

The Ifugaos have a rule in adultery cases: "Man to man and woman to woman," meaning that the paramour indemnifies the husband and the woman in the case, the offended wife. In Kalinga the offended wife receives nothing—"she can only scold and slap her husband or beat or stab the other woman."

95. Adultery discovered in flagrante; *homicide; payments and intermarriage of groups (1918).*—Naganag caught his wife and his second cousin in adultery. He slew Kacinto on the spot. In the Court of First Instance he received a sentence of two years' exile to Bontok. On returning from exile, he and his group paid the following weregilds and/or *pakan:*

> 1 gusi worth 10 carabaos
> 1 field worth 10 carabaos
> 1 field worth 8 carabaos
> 1 gusi worth 7 carabaos
> 1 gusi worth 6 carabaos

1 earring (gold) worth 8 carabaos
1 earring (gold) worth 7 carabaos
1 gong worth 1 carabao
Blankets, gee-strings, Chinese bowls,
    head axes, etc., in great number

After these payments, Naganag married the first cousin of his victim. In this instance the payments appear to have been made in order to make peace within the family and facilitate the marriage to his victim's cousin.

DaLadag.—Sometimes a husband is too proud to accept weregilds and will be satisfied with nothing less than a token wounding of the culprit, often a hacking of the head or a cut on the arm, called *daLadag:*

96. Adultery; weregild refused; token wounding (ca. *1918*).—At the village spring in Balensiagao region, Malannag, of Dalimugao village, was seen giving a light to Aknay, the wife of Awingan, a pangat, keeping the cigar in his mouth as he did so. The two were suspected of amorous relations, and Awingan, without investigation, set out to kill Malannag. His kindred intervened and restrained him. Malannag offered weregild, but the pangat refused them. Then Malannag's party offered him for token wounding [*daLadag*]. Both men had strong kinship groups. The people of the whole region assembled to witness the event.

The male cousins of Awingan held Malannag and the male cousins of Malannag held Awingan so as to restrain him from seriously wounding Malannag. Awingan with a head ax made a small incision in Malannag's forearm. Then all the people shouted, Whoo! *Nagangput di daLadag* ["The *daLadag* is finished"].

Incest (*putut*) is said never to occur. It is said that there is no case in the memories of Lubwagan's old men of incest even between first cousins. I sent an informant repeatedly to different barrios to find a case if possible, for the settlement of such a case would have been interesting,[10] but he never succeeded in doing so. All he could find was the following case from Abra:

10. I am compelled to believe the crime very rare. Inasmuch as kinship avoidances are believed by some authorities to have been invented or, at least, to function to prevent incest, it is interesting to note, in this connection, that the Kalingas have none.

97. Incest in Abra; father punishes.—Bawalan and his sister would go on trading trips together. Since they never took another companion along, they began to be talked about, and after some months people's suspicion was confirmed by the pregnancy of the girl. On being questioned, both kept silent; and their demeanor, it was concluded, was further evidence that the brother was responsible for his sister's condition. The punishment was inflicted by the father, not by the *lakay*, or village chief, as is the custom in those parts for other offenses.

The father took all the son's rice fields away from him and gave them to the sister, the mother of the child.

Q. But I asked you for a Kalinga case?

A. Nothing like that ever happened here. I never heard of a single case.

Q. It must have happened between first cousins.

A. No—not even between first cousins; a man may marry a second cousin; but he may not debauch her; we call such an act *ina-aso-da*, "they did like dogs," or *putut*.

Q. If such a case as the one from Abra were to happen here, do you think the arrangement of it would follow the same pattern as there?

A. It is hard to say—that would depend on the father in the case. He would consult with the kindred on both sides and then would do what he thought best. Myself, I like the way the Abra father arranged the case. The brother's field went to the child; the sister still had her fields. Now if the brother, stripped of his fields, should go away somewhere, to the mines to work, maybe somebody would marry the sister; maybe they would not blame her very much—they would certainly blame the brother more. Yes, it was a good arrangement.

Two instances of incest between a man and his first cousin's daughter occurred in regions near Lubwagan, the man being in each case a graduate of the intermediate school:

98. Incest (1930).—A-n, of Ginaang, had incestuous relations with his cousin's daughter. The two kept the matter hidden from everybody because they "would go into ambush." Finally the girl was "pregnated" by him and on being questioned confessed the truth. They were forced to marry. But A-n was so often "insulted" by his townmates that he went to Manila on the pretext of continuing his studies, but really in order to earn. A year or two later he returned and married a woman from Kagayan. The pangats decided that A-n ought to give the girl two large fields, which he did.

99. Incest (1941).—This case, that of a young man in Kagalwan, was the same as the foregoing except that the boy went to Baguio, where he is at present working in the mines.

Malicious killing of animals is punished with *sukat*, the penalty applied in cases of theft and other property damage constituting tort.

100. Malicious killing of animals; sukat (1919).—A carabao belonging to Maganum broke into the hill farm of Pangat Wakas and did great damage. Wakas in great anger hamstrung the animal instead of going to the owner and asking damages. When Maganum went to his pasture land, he missed the carabao and, searching for it, found it lying in Wakas' hill farm, unable to walk.

Maganum armed himself with spear, head ax, bolo, and shield and proceeded toward Wakas' house, but many people grabbed him and held him. The mutual kindred called two or three pangats and went with them to Wakas and persuaded him to pay *sukat*, that is, three carabaos, and to slaughter a fourth for a feast, *palanos*, to the pangats and to Maganum's kindred.

Insult ("subog"); false accusation and slander ("likot").— These offenses are not punished by indemnity or formally at all, as they are among the Ifugaos. If an Ifugao accuses another man and challenges him to submit to an ordeal, there is usually an agreement beforehand about the indemnity to be paid him should the ordeal show him innocent. This is not the case among the Kalingas.

The Kalinga is a braggart, especially in his cups. His sneering and boasting often lead to the revival of blood vengeance and to his own death. The following is an instance that happened in Talgao during the month in which I am writing this (March, 1941); there have been two or three recent similar cases.

101. Murder (March, 1941).—A group of young men were assembled at night in a house in Sumadel where they habitually slept [*o-obogan*] and were chanting improvisations. One of them began to boast of his valor [*panalpaliwat*] and insulted Ma-ulat, singing that his uncle had killed Ma-ulat's cousin and that Ma-ulat and his kindred had been afraid to do anything about it. Ma-ulat went out without saying a word and sharpened his head ax. When he came back to the dormitory, the inmates had fallen asleep and the fire had burned down, so he struck a match for a light to make sure he got the right man. He beheaded the man with a single blow of the ax, then ran away. The councilor and houseowner summoned the men of the place and ascertained that Ma-ulat was missing; then the councilor sent to Tinglaiyan to summon police and constabulary. Ma-ulat was arrested.

Rape (pugud).—The Kalinga takes a very realistic and common-sense attitude toward this offense. Such a thing as the overpowering of a woman by a gang does not occur, and as between one man and one woman, he is quite certain that penetration could not occur without the woman's consent. If he defined the crime as "any degree of penetration" after the fashion of our statutes, I think he would still be skeptical about the impossibility of the woman's preventing that if she were so minded. He recognizes, of course, that a woman may be terrorized into submission.

Violation of a woman of an enemy family is sometimes construed as the next best thing in the way of vengeance to killing her.

102. Rape as a vengeance (1927).—Liban of Bangad was a graduate of an intermediate school. A relative of his, long ago, had been killed by the father of a certain girl of Bangad, and Liban hated the girl and would have liked to kill her, but was deterred by fear of imprisonment. Accordingly, on meeting the girl in a secluded place, a stream well distant from the town where she was washing camotes, he raped her, frightening her into submission by threats of killing her in revenge.

She complained to her father, and a demand for a *multa* of six blankets was made on Liban's kinship group. Liban was willing to pay them, but a conservative old uncle persuaded him to refuse, as he considered that the family was entitled to at least a minor revenge for the relative of theirs who had been slain by the girl's father.

The girl's father brought her to Lubwagan, where, after a medical examination, a complaint was sworn out before the justice of the peace. The case was tried before the Court of First Instance and Liban received twelve years.

Twelve years, when he might have gotten off by paying six blankets! But it was not only of his uncle's conservatism that Liban was the victim; he was the victim of his own timidity and unawareness. Had he only kept tab on the sentences of Philippine judges, he would have known that he would probably have received a much lighter sentence had he pursued his original inclination and murdered her.

103. Rape of a married woman; her vengeance (ca. *1910*).—While getting water from the village spring, Onek of Limos was assailed by a man from Ginaiyon who, under threat of killing her, took her into the jungle and raped her. After the deed, Onek told the man, "Now that you have taken my honor, let us continue the relations here in this place, and do you build a shack for our nest." Then the two appointed a rendezvous.

Onek said nothing to her husband, but on the appointed day she told a first cousin of hers, and he followed at a distance and went into hiding near the shack the man had built. Onek went into the shack and found the man waiting. She told him, "Not until I have prepared betels for us to chew." She then took the man's head ax and began to split betels, and, when the man turned his eyes away, she tried to split the fellow's head, at the same time screaming for help. Her cousin came and helped her dispatch the man. Then she went home and told her husband.

This case is said to have been investigated by Governor Hale, who absolved the woman and her cousin. The peace pact between Limos and Ginaiyon was not affected, since the two wrongs canceled each other.

Attempted rape of an unmarried woman is about as serious as the accomplished offense.

104. Attempted rape; settlement (*1939*).—A girl, X, of Linas barrio Lubwagan, was born with two arms but one of them ended just below the elbow. One day when she was about fifteen years old, she went to water a field at Malbuan, near Dugnak. A man, Banau, thirty years old, caught her and attempted to rape her. Finally, people came near the place, then the man ran away. The girl went home and told her father. The father went to Pangat Galamoy, also of Linas, who consulted with the other pangats of the barrio, Damag, Kanao, and Palaiyok [now deceased]. They decided that the offender ought to pay a *multa* of 40 pesos. However, some of Banau's kindred were also related to the girl's father and interceded. Accordingly, the culprit was let off from the penalty on his promise not to repeat the offense and warned that if he did the *multa* would be 100 pesos and/or prosecution in the government court.

Q. Was the case considered more serious because the girl had only one hand?

A. Not in the least; all a woman needs in order to defend herself against being raped is a pelvis.

Theft of a minor object within the town is paid by *multa* if arranged informally; by *sukat* if the case is settled by a go-between or several pangats. If committed against an alien, the punishment is more severe (see Case 60).

Sorcery (*"opas"*).—The Kalinga is too much of a realist, too little of a mystic, to concern himself very seriously about this offense. It is usually practiced against somebody who has killed or wounded a relative. Priestesses belonging to the offended group are assembled; they ring plates and "curse the fellow," and sometimes one of his hairs comes into a plate and rites are made over it. "But nobody believes it will work. Maybe somebody dies from sorcery once in a while—you never can be sure." Indemnities are never levied when sorcery is suspected; "all you can do is to try to kill the fellow in the same way—if you think it worth your while to try."

Probably the low credence in sorcery is connected with the fact that it is mainly the old women who practice it.

Poisoning (*"kodEt"*).—People thoroughly believe in the effectiveness of poisons. The death of my old friend, Goyao, father of Naganag, about two years ago was attributed to poisoning at a drink fest he attended in Lubo. Formerly, it is said, poisoners were sometimes boloed, "but now, if you suspect a man, all you can do is to try to poison him in retaliation." There are a few persons who are reputed to know how to make poisons, and they may be hired to prepare a poison for one or themselves to introduce it into the food of an enemy if he lives in the same region. No person having children will ever try to administer poison because of the belief that, if he succeeds in this kind of killing, one of his own children is sure to die. Formerly there was a man in Tanglag, Tuling, who could "call a worm" which "shed its hairs for him," and the man picked these up and used them for poison. He had no children and died without heirs nearer than second cousins—his life had been devoted to caterpillar hairs.

CRIMES

There are only two offenses which correspond to the definition of a crime, namely, that it is an offense against the sovereign power of a political unit. One of them is an offense against the moderative or mediative authority of the region, namely, an aggression by one kinship group against another while a controversy between the two is being mediated. It is punished by what may safely be called an execution rather than a retaliation, or would be so punished if it occurred—it is said never to do so. The other is an offense against the foreign relations of the region, namely, the killing or wounding of a citizen of another region with which there is a peace pact. Its punishment, too, must be regarded as an execution, although there still remain in the punishment some of the features of a retaliation.

Chapter VI

CONCLUSION

$\mathbf{K}$ALINGA social organization embraces units of two kinds: a tribal, the kinship group, and a territorial, the regional state. The latter unit is composed of the tribal ones—as many as there are groups of brother-sister in the population.

The following traits of the regional state are readily perceived to be continuations from tribal, or blood-tie, society: (1) the high degree of sovereignty in domestic affairs that is held by the kinship units; (2) the right retained by kinship units to demand exclusion from any pact concluded by the regional state and the ability of a very few of them to veto such a pact; (3) the fact that the state's restriction of the sovereignty of the kinship groups is vested ultimately in the strongest of these and proximately in their leaders; (4) the persistence, even in the two crimes that are state-punished, of the collective retaliation that is characteristic of kinship society; (5) the fiction of a kinship between reciprocal pact-holders: namely, the kinship obligations between them, the *lotok* indemnity with which a pact-holder is rewarded as if he had avenged a feudist wrong (p. 200), the marriage prohibitions between their children, and the exchange of spears by which a pact-holder, in punishing a wrong against the region for which he holds the pact, symbolically if not actually, uses that region's spear; (6) the demand for a victim (*kompaLa* [see p. 177]) from another region as the price of forbearance

from attacking it (*duwaL* [see p. 193]), both being obviously
extensions of the practice by kinship groups of demanding
the *daLadag* victim (p. 246) as an atonement of wrong; (7)
the persistence in some regions of the intervention of a
third-party pact-holder when a kinsman who is not his subject has been wronged; and (8) the practice of balancing
the debt of life when regions make peace—though here the
statelet has humanely risen above the hard-and-fast balance of blood-feud calculation, since a wound inflicted by
one region balances any number of lives taken by another.

There are two aspects of the regional state: a domestic
and a foreign. The Kalinga is barely conscious of his state
in the former aspect, for it hardly asserts a sovereignty and,
in fact, exercises only moderative and mediative functions.
It exercises no legislative powers (although a faint beginning is possibly to be seen in the action of the pact-holders
that time they threw their influence on the side of holding
agents to full responsibility [see pp. 134–35]). Its judicial
powers are limited to the efforts of the pangats to interpret
the custom-law and of go-betweens to "keep the indemnities regular." Its most conspicuous exercise of police power
is the enforcement by go-betweens of the law against interruption of mediation by an act of violence. But it would be
a mistake not to recognize the pangats' moderative and
mediative activities as exercise of a police power, *and one
that is backed by force*, even though only a psychological
compulsion, "influence over the people," is employed. For
that influence is grounded partly in trust of the pangats as
men whose vision exceeds the narrow one of their kinship
groups but mainly in fear of them as dangerous men who
have killed a number of people. Thus, there *is* a sanction of
force, clumsily and indirectly applied, it is true, but none-
theless force. If, however, a case requires direct force, it is
the offended kinship group that applies this—the state, in

its domestic aspect, has neither the puissance nor the mechanism for executing settlements between its member-groups and regards these as private wrongs unless they threaten the peace.

Taking a last general look at this domestic aspect, we note that the Kalinga state is a composite, not an integrated, unit. Its components are homogeneous, have surrendered but a minimum of their independence, and are with difficulty held in subordination. Employing a political term, we might call it a "confederation" if we first brushed away from that word all connotation of a union consciously and voluntarily entered into.

The Kalinga state is developed much more highly in the aspect of its foreign affairs than in its domestic aspect. Its defined boundaries, citizenship, quasi-naturalization, provisions for change of citizenship (in which it is considerably more humane than a few of the modern nations), treaties and the mechanism for enforcing them, declared wars that are definitely above the blood-feud level of the kinship units, its preservation of its neutrality—these are the marks of no mean sovereignty. If in Ifugao the state is just germinating, then in Kalinga its domestic aspect is just pushing its seed leaves into the light, but its foreign relations aspect is full knee-high.

Nevertheless, even in the last aspect, the Kalinga state is still a composite one, for its member-units may remain outside it at will and may demand not to be bound by its treaties and pacts.

Epilogue

WHILE this volume was being prepared for publication after Barton's death, a copy of the *Baguio Midland Courier* for October 26, 1947, was received from his friend, Laurence L. Wilson, which contained a column which Barton would have appreciated. It is appended to indicate that life still goes on in Kalinga in its customary fashion.

KALINGA TRIBAL WAR IS NARROWLY AVERTED

A feudal war in Kalinga between the villages of Mabongtot, Lubuagan and Mangali, Tanudan was recently averted by the timely intervention of Lt. Mario Bansen and Mr. Antonio Kanao, mayor of Lubuagan.

According to information these two villages had continuously fought each other in the past, but in recent years there had been a peace pact or "bodong" between the two. However, last August the Mabongtot chief who had made the pact with Mangali died, in which case a successor had to be appointed and a new pact made. Otherwise the old feuds would come back into play.

In this particular case no effort was apparently made to renew the pact between the two villages and trouble started when an attempt was made on the life of the mayor of Tanudan. From then on the situation got worse until both villages were prepared to fight it out on the traditional battleground as their forefathers had done, except that now they have the better tools and ways of killing each other that modern, civilized warfare has brought them. Foxholes and shells of various calibers were found on their proposed battleground when this was inspected.

Fortunately, the intervention of Lt. Bansen and Mayor Kanao averted any actual bloodshed, and now it is reported that a new pact is in the making. The village chieftains have already exchanged spears which is a sign for truce. The first ceremonies for the new bodong are scheduled for this week.

Glossary

AbeLyan—(1) Engagement; (2) affianced persons.

Abuyog—Trading partner.

Adugan (i-adug)—To watch over; *spec.* sit-down collection of debt.

Agabak—Bastard.

Agamang—Dormitory for the unmarried (Ifugao).

Aiyaiyam—Property in animals; *lit.* "pets."

ALan—Ghoul spirit.

Alang—Term applied to the air-burial scaffold; also the victim slain so that a corpse exposed in the scaffold may be interred.

Alasiu—Truce between regions; period after spears have been exchanged during which a peace pact is negotiated.

Amano—Equilibrium of vengeance; balance of accounts in revenge.

Ambagduan—A line crossing the river at right angles; *fig.* "everywhere."

Among da papangat—Assemblage of the pangats.

Anao—Raincape made of palm leaves.

Angkat—Manner of selling in which the agent keeps all above a fixed price.

Anito—Soul of deceased person; malicious spirit.

Apa—Prohibition laid on use of the unowned under certain conditions.

Apin—The lining of leaves placed in a pot in which rice is to be cooked.

Apon—Textile gifts in a sale, symbolic of wrappings in which goods received in exchange will be carried home.

Atod—Gifts by husband's family to the family of his wife.

Awat—An excusable injury; accident.

Baga—Saying; *spec.* proposal of marriage.

Baiyad—(1) Indemnity paid to kindred of deceased spouse by widowed person who remarries before customary lapse of time of widowhood; (2) almost any indemnity except weregild, *sukat*, or *multa*.

Baiyong—A kind of altar; guardian stones.

Baiyuga—Ransom (Magnao term).

Bakdoi—A stick or pole laid or planted to determine a line between warriors of different regions engaged in battle over which it is believed to be certain death to trespass—any neutral observer may lay and declare it.

Baknang—Wealthy or well-to-do person; person of middle class.

Balingbing—A split bamboo, with tapered free ends, beaten as a musical instrument.

Baluknit—War or battle between regions.

Banat—(1) A gift sent as a proposal of marriage; (2) a pledge of property, especially of a field in which possession and use are given until the debt is repaid; (3) object sent as a bid for peace between regions (a spear or Chinese bowl)

Bangibang—A stick beaten during processions at the funeral of a murdered or beheaded man (Ifugao).

Bansak—Gifts corresponding to the *hakba* of the Ifugaos from the kin of the groom to the kin of the bride—customary in the Magnao-Naneng District but not in Lubwagan.

Basi—A fermented beverage made from the juice of sugar cane.

Basig—Childless.

Basigan—To fulfil toward a childless person the obligations of a child.

Bawbanagan—Corner of Kalinga house in which valuable heirloom gusi stands.

Bibiyu—Companion; *spec.* period at which Kalinga attains his "majority."

BiLag (biyag)—Prisoner of war; captive.

Bilay—A share of cooked meat.

Biling—A game of chance; "odd or even."

Binglai—Master's share of crop from rented field.

Biyao (biyo)—Pact of trade (Ifugao).

Biyu n di so-ol—The lesser and more numerous presents to a seller's kindred.

Bolo—A knife of varying form, about 20 inches long, carried in a scabbard and used in fighting and work.

Budong—Peace pact. See also *Mangdon si budong*.

Buguy—An offense against the peace pact.

Bulaiyao—A flying demon which preys on mankind and is believed able to "turn its fire on or off."

Bunong—Contributions of relatives and neighbors to a feast.

BUtok—A small bundle of unthreshed rice, about the size of a man's thumb where it is tied, just below the heads.

Butut—"Big-belly," the penalty for eating with father's slayer or for not enforcing an *apa* or peace pact.

Buwa—Division of the acquired property when spouses divorce.

Buyon—Rite of divination to determine a culprit or the most feasible victim of vengeance.

Camote—The tropical sweet potato, a plant native to Central America.

Dagdagas—Mistress.

Dai-ing—Folktale, story.

Daiya—The upstream region; direction upstream.

Daiyag—The right of a man in urgent need of an animal for sacrifice to wound any animal and take it—he is obligated to pay it back with "increase" interest later.

DaLadag—Token wounding of a culprit.

Dalan—A measure of unthreshed rice equal to 2 *lakom*, 10 *iting*, or 60 *bUtok*, and giving approximately 4 *gantas* of rice at first harvest or 2.4 *gantas*, second harvest.

Dalum di pita—The underworld.

Dalus—An indemnity due for violation of a region's neutrality.

Dangdango—Style of oratory used in discussions at the drinking of the pact.

Dauwai—A kind of confection.

DikEt—Glutinous, fermentable rice; *spec.* cakes made of such rice, symbolic on account of their stickiness of loyalty.

Dinongan—Mourning observances of kindred and surviving spouse.

Dinson—Head-hunting or slaying immediately after death of a pangat.

Diom—The lower half of a slaughtered animal.

Dolnat—"Pact-warming" feast.

Dosa—Weregild.

Du-u—Ordeal by hot water or by chewing dry rice.

DuwaL—A victim delivered to be killed in order to prevent an attack on a town.

Ebgan—Dormitory for the unmarried (Kankanai).

Fiat—The "clinching phrase" or declaration by which the magic inherent in myths is directed to a particular case and made active.

Gaiyagai—Challenge to battle.

Gaiyamos—Free-for-all scramble over carcass of slaughtered animal in which each man hacked off for himself whatever meat he could—now obsolete.

Gaiyauwa—Present sent by purchaser to an influential relative of the seller who does not come to ask for *so-ol*.

Gatad—The "base" in a series of purchase payments—it goes to the seller.

Gatang (ginatang)—Acquired property.

Gopas—Rupture of peace pact.

Gunsud—Fees or presents to the go-between.

Gusi—Valuable jars, used for containing rice wine or basi and constituting media of exchange and accumulation.

Hakba—Gifts by groom's family to the bride's (Ifugao).

I-adug—Sit-down collection.

Idang—Divorce.

Ilang (INang)—A share in meat distribution; a spit for holding meat.

Impakan—The giver of a pig in charge to a caretaker who will feed it for a share of the increase.

Ina-aso-da—"They did [were] like dogs," an expression of incest.

Inanak—Adopted child.

Intokom—Adultery.

Inum di budong—"Drinking of the pact."

Iting—A bundle of unthreshed rice consisting of six little bundles.

Ka-asauwa—Newlyweds.

Kaboy—A kind of blanket.

Kabunyan—Name of the supreme god.

Kadangyan—Wealthy aristocrat.

Kaga—A medium-sized pig worth about 10 pesos.

Kaiyingan—Forest clearing.

Kaiyu—War expedition.

Kalibit—A bamboo harp, consisting of strings raised from a segment of bamboo.

Kalilintog—"The peacemakers," a term applied to the pangats collectively.

Kalpaiyan—Textiles symbolic of rope used for leading away an animal received in exchange.

Kamalanan—Special rank and title of the oldest pangats.

Kandauwan—The central portion of the floor of a Kalinga house.

Kapoón—Descendants of a distant ancestor; *spec.* the kindred that are outside the family circle.

Kapús—The poor.

Katotokon—Individual who has just received his inheritance.

Kidul—Thunder-god.

Kilat—God of lightning.

Kilib—Private revenge; blood feud; head-hunting expedition.

Kinship terms—See pages 68–69.

Koipa—A beginning of the work of clearing a hill farm—it establishes a prior right to cultivate.

KompaLa—A victim formerly exacted from a defeated town to be ritually wounded.

Lagod—Downstream; region downstream.

Lakom—A measure of unthreshed rice equal to 2 *iting* or 12 *bUtok*.

Langdo—Secondary mourning.

Lobloba—Didactic wounding—the wounding of the little son of a pangat with the aid of his father.

LoLak—A generation.

Longos—The upper half of a carcass.

Lonok—Ratification of the peace pact.

Lotok—Payment due an avenger from the relatives of the person avenged.

Lumawig—Local god of the Mangali-Lubo district.

Mabitil—Poor man, "likely to become hungry" (Ifugao).

Mabón—"Can be sent on errands"; an age period in the growth of a child.

Ma-imis—Age at which a baby begins to smile.

Maka-ubog—To sleep with age-mates of the same sex.

MaLnos—Newborn.

Mambaga—"Bespeaker"; *spec.* "messenger" in marriage proposals, dunner in case of debt.

Mambanat—Person who carries a bid for peace.

Mamlak—Seller.

Mamlindao—Hunting-spirits or hunting-demons.

Mampa-angkat—One who gives property to be sold for a fixed price, agent to keep all above that price.

Mana-agi—Relatives collectively.

Manadaldalan—Age period during which child is learning to walk.

Manangkon—One who cares for and pastures cattle for a share in the increase.

Mandapat—"Uniter(s)," the period when a newlywed couple begin marital relations.

Manga-alisig—Priestess; medium.

MangaBeLyan—Relationship between persons whose children have married.

Mangaikaiyu—Period during which getting wood is the duty of a boy or the corresponding age period of a girl.

Mangiwatwat—"Distributor"; *spec.* a tactful, quick-witted person who distributes for a purchaser the presents to the seller's kindred.

Manganan—A field not allotted to the children but retained by parents to supply their food (Kankanai).

Mangdon si budong—Peace pact-holder.

Mangi-ugud—Go-between, mediator.

Mankikipkip—"Time of trapping fish."

Manlilintog—Peacemaker(s); term applied to the pangats, collectively.

Manlukbub—Age during which a child is learning to creep.

Manoddak—"He runs around"; an age period in the development of the child.

Mansiksikad—"He stands up"; an age period in the development of the child.

Mantauwag—One who acts as agent in selling.

Ma-ongaiyan—A payment made to owner of an animal seized for the debt of his neighbor "for its tiredness."

Mimiting da papangat—Meeting of the pangats.

Mongo—A kind of pea raised in hill farms.

Multa—A small indemnity levied as a rule when a case is settled "informally."

Nabaiyat—Relatives outside the kinship group (Ifugao).

Nabalu—Widow or widower.

Namakan—One who feeds and cares for a sow for a share in the increase.

Natumok—Members of the middle class (Ifugao).

Na-unat—Withdrawal of a go-between from a case.

Ngato—The skyworld.

Numbaluan-na—"For widowing him (her)"; vengeance taken for death of spouse by widowed spouse and/or kindred.

Obog—Any private house in which children and unmarried youths habitually sleep.

Odon—Property except animals.

Olag—Dormitory for unmarried women and girls (Bontok).

Opas—Sorcery.

Otod—Gifts made by kindred of husband to kindred of the wife.

Pa-anak—Interest.

Pa-anao—Textiles given to seller and his companions symbolic of water capes to protect the things received in exchange from rain on the homeward journey.

Pabaál—A present given to the agent who purchases for one in a foreign region.

Padak—See *Pagek*.

Padalkoy—Glutinous rice cakes, *diket*, presented to seller and his companions for a snack on the road home.

Pagek—Stones buried as landmarks along the boundary of a field.

Pagud—Shelf on which valuable jars and bowls are kept.

PaiLdus—See *Purdus*.

Pa-inúm—A drink given to an agent who purchases for one in a foreign region; drinks provided for celebrating a purchase.

Paiyak di mamlak—"Wings of the seller"; presents to seller's kindred.

Paiyao—Irrigated rice field.

Pakán—Gifts to offended person for making peace so that the offender and offended may eat together.

Palanos—A ritual feast at which an animal is killed.

Palin—Oath.

PaLnok—Gift to the seller and his wife.

Palpaliwat—Boastful recital of exploits.

Paltik—Illegally manufactured and owned firearms which abound all over the Philippine Islands.

Pangat—The most influential men of the kadangyan class whom popular appraisal has elevated to a special rank which is endowed with political functions; *pangat di so-ol*, the larger of the *so-ol* presents to the kindred of the seller.

Pasoksok—(1) A bribe; (2) gift to curry favor; (3) payment demanded by one who detects a culprit in the commission of an offense.

Patali—Textiles symbolic of ropes with which to lead home animals received in exchange.

Patanggok—A simple musical instrument made from a bamboo node and played by beating it against some other object.

Patay—The first of a series of payments made in purchasing a field or other property—it is always a Chinese bowl.

Patoi—Killing or wounding.

Peso—The principal unit of Philippine currency—worth half a U.S. dollar.

Pias—A share of meat sent to an absent person.

Pili—Property-guardian spirit (Ifugao).

Pinading—A kind of local spirit, derived sometimes, perhaps always, from a soul of the dead.

Piyokyas—Vengeance for slaying of spouse taken by widowed spouse and/or his kindred.

Posipos—Feast and ritual to secure recovery from sickness.

Presidencia—Municipal building.

Presidente—Former title of the mayor of a region.

Pugud—Rape.

Purdus—A runo reed having its blades tied in a knot (Ifugao, *pudung*).

Putut—Incest.

Puwak—A measure of unthreshed rice equal to 5 *dalan*.

Puyong—An adopted relative; a servant who is taken as a member of the household.

SalDa—A form of pawning or pledging property whereby ownership of the property passes to the creditor after a definite period if the debt remains unpaid.

Sangi—Bamboo stake with its upper end split and holding a pig's jawbone—the symbol of *apa*.

Saosao-ay—A form of oratory.

Sapata—An oath taken on a decorated jar of basi.

Sarong—A rectangular piece of cloth wrapped by the women around the hips as a skirt.

Singising—Chinese bowls used in the rites performed by mediums.

SinpaRsoo—One generation.

Sipat—(1) The smaller units in the *pakan* payments given to the distant kindred so as to remove the taboos against their eating with an offender against their kinship group; (2) spear sent as a bid for peace.

Sipi—Elevated strips of floor along the sides of a Kalinga house.

Siwat—Ransom (Lubwagan term).

So-ol—Gifts to the kindred of the seller of property.

Sukat—An indemnity normally three times the value of property stolen or carelessly or maliciously destroyed or injured.

Sumina—The "going separate" of a married pair to establish a household of their own.

Suyung—The upstream region.

Tagabu—"Inside" tenant, who lives in master's household.

Tagaipai—A creeping plant (*Drymaria cerdata* [Linn.] Willd) used in religious rites.

Taliwan—Seizure to cover debt.

Tawid—Inherited property.

Tobtobwak—Rotation in the use of an irrigation ditch.

Tokdai—A system of selling in which the agent's fee is one of *so-ol* payment.

Tokom—Present due one under certain conditions, who has not intervened in an offense against a nonrelated person (Ifugao).

Tongali—A nose flute.

Tubyao—Tenant who lives in his own house.

Tugtugao—Wedding feast.

Tungu—A feast given by an offender in expiation of his offense.

Ubog—The sleeping-together of age-mates of the same sex.

UnLaLim—Folktale.

Unoi—First rice crop—planted in January–February.

Utong—Animals sacrificed for the soul of recently deceased person.

Uyak—Second rice crop—planted during July–August.

Uyon—Largest unit in rice measure, it gives about 40 *gantas* if first-harvest rice, 24 *gantas* if second.

Yabyab—"Fanning" rites performed the day following burial.

INDEX

Index

1. Ordinarily the cases follow, or are included in, the page numbers just preceding the case numbers.

PLATES

PLATE II

A Village of the Lubwagan Region

PLATE III

A View of the Region of Guinaang

PLATE IV

The Central Village of Bangad—Fearfully Crowded Due to Immigration Following the Outbreak of War with Tinglaiyan

PLATE V

OCTAGONAL KALINGA HOUSE—DWELLING OF THE WEALTHY

PLATE VI

SQUARE KALINGA HOUSE—DWELLING OF THE COMMONERS

The sharpened bamboos are reared to protect a pregnant woman against fetus-devouring deities.

PLATE VII

A KALINGA MAN AND WOMAN

In the springtime, and at all times, the Kalinga mind lightly turns to thoughts of killing.

PLATE VIII

A Kalinga Male of Decided "Dravidian" Type—and Again the Typical
Manifestation of Kalinga Humor

PLATE IX

ANOTHER DRAVIDIAN TYPE
The man is a pact-holder from eastern Kalinga

PLATE X

RIOTOUS ADORNMENT OF THE KALINGAS OF THE EAST

PLATE XI

KALINGA CHILDREN AND THEIR CARETAKERS

PLATE XII

KALINGA WOMAN SCOURING THE FLOORS OF HER HOUSE

She lugs them to the stream for this purpose at least twice a week

PLATE XIII

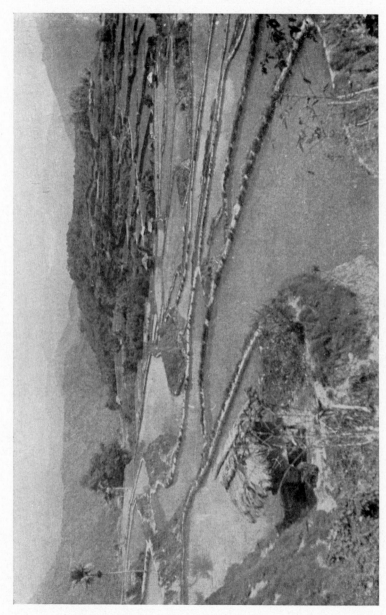

FIELDS JUST BELOW LUBWAGAN VILLAGE

PLATE XIV

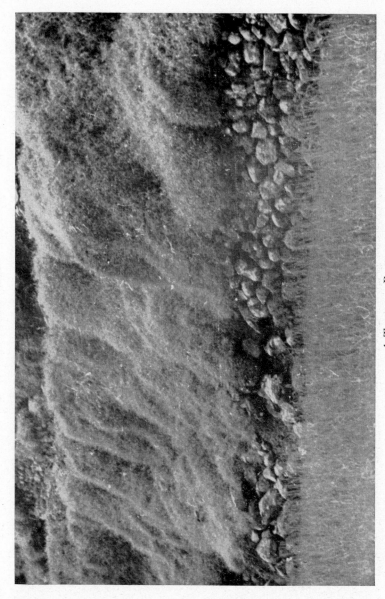

A TERRACE BANK

Above the stone wall, the bank is covered with heavy grass that protects it from erosion

PLATE XV

A Man Chipping Away a Large Stone in Order To Enlarge the Area of His Rice Field
His wife and a helper carry away the rubble in baskets and bring back good soil to fill in

PLATE XVI

Preparation of a Field for Planting by Driving Water Buffalo Around and Around

PLATE XVII

VEGETATION BEING RAKED UP OUT OF THE UPPER MUD AND THRUST DOWN DEEP AFTER THE
FIELD HAS BEEN TRAMPED INTO CONDITION

PLATE XVIII

A Kalinga Dance—It Isn't What It Used To Be

PLATE XIX

SOME OF THE MIDDLE-AGED WOMEN DANCING IN NATIVE COSTUME

PLATE XX

A Meat Distribution, Following a Sacrifice To Cure Sickness
The shares of meat are suspended from the two poles at the left

PLATE XXI

A Kalinga Having a Swig of Sugar-Cane "Basi"

PLATE XXII

PLATE XXIII

A Pact-holder from Northwestern Kalinga

PLATE XXIV

THE WIFE OF PANGAT DUGYONG DEMONSTRATES HER PLANTING-STICK

PLATE XXV

A Dalupa Man Arguing the Case for His Town to a Group of Lubwagan Men

PLATE XXVI

A Death Chair; across the Seat a Fly Switch

PLATE XXVII

CAIRN TYPE GRAVE, WITH TENT SHELTER

PLATE XXVIII

PLATE XXIX

LUBWAGAN VILLAGE FROM THE ROAD